DATE DUE

SE 23 '94			
NOV 0 4 1994			
Jan 23, '95			
NO 3 '95			
DE 5 '96			
JE 19 '98			
OC 5 '99			
OC 26 '00			
OC 9 '06			
NO 6 '06			
MY 29 '07			

DEMCO 38-296

CURRICULUM DEVELOPMENT IN VOCATIONAL AND TECHNICAL EDUCATION

CURRICULUM DEVELOPMENT IN VOCATIONAL AND TECHNICAL EDUCATION
Planning, Content, and Implementation

FOURTH EDITION

CURTIS R. FINCH

JOHN R. CRUNKILTON

Virginia Polytechnic Institute
and State University

ALLYN AND BACON
Boston   London   Toronto   Sydney   Tokyo   Singapore

Copyright © 1993, 1989, 1984, 1979 by Allyn and Bacon
A Division of Simon & Schuster, Inc.
160 Gould Street
Needham Heights, Massachusetts 02194

Library of Congress Cataloging-in-Publication Data

Finch, Curtis R.
    Curriculum development in vocational and technical education :
planning, content, and implementation / Curtis R. Finch, John R.
Crunkilton. — 4th ed.
        p.   cm.
    Includes bibliographical references and index.
    ISBN 0-205-14616-3
    1. Vocational education—Curricula.   2. Technical education—
Curricula.   3. Curriculum planning.   I. Crunkilton, John R.
II. Title.
LC1048.C48F56   1992
375'.0086—dc20   92-25888
                                                                       CIP

Printed in the United States of America

10   9   8   7   6   5   4   3   2   1   96   95   94   93   92

To our parents, wives, and children

Contents

Preface to the
Fourth Edition

This book is meant to fill an obvious void in the professional vocational and technical education literature. For some time there has been a need for a book that presents sound, usable principles for curriculum development in vocational and technical education. We have accepted the challenge to meet this need and the result of our effort can be seen herein. Persons who will find this content directly applicable to their professional areas include vocational and technical teachers, curriculum coordinators, principals, directors, and state education agency staff, as well as training specialists in the private sector. Much of the material has relevance to anyone who is involved in curriculum development work.

The content focuses on vocational and technical education curriculum development from a general perspective. Basic curriculum principles and strategies are presented that apply to a number of vocational service areas. These, in turn, are supplemented by practical examples that deal with curriculum development in specific areas. Concerns associated with secondary and postsecondary curriculum development are discussed as appropriate to ensure that both of these important areas are adequately covered.

Based on valuable input from persons who used this book, comments from others, and various changes in the field, we have incorporated several changes into the fourth edition. These changes include consideration for strategic planning in curriculum planning and inclusion of various curriculum design and implementation strategies.

Section I of this edition focuses on curriculum development in a more general context. Chapter 1 conceptualizes curriculum as related to vocational and technical education. Contemporary designs for curriculum development are provided in Chapter 2. These include systems and models that may be applied to a range of vocational and technical education and training settings.

Section II deals with the essentials of curriculum planning. Chapter 3 serves as a foundation for this planning in that it emphasizes the importance of systematic decision making in curriculum planning. The next two chapters describe how information may be collected and assessed as part of this decision-making process: Chapter 4 enumerates the ways that school-related data may be gathered, whereas Chapter 5 deals with community-related data in a similar manner.

Section III represents the next logical step in curriculum development, since it deals with establishing curriculum content. Once a decision has been made to proceed with the development of a curriculum or program, content must then be formalized. Chapter 6 describes the various strategies a curriculum developer may use when content is being established. The process of actually deciding what content to include is presented in Chapter 7. This is followed by Chapter 8, where the formulation of specific curriculum goals and objectives is detailed.

The actual business of implementing the curriculum is described in Section IV. Chapter 9 deals directly with the identification and selection of relevant curriculum materials. If high-quality materials cannot be located, Chapter 10 may be used as a guide for developing them. Chapter 11 presents a variety of strategies that may be used to implement the curriculum. The final chapter deals with an area often neglected by curriculum developers: systematic evaluation of the vocational and technical education curriculum.

Collectively, these chapters provide the professional vocational and technical educator with a detailed set of guidelines for use in the systematic development of high-quality vocational and technical education curricula. The content serves as a resource and reference to be utilized whenever any vocational and technical curriculum is being planned, content is being established, and curriculum implementation is taking place.

Curtis R. Finch
John R. Crunkilton

Acknowledgments

We wish to express our appreciation to a number of educators who took the time and effort to offer their valuable suggestions for this edition. They are William Callahan, Minuteman Regional Vocational High School, Lexington, MA; Dr. James E. Christiansen, Texas A&M University, College Station, TX; Dr. Kenneth Gray, Pennsylvania State University, University Park, PA; and Marie Kraska, Ph.D., George Wallace Center, Auburn University, AL.

CURRICULUM DEVELOPMENT IN VOCATIONAL AND TECHNICAL EDUCATION

SECTION I

CURRICULUM DEVELOPMENT IN PERSPECTIVE

Before curriculum development can take place it is important to understand the comprehensive nature of curricula and the many ways they can be designed. The curriculum developer is in a key position to effect improvement in vocational and technical education but may not be able to do so if he or she does not understand fully the context within which a curriculum must operate.

Section I of this book focuses on the conceptual nature of curriculum development, and succeeding sections build on this basic framework. In Chapter 1, a brief historical perspective is provided, as well as a view of what constitutes education. Then the characteristics of and a rationale for curriculum development are discussed. These set the stage for later sections dealing with planning, content, and implementation.

The primary thrust of Chapter 2 is on describing how systematic curriculum design may be utilized in vocational and technical education. Systems concepts from engineering and science may be readily adapted to education; however, educators have tended to disregard systems and models. This chapter explains what constitutes systematic curriculum design and shows how systems and models can be applied in vocational and technical school settings. Although both these two chapters are basic to curriculum development, it is not necessary to read them before proceeding with the remainder of the book; however, the basic concepts presented in these first chapters may contribute to a better understanding of curriculum planning, content, and implementation.

1

1

Curriculum Development: An Overview

Introduction

Ever since the term *curriculum* was added to educators' vocabularies, it has seemed to convey many things to many people. To some, curriculum has denoted a specific course, while to others it has meant the entire educational environment. Whereas perceptions of the term may vary, it must be recognized that curriculum encompasses more than a simple definition. Curriculum is a key element in the educational process; its scope is extremely broad, and it touches virtually everyone who is involved with teaching and learning.

This volume focuses on curriculum within the context of vocational and technical education. In no other area has greater emphasis been placed upon the development of curricula that are relevant in terms of student and community needs and substantive outcomes. The vocational and technical curriculum focuses not only on the educational process but also on the tangible results of that process. This is only one of many reasons why the vocational and technical curriculum is distinctive in relation to other curricular areas and why vocational education curriculum planners must have a sound understanding of the curriculum development process.

Historical Perspectives

Several factors have appeared to cause the differences that currently exist between the vocational and technical curriculum and curricula in other areas. Perhaps the foremost of these is historical influence. History has an important message to convey about antecedents of the contemporary vocational and technical curriculum and provides a most meaningful perspective to the curriculum developer. Curriculum as we know it today has evolved over the years from a narrow set of disjointed offerings to a comprehensive array of relevant student learning experiences.

Early Foundations of Curriculum

Education for work has its beginnings almost four thousand years ago. This earliest type of vocational education took the form of apprenticeship. Organized apprenticeship programs for scribes in Egypt are recorded as early as 2000 B.C. At about that time, schools were established that provided two stages of training:

> The first or primary stage consisted of learning to read and write ancient literature. The second was an apprenticeship stage during which the learner was placed as an apprentice scribe under an experienced scribe, usually a government worker (Roberts, 1971).

Thus, the earliest form of education for work was organized in such a way that basic knowledge could be developed in a classroom setting and applied skills could be developed "on the job."

Even as organized apprenticeship programs began to flourish, this same basic arrangement persisted. Apprenticeship programs initiated in ancient Palestine, Greece, and other countries followed a similar pattern with youngsters learning a craft or trade through close association with an artisan. Although apprenticeship programs expanded rapidly as various skilled areas became more specialized, reliance continued to be placed on training in the actual work setting—which, in most cases, consisted of conscious imitation. The apprenticeship form of instruction thus remained virtually unchanged until the nineteenth century.

Alternatives to Apprenticeship

By the sixteenth century, alternatives to apprenticeship were being strongly considered. The educational schemes of philosophers such as Comenius and Locke proposed inclusion of manual arts. Samuel Hartlib set forth a proposal to establish a college of agriculture in England. These and other events in the Realism Movement resulted in trade subjects and practical arts being introduced into formal education. The Age of Reason, likewise, became a catalyst for shifting away from the traditional apprenticeship system. Rousseau's concern about the value of manual arts in education served as a model for other educators such as Pestalozzi, Herbart, and Froebel. As Bennett (1926) indicates, Rousseau's "recognition of the fact that manual arts may be a means of mental training marked the beginning of a new era of education."

With the advent of the Industrial Revolution in the early 1800s, apprenticeship began a steady decline. The great demand for cheap, unskilled labor obviously could not be met through apprenticeship programs, and many newly established industrial firms did not desire persons with such extensive training as was provided through the traditional learner-artisan relationship. However, as the Industrial Revolution progressed, owners and managers soon began to realize that skilled workers would be a definite asset to an organization. This increased demand almost seemed to correspond with the rapid decline of formal apprenticeship programs in many skilled areas.

Toward Systematic Curriculum Development

Perhaps one of the earliest forms of systematic curriculum building in vocational education may be attributed to Victor Della Vos, director of the Imperial Technical School of Moscow. At the Philadelphia Centennial Exposition of 1876, Della Vos demonstrated a new approach to teaching the mechanical arts that "became a catalyst for vocational education in the United States" (Lannie, 1971). Rather than learning through conscious imitation, the Russian system utilized shops where formal instruction in the mechanical arts could be provided. This system attempted to teach mechanical arts fundamentals

> (a) in the least possible time; (b) in such a way as to make possible the giving of adequate instruction to a large number of students at one time; (c) by a method that would give to the study of practical shopwork the character of a sound, systematical acquirement of knowledge; and (d) so as to enable the teacher to determine the progress of each student at any time (Bennett, 1937).

Using these basic principles, Della Vos set up separate shops in the areas of carpentry, joinery, blacksmithing, and metal turning where students completed graded exercises that were organized logically and according to difficulty (Lannie, 1971). The Russian system, which was noted by many Americans, had a most substantial impact on Calvin Woodward and John Runkle. Woodward initiated a manual training school at Washington University in Saint Louis that closely paralleled the system developed by Della Vos. Runkle, who served as president of Massachusetts Institute of Technology, favored the Russian system to the extent that practical shop instruction was initiated for engineering students, and a secondary school of mechanical arts was established on the M.I.T. campus. These pioneer efforts served as important precursors of the contemporary vocational and technical curriculum.

The successes of Runkle and Woodward generated great interest in this form of instruction, and soon manual training began to spring up in a number of schools around the United States. Shopwork was even introduced into the elementary schools and, by the late 1800s, it was a formal part of many grammar schools across the nation. However, this progress did not serve as the best substitute for apprenticeship. Manual training and other forms of practical arts such as domestic science represented course work "of a vocational nature but these courses were incidental or supplementary to the primary function of the school" (Roberts, 1971). In response to this deficiency, schools began to organize so that students could be prepared to enter work in a variety of occupational areas. During the late 1800s and early 1900s, technical institutes, trade schools, commercial and business schools, and agricultural high schools began to flourish. Many of the offerings provided in these schools were similar in scope to those found in today's comprehensive high schools and community colleges. However, the standards associated with these programs were quite lax or even nonexistent. Quality was at best a local matter and, more often than not, did not extend beyond the concern of the individual instructor. The result was a considerable amount of inconsistency in quality among programs across the nation.

By 1900, a rather strong public sentiment for vocational education had developed. As the Industrial Revolution continued to expand, a need for skilled workers increased. This need was expressed by both businesspeople and labor leaders. Rural America began seriously to question the relevance of traditional education and sought to have agriculture play a more important role in the school program. These feelings were more formally presented to the federal government by way of national organizations. Groups such as the National Society for the Promotion of Industrial Education and the Association of Agricultural Colleges and Experiment Stations led the way in terms of securing federal aid for vocational education. The culmination of their efforts was passage of the Smith-Hughes Act in 1917.

The Smith-Hughes Act and subsequent federal legislation have had profound effects on the public vocational and technical curriculum. Not only has legislation provided funds for high-quality education, but state and local education agencies have been required to meet certain standards if they want to qualify for these funds. Since legislation has stipulated that vocational education be under public supervision and control, the standards associated with federal funding have had great impact on curriculum development in vocational education. Types of offerings, targeted groups of students, scheduling, facilities, equipment, and numerous other factors have been incorporated into federal legislation supporting vocational education. These factors have, in turn, affected curriculum planning, development, and implementation, since they have required the local developer to be responsive to national-level concerns.

The point should be made that the Smith-Hughes Act and more recent legislation have supported the concept of providing students with a broad experiential base in preparation for employment. This contrasts greatly with many of the early vocational offerings, which were more or less separate entities, often consisting of single courses. A major impact of federal legislation on vocational and technical curricula, then, has been in the area of quality control. The various vocational education acts have assisted greatly in the establishment of minimum program standards.

Contemporary Perceptions of Education

The present-day curriculum may be perceived as being a basic part of the broader area known as education. Education itself is often viewed as an amorphous term that defies description and explanation. In actuality, education is a concept that each curriculum developer needs to define and refine before the curriculum development process is carried out.

Education and Its Elements

In contemporary society, education may be viewed as comprised of two basic elements: formal education and informal education. *Formal education* is that which occurs in a more structured educational setting. Representative of this element would be school and school-related activities such as taking a course, participating in a school athletic event, holding employment as part of a formal cooperative vocational education program, or being involved in a student club or organization. *Informal education* (often called nonformal education) consists of that education which typically takes place away from the school environment and is not a part of the planned educative process. Part-time volunteer work in a hospital, babysitting, taking a summer vacation in Europe, and waiting on tables might be considered as informal education activities. Central to this element is the fact that a person chooses to engage in a nonschool activity, and this participation results in some form of education. Also central to this element is that education extends far beyond the four walls of the school and encompasses more than what is under a teacher's direction. Career awareness, exploration, and preparation may take place through one's personal initiative or by way of a parent's encouragement. Education in its formal and informal spheres encompasses a great portion of one's life. From early childhood through adulthood, opportunities exist for participation in formal and informal education, and the extent of a person's participation often corresponds with his or her capabilities to perform various roles in later life.

Goals of Education

Superimposed on the formal and informal elements of education are two categories that reflect the broad goals associated with it. These two types of education may be referred to as *education for life* and *education for earning a living*. As may be noted in Figure 1–1, the two are not mutually exclusive. Dealing with these two broad goals as separate entities is sometimes quite difficult, if not impossible. Each must be considered in light of the other. Basic preparation for life as part of one's high school education may serve as a foundation for postsecondary education or earning a living. Likewise, education for earning a living, received early in one's life, might serve to let an individual know that a certain occupation would or would not be satisfying to that person. However, a con-

FIGURE 1–1. *Education in our society*

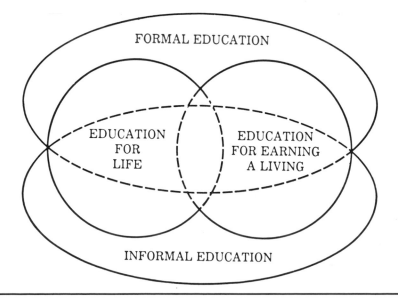

tinued interest in the field, together with education in that area, might nurture a strong avocational involvement.

One should remember that each of these types of education can be facilitated in formal and informal ways. For example, a youngster who takes a part-time job as a service station attendant to earn some extra money might find that some of this experience makes a direct contribution to a formal school-based auto mechanics program. On the other hand, this same experience could make the student a better citizen by serving as a realistic example of how our free enterprise system operates. Whether the experience is preparation for life or for earning a living, education may be provided through formal or informal means. Although informal education may not be as deliberate and systematically structured as formal education, it nonetheless serves as an important contributor to the outcomes of education.

Toward a Definition of Curriculum

How, then, may we define curriculum? Referring to Figure 1–1, it can be noted that formal education, which includes education for life and education for earning a living, represents a vast array of learning activities and experiences. These learning activities and experiences are not merely specific class sessions or courses but extend to or through the entire educational spectrum of a particular school or schools. Within this context, curriculum may be perceived as being rather global in nature and representing a broad range of educational activities and experiences. Thus, curriculum may be defined as *the sum of the learning activities and experiences that a student has under the auspices or direction of the school.* Acceptance of this generic definition commits the curriculum developer to accept two additional supporting concepts. First, the central focus of the curriculum is the student. In fact, one may interpret this to mean each student has his or her own curriculum. This interpretation is a sound concept, since students often select courses, experiences, and noncredit activities that align with their unique personal needs and aspirations. This fact might be pointed out by asking, "How often can it be found that two students have had exactly the same set of educational experiences?"

A second supporting concept has to do with the breadth of learning experiences and activities associated with a curriculum. Formal courses are not the only items considered to be a part of the curriculum. Clubs, sports, and other *cocurricular* activities are significant contributors to the development of a total individual and to curriculum effectiveness. Learning and personal growth do not take place strictly within the confines of a classroom or laboratory. Students develop skills and competence through a variety of learning activities and experiences that may not necessarily be counted as constructive credit for graduation. Student vocational organizations, social clubs, and athletics are but a few of the many experiences that extend beyond the prescribed set of course offerings of a school. These experiences have the power to make contributions to student growth in ways that cannot be accomplished in classroom and laboratory settings.

Accepting the foregoing implies that we must consider a curriculum as encompassing general (academic) education as well as vocational and technical education. Realistically, whether at the secondary or postsecondary level, the curriculum includes courses and experiences associated with preparation for life and for earning a living. This more global definition of curriculum enables us to consider not only what might be offered in vocational and technical education, but how those learning activities and experiences should relate to the student's more general studies.

The foregoing concepts also support the notion that a curriculum should focus on developing the whole person. It is not enough to have the curriculum include courses and experiences that are exclusively related to vocational education. General studies are clearly a part of every curriculum as they serve to provide the student with a broad knowledge base both for life and for earning a living. Likewise, the curriculum builder must keep in mind how general and vocational studies are intertwined. Life-related content such as mathematics, communication skills, and science is a meaningful contributor to content for earning a living and vice versa. Thus, as the curriculum is being designed and implemented, consideration must be given to how these two content areas may be closely integrated rather than segregated from each other.

Curriculum and Instruction

In order to clarify this definition of curriculum it is important to examine how it may be distinguished from the concept of instruction. Whereas curriculum constitutes a broad range of student experiences in the school setting, instruction focuses on the delivery of those experiences. More specifically, instruction may be perceived as *the planned interaction between teachers and students that (hopefully) results in desirable learning*. Sometimes, serious questions may be raised as to what exactly constitutes curriculum and what constitutes instruction. Some educators feel that any curriculum includes instruction; others contend that sound instruction includes a sound curriculum.

A brief description of curriculum development and instructional development should aid in clarifying these apparent differences of opinion. Curriculum development focuses primarily on content and areas related to it. It encompasses the macro or broadly based activities that impact on a wide range of programs, courses, and student experiences. In fact, the curriculum should define the institution's mission and goals. Curriculum activities are typically conducted prior to and at a higher level than instructional development. In contrast, instructional development is more of a micro activity that builds on curriculum development through planning for and preparation of specific learning experiences within courses.

Naturally, when curriculum development is taking place, the instruction that is to be built on this framework must be kept in mind. Likewise, principles of learning are not avoided when a curriculum is being developed; they are merely considered from a higher level of generalization. Anyone who is developing instruction must be constantly aware of the content to be included in that instruction. In the case of instruction, content that has already been derived as part of the curriculum development process is further explicated and specific strategies are designed to aid the student in learning this content. Figure 1–2 provides a visual description of possible shared and unique areas associated with instructional development and curriculum development. Although each area focuses on a number of rather unique concerns, many aspects of

FIGURE 1–2. *Possible shared and unique aspects of instructional development and curriculum development*

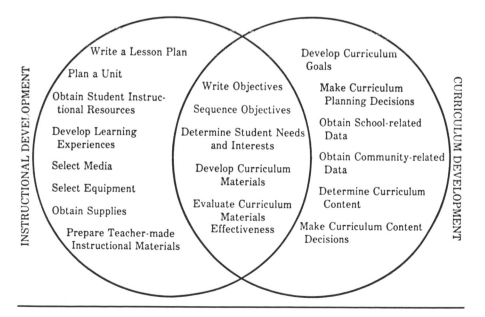

development could be classed as either curriculum or instruction. The shared aspects of curriculum and instructional development sometimes become unique to one area or the other based on the person or persons involved in the development process as well as those who will eventually benefit from this development. If one teacher were writing objectives for his or her course, this activity might be classed as instructional development. However, if a group of teachers were writing objectives for use in their courses and, perhaps, other teachers' courses, the activity might be considered as curriculum development. The distinguishing differences between these two areas become the scope of the development process and the extent of generalizability. If the developmental process involves a number of professionals and the product of this effort will be usable by a number of teachers, the process is more correctly termed curriculum development. Instructional development is best viewed as usually involving one professional (typically a teacher) in the process of preparing for his or her own classes. Although the distinctions between curriculum development and instructional development are not as clear as many would like them to be, they serve fairly well to identify each process.

Characteristics of the Vocational and Technical Curriculum

It should be noted that most discussions presented in this book will center on the vocational and technical education curriculum. One must, however, recognize that from a conceptual point of view the *ideal* curriculum is neither "academic" nor "vocational and technical." Vocational and technical curriculum terminology is used throughout this text merely as a means of emphasizing this area of study within the total curriculum and highlighting the unique aspects of vocational and technical education curriculum building.

Even though vocational and technical education is included within the overall framework of education, the vocational and technical curriculum has certain characteristics that distinguish it from the rest of the educational milieu. These characteristics represent a curricular focus that may be best associated with curriculum building, maintenance, and immediate and long-term outcomes. Whereas each of these characteristics is, to a greater or lesser degree, associated with other curricula (e.g., general or academic), their influence on the vocational and technical curriculum development process is important to note. Collectively, they represent the potential parameters of any curriculum that has as its controlling purpose the preparation of persons for useful, gainful employment. These basic characteristics of the vocational and technical curriculum include orientation, justification, focus, in-school success standards, out-of-school success standards, school-community relationships, federal involvement, responsiveness, logistics, and expense.

Orientation

Traditionally, the vocational and technical curriculum has been product- or graduate-oriented. Although a major concern of vocational education has been to provide a means for each student to achieve curricular outcomes, the ultimate outcome is more far-reaching that the educational process. The ultimate success of a vocational and technical curriculum is not measured merely through student educational achievement but through the results of that achievement—results that take the form of performance in the work world. Thus, the vocational and technical curriculum is oriented toward process (experiences and activities within the school setting) and product (effects of these experiences and activities on former students).

Justification

Unlike its academic counterpart, the vocational and technical curriculum is based on identified occupational needs of a particular locale. These needs are not merely general feelings; they are clarified to the point that no question exists about the demand for workers in the selected occupation or occupational area. Thus, curriculum justification extends beyond the school setting and into the community. Just as the curriculum is oriented toward the student, support for that curriculum is derived from employment opportunities that exist for the graduate.

Focus

Curricular focus in vocational and technical education is not limited to the development of knowledge about a particular area. The vocational and technical curriculum deals directly with helping the student to develop a broad range of knowledges, skills, attitudes, and values, each of which ultimately contributes in some manner to the graduate's employability. The vocational and technical education learning environment makes provision for student development of knowledges, manipulative skills, attitudes, and values, as well as the integration of these areas and their application to simulated and realistic work settings. The vocational and educational curricular focus also includes the integration of academic studies such as mathematics, communication skills, and science with applied studies so that students are better able to link these academic content areas to applied vocational and technical education content. Integration arrangements of this sort are detailed in Chapter 11.

In-School Success Standards

Although it is important for each student to be knowledgeable about many aspects of the occupation he or she will enter, the true assessment of student success in school must be with "hands-on" or applied performance. For example, knowledge of the metric system is important to the extent that it contributes to student success in applied situations such as cutting metric threads on a lathe, administering medication, or repairing a car. In-school success standards must be closely aligned with performance expected in the occupation, with criteria used by teachers often being standards of the occupation. The student may be required to perform a certain task or function in a given time using prescribed procedures, with each of these standards having its parallel in the work world.

Out-of-School Success Standards

The determination of success is not limited to what transpires in a school setting. A vocational and technical curriculum must also be judged in terms of its former students' success. Just as a college preparatory or community college transfer curriculum is judged on the basis of graduates' success in a four-year college or university, former vocational and technical students should demonstrate their success in the world of work. Thus, there is a major concern for the product or graduate of the curriculum, particularly with respect to employment-related success. Although success standards vary from school to school and from state to state, they quite often take the form of affective job skills, technical skills, occupational survival skills, job search skills, and entrepreneurial skills (Wentling and Barnard, 1986). There are certainly other standards that could be added to this list; however, the above items are out-of-school success standards that vocational and technical education as well as business and industry leaders rank as being very important curricular outcomes.

School-Community Relationships

Although it is certainly recognized that any educational endeavor should relate in some way to the community, vocational and technical education is charged with the responsibility of maintaining strong ties with a variety of agriculture, business, and industry-related areas. In fact, strong school-community partnerships exist in many locales. Since there are a number of potential "customers" in the community who are interested in products (graduates), the curriculum must be responsive to community needs. Employers in the community are, likewise, obligated to indicate what their needs are and to assist the school in meeting these needs. This assistance might consist of employers serving on curriculum advisory committees, donating equipment and materials to the schools, or providing work stations in the community for students enrolled in cooperative vocational education. Whatever relationship exists between the vocational curriculum and the community, it should be recognized that strong school-community partnerships may often be equated with curriculum quality and success.

Federal Involvement

Federal involvement with public vocational education has existed for many years. Ever since the passage of the Smith-Hughes Act in 1917, schools that were qualified and desired reimbursement for the operation of vocational curricula have had to meet certain federal requirements. These standards are basically developed and monitored at the state level, but each state must have its plan of action approved at the federal level before funding is allocated. This, of course, means that if federal reimbursement is desired for an offering, state and federal requirements must be adhered to. The extent to which federal involvement affects the curriculum may constitute a distinct asset or a liability. Requirements such as certain clock hours of vocational instruction and certain types of equipment to be used in the shop or laboratory might foster a higher level of quality. On the other hand, there may be certain requirements that place undue restrictions on curriculum flexibility, and thus hinder attempts at innovation or at meeting the needs of certain student groups.

Responsiveness

Another basic characteristic of the vocational and technical curriculum is its responsiveness to technological changes in our society. Two hundred years ago, programs and their content that prepared people for work were quite stable. Typically, the skills and knowledge developed in an apprentice program would be useful for the rest of one's productive life. Today, however, the situation is quite different. The Industrial Revolution and, more recently, the integration of technological concepts into our everyday life have had a profound impact on vocational and technical education curricula. The contemporary vocational curriculum must be responsive to a constantly changing world of work. New developments in various fields should be incorporated into the curriculum so that graduates can compete for jobs and, once they have jobs, achieve their greatest potential.

Logistics

Bringing together the proper facilities, equipment, supplies, and instructional resources is a major concern to all persons involved in the implementation of vocational curricula. The logistics associated with maintaining any curriculum are often complex and time-consuming, but the sheer magnitude of most vocational curricula makes this factor quite critical to success or failure. Some logistical concerns are associated with any curriculum. Physics and chemistry equipment and materials must be available for experiments. Recording devices must be in proper working order when language laboratories are being used. Textbooks must be on hand when mathematics and history classes begin. However, all of the above types of items, and many more, might be needed in vocational laboratories across the country. The highly specialized equipment needed to operate quality programs usually requires regular maintenance and must be replaced as it becomes obsolete. Materials used in the curriculum must be purchased, stored, inventoried, replaced, and sometimes sold. The need for coordination of cooperative vocational programs with businesses and industries in a community working closely to establish and maintain relevant work stations for students presents a unique set of logistical problems. The logistics associated with operating a vocational and technical curriculum are indeed complex, and these complexities need to be taken into account when a curriculum is being established and after it becomes operational.

Expense

Although the cost of maintaining a vocational curriculum is not inordinately high, the dollars associated with operating certain vocational curricula are sometimes considerably more than for their academic counterparts. This expense may depend on the particular area of instructional emphasis, but there are some items in the vocational curriculum that show up quite regularly. These include basic operating costs such as heating, electricity, and water; purchase, maintenance, and replacement of equipment; purchase of consumable materials; and travel to work locations that are away from the school. Some of these costs are necessary to operate any school; however, the vocational and technical curriculum may often require greater basic operating expenditures because of facilities that have a large square footage or equipment such as welders, ovens, or computers that require large amounts of energy for their operation. Equipment must be updated periodically if the teacher expects to provide students with realistic instruction, and this updating process can be most expensive for a school to carry out. The ever-increasing costs associated with the purchase of high-quality equipment make this area one of tremendous concern to vocational educators. Finally, the purchase of consumable materials requires a sustained budgetary commitment to the curriculum. Dollars need to be available to buy consumables as they are used by students throughout the school year. These items are not limited to pencils and paper; they might include such diverse items as oil, flour, shampoo, steel, wood, or fertilizer.

A Rationale for Curriculum Development in Vocational and Technical Education

The uniqueness of the vocational and technical curriculum raises a critical question. What is the basic direction that curriculum development in vocational and technical education should take? History tells us that, traditionally, curricula have been developed in a somewhat haphazard manner with little consideration given to the impact of the development process. Another point is that a vocational and technical curriculum soon becomes outdated when steps are not taken to keep it from remaining static. Finally, it must be recognized that the vocational and technical curriculum thrives on relevance. The extent to which a curriculum assists students to enter and succeed in the work world spells out success.

As a curriculum is being developed, the vocational educator is obligated to deal with these concerns in such a way that quality is built into the "finished product" or graduate. Any curriculum that is not developed systematically, or that becomes static or irrelevant, will soon have an adverse effect on all who come in contact with it. In order to avoid this difficulty, curriculum developers must give consideration to the basic character of the curriculum and build in those factors that contribute to its quality. Whereas some of these factors might apply equally well to any sort of curriculum development, they are especially relevant to vocational and technical education. As the development process is going on, outcomes of this process must be made clear. It is hoped that these outcomes will lead to a vocational and technical curriculum that is data-based, dynamic, explicit in its outcomes, fully articulated, realistic, student-oriented, evaluation-conscious, and future-oriented. Each of these is important to the success of the contemporary vocational and technical curriculum, and, as will be seen, each is congruent with the character of vocational and technical education described in the chapters to follow.

Data-Based

The contemporary vocational and technical curriculum cannot function properly unless it is data-based. Decisions about whether or not to offer a curriculum need to be founded upon appropriate school- and community-related data. Curriculum content decisions should be made after a variety of data, such as student characteristics and the nature of the occupation being prepared for, have been assembled and examined. The quality of curriculum materials is determined after data have been gathered from teachers and students who use them. In fact, the use of data as a basis for curriculum decisions cannot be overemphasized. The reason for this is that developers of traditional curricula have often neglected to place emphasis on the relationships that should exist between data and curriculum decisions.

Dynamic

It might be said that a static curriculum is a dying curriculum. Just as vocational and technical education is in a dynamic state, its curricula must, likewise, be dynamic. Administrators, curriculum developers, and teachers must constantly examine the curriculum in terms of what it is doing and how well it meets student needs. Provision must be made for curricular revisions, particularly those modifications that are tangible improvements and not just change for the sake of change. This does not mean that once each year or so the curriculum is checked over by a panel of "experts." Provision must be made to redirect, modify, or even eliminate an existing curriculum any time this action can be fully justified. The responsiveness of a curriculum to changes in the work world has much bearing on the ultimate quality of that curriculum and its contribution to student growth.

Explicit Outcomes

Not only must the contemporary vocational and technical curriculum be responsive to the world of work, it must also be able to communicate this responsiveness to administrators, teachers, students, parents, and employers. Broadly stated goals are an important part of any curriculum; however, these goals are only valid to the extent that they can be communicated in a more explicit manner. Although it is recognized that we cannot state all curricular outcomes in specific measurable terms, many of these outcomes may be written down in such a manner that the broad curricular goals are made more quantifiable. To the extent that outcomes are explicit, we will be able to tell whether students achieve them and how the outcomes relate to a particular occupation. This is perhaps the most commanding reason for ensuring that curriculum outcomes are clear and precise.

Fully Articulated

Although courses and other educational activities contribute to the quality of a curriculum, the way that they are arranged in relation to each other makes the difference between experiences that are merely satisfactory and experiences that are superior. Curriculum articulation may involve the resolution of content conflicts across different areas or development of a logical instructional flow from one year to the next. Articulation might extend to determining the ways cocurricular activities, such as student vocational organizations, lend support to the rest of the curriculum or deciding which mathematics concepts should be taught as a prerequisite to a particular technical course. It may include the articulation of curriculum content between vocational and technical and general education courses.

Curriculum articulation also takes place throughout levels of schooling. Reduction or elimination of instructional duplication at the secondary and postsecondary levels might be a major concern of the curriculum developer as well as those who are funding the offerings. Articulation across levels also enables both the secondary and the postsecondary instructor to teach what is best for his or her particular group of students and to do this in a more efficient manner. In this regard, articulation may extend to formal tech prep and 2 + 2 agreements that establish sound curriculum linkages.

Realistic

The vocational and technical curriculum cannot operate in a vacuum. If students are to be prepared properly for employment, the curricular focus must be one that is relevant. Content is not developed merely on the basis of what a person should know but also includes what a person should be able to do. Vocational curriculum content is typically based upon the actual worker's role with relevant tasks, knowledges, skills, attitudes, and values serving as a foundation for what is to be taught. Great emphasis must be placed upon practicality. Since the bulk of a worker's time is spent in applied areas, many student experiences must, likewise, be of a practical nature. Hands-on experiences in a laboratory or cooperative educational setting provide the student with a relevant means of transferring knowledges, skills, and attitudes to the world of work.

Student-Oriented

Most curricula are, to some extent, student-oriented, and curricula in vocational and technical education are certainly no exception. Currently there is a great deal of concern about how a curriculum can best meet students' needs. Various approaches such as team teaching, differential staffing, and individualized instruction have been used by teachers to help meet these needs. But, regardless of the approach a teacher uses, a basic question has to be answered: To what extent will the approach actually assist students in preparing for employment?

Another aspect of student orientation deals with the teaching-learning process. Not only must the curriculum meet group needs, but there is an obligation to meet the individual student's needs. In order for these needs to be met in an expeditious manner, arrangements could, for example, be made to provide instruction that accommodates various students' learning styles, to develop individual training plans, or to make available alternate paths for the achievement of course objectives. Whatever the means used to assist students, a basic concern should be with the individual and how he or she may be helped in the best possible ways.

Evaluation-Conscious

Evaluation is perceived by many to be an activity that comes periodically in conjunction with accreditation procedures. Realistically, administrators and teachers cannot wait that long to find out how successful they have been. Curriculum evaluation has to be an ongoing activity—one that is planned and conducted in a systematic manner. Anyone who is involved with the vocational and technical curriculum should be aware that evaluation is a continuous effort. As a curriculum is being designed, plans must be made to assess its effects on students. Then, after the curriculum has been implemented and data have been gathered, school personnel may actually see what strengths and weaknesses exist. Although most educators recognize that evaluation is not a simple activity, it is one that should be carried out concurrently with any curriculum effort.

Future-Oriented

Educators, particularly vocational and technical educators, are very much concerned about the future. What technological changes might affect the need for graduates? What types of school laboratories will be needed twenty years from now? What sorts of continuing education will be needed by students who are in school right now? These and other questions are often raised by vocational educators who think in futuristic terms (Finch and Crunkilton, 1985; Finch, 1986). Persons responsible for the contemporary vocational and technical curriculum need to ensure that ongoing curricula are considered in relation to what will or may occur in the future. As decisions are being made about curriculum content and structure, thought should be given to the future results that might come from those decisions. Any curriculum that hopes to be relevant tomorrow must be responsive to tomorrow's as well as today's needs. The extent to which a curriculum is successful twenty, thirty, or even forty years from now will be largely dependent on the future-oriented perspective associated with it.

Utilizing Sections I, II, III, and IV

This section sets the stage for those that follow. It gives an overview of curriculum development in vocational and technical education by providing a brief historical framework as well as discussing contemporary perceptions of the curriculum and how the curriculum may be designed in a systematic fashion. Chapter 1 points out that curriculum development involves few absolutes. It is one thing to build a chair or table to meet certain specifications and quite another to build a curriculum that may involve and affect numerous teachers, students, and employers. Chapter 2 focuses on several contemporary designs for curriculum development. These designs, in turn, serve as general frameworks for curriculum planning, content, and implementation.

The sections that follow relate to a common theme: decision making. The authors believe that, in order to develop and implement a sound curriculum, one must recognize the value of making realistic, systematic decisions. Decision making will be emphasized in each of the three sections, since it relates to many aspects of the curriculum development process.

Figure 1–3 provides a summary of the curriculum development process. Each of the blocks represents a section in the book that a reader might refer to if interested in one particular aspect of curriculum development. Section II deals specifically with planning a curriculum. This section would be relevant to persons who are developing a new curriculum or updating an existing one. The establishment of alternate decisions regarding the curriculum serves as a base for this section. Details about gathering school- and community-related data are provided so that the curriculum developer may obtain meaningful information to aid in the decision-making process.

Section III focuses on the establishment of curriculum content. It is at this point that one has decided to develop the curriculum. This section

FIGURE 1–3. *Curriculum development in vocational and technical education*

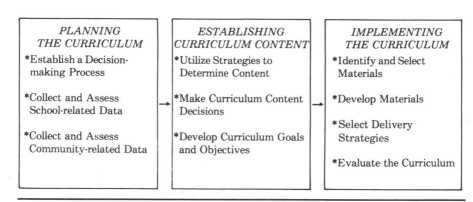

would be of particular value to individuals who are ready to decide about content to be included in the curriculum. It contains details about the ways curriculum content may be determined and the procedures used to develop curriculum goals and objectives.

Section IV is concerned with various aspects of implementing a curriculum. Persons who have gone through the planning and content-establishment stages would find this section most meaningful. It first deals with the identification and selection of materials, since this is often the most inexpensive route to take. The development of curriculum materials is also detailed. Since one must consider the most effective ways to provide the curriculum, several delivery strategies are presented. A final aspect of Section IV is curriculum evaluation. Whereas the development process is certainly important, the quality of a curriculum is determined only through evaluation in realistic settings.

Related References

Bennett, Charles A. *History of Manual and Industrial Education up to 1870.* Peoria, Ill.: Charles A. Bennett, 1926.

―――. *History of Manual and Industrial Education, 1870 to 1917.* Peoria, Ill.: Charles A. Bennett, 1937.

Davis, O. L., Jr. ed. *Perspectives on Curriculum Development, 1776–1976.* Washington, D.C.: Association for Supervision and Curriculum Development, 1976.

Finch, Curtis R. *Possible New Directions for Vocational Education Curriculum Development.* University Council for Vocational Education, 1986.

Finch, Curtis R., and Crunkilton, John R. "Is Your Curriculum Ready for the Nineties?" *VocEd*. 60, no. 2 (1985): 31–32.

Lannie, Vincent P. "The Development of Vocational Education in America, A Historical Overview," in Carl Schaefer and Jacob Kaufman, eds., *Vocational Education: Social and Behavioral Perspectives*. Lexington, Mass.: D.C. Heath, 1971.

Roberts, Roy W. *Vocational and Practical Arts Education*. New York: Harper and Row, 1971.

Wentling, Tim L., and Barnard Wynette S. "An Analysis of Perceived Emphasis on Vocational Education Outcomes." *Journal of Vocational Education Research* 11, no. 4 (1986): 81–94.

2

Contemporary Designs for Curriculum Development

Introduction

Educating youth and adults is no longer a simple process. It has, in fact, become very complex. Contemporary educators must give consideration to a multitude of curriculum-related factors ranging from federal and state regulations to cost, content, and accountability. Each of these factors has the potential to limit or nullify curricular success; and collectively, the factors that have an impact on a curriculum may pose a serious problem to educators in general and vocational educators in particular.

In an effort to counteract potential problems and to ensure that curricula maintain their relevance, many curriculum developers have moved toward more systematic design. This chapter provides an introduction to such systematic design efforts. It is by no means a complete discourse, but rather a sampling of what exists in this dynamic area. First, the basic concepts of systematic curriculum design are discussed. These concepts set the stage for the presentation of selected systems and models which have relevance to a range of vocational-education offerings. A perspective on how models and systems can have an impact on the field is also presented. In order to be successful, systematic design efforts must stay relevant to the day-to-day operation of vocational programs and courses.

A Systems View of Curriculum Development

Systematic Curriculum Design

In a basic sense, much of what happens in education is tied to various systems. The school library, for example, employs a systematic process to account for books and related resource materials. Without such a system, the potential would exist for great losses due to forgetful borrowers. The climate-control system in a school can affect temperature changes in various classrooms and laboratories. Schools are thus surrounded by systems that contribute in many ways to education's success. It may be beneficial at this juncture to take a closer look at systems concepts as well as the way these concepts apply to systematic curriculum design.

If we accept the systems concept as a potentially useful framework for curriculum development efforts, it is important first to understand what comprises a system. Likewise, the notion of educational systems must be explored. It may also be helpful to distinguish between curriculum and instructional systems. And finally, the basic characteristics of curriculum models should be explored.

Systems Fundamentals

An everyday explanation of a system might be "an organized way of doing something." This definition, although adequate for simple activities, does not convey some basic precepts of a true system. To communicate this scope, we must define a system as *a collection of elements, interacting with each other to achieve a common goal.* Since there is great concern about dynamic as well as static systems, one should note that interactions within a system may cause change over time. Such changes make a system more dynamic.

In order to illustrate basic systems concepts, it may be useful to examine the previously mentioned school heating system. As noted in Figure 2–1, a thermostat detects a difference between the actual temperature and the desired temperature. It signals the controls to operate a furnace. Once actual and desired temperatures are equal, the thermostat once again signals the controls, this time to turn off the furnace. In reality, most systems are not this simple. Changes may occur outside a system which affect that system. If a door near the thermostat is inad-

FIGURE 2–1. *School heating system*

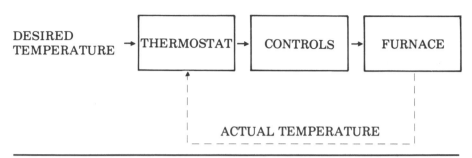

vertently left open and cold air enters the building at that spot, the furnace will operate even though other parts of the building may be at the proper temperature. Changes occurring outside the system occur in what may be called the *system environment*. Thus, it is important when designing systems to determine where the boundary exists between a system and its environment.

Educational Systems

Applying these basic notions to education may lead to the system provided in Figure 2–2. Students entering the program represent *input* to a means of *process* (a vocational program). *Output* from this process is in the form of program graduates. Assessment of program graduates (e.g., contributions to society, job satisfaction, competence attained) serves as *feedback* for system adjustment. For example, a lack of graduate competence in certain areas may necessitate the adjustment of learning

FIGURE 2–2. *Vocational program system*

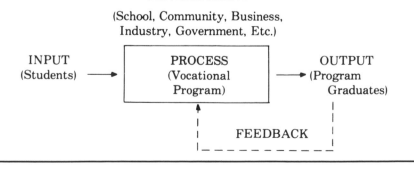

experiences or revisions to the competencies themselves. It is important to keep in mind that input, output, and feedback can have a major impact on a particular educational system. Likewise, the *environment* within which an educational system operates must be taken into account. School, community, business, industry, and government are among many factors external to a vocational program that can influence input, system operation, and output. Figure 2–3 contains a brief glossary of systems-related terms.

The systems approach to education deals with a variety of areas. Examples would be planning systems, instructional systems, implementation systems, curriculum systems, and evaluation systems. However, regardless of the system, basic systems concepts should prevail. To further illustrate how systems concepts are applied to vocational education it may be beneficial to examine a system for implementing competency-based education (CBE). Input to the system would consist of a program that is not currently competency-based. Each of the system components is designed to facilitate implementation; components build upon one another with the earlier components serving as a basis for later work. System output would be an implemented competency-based education program. Feedback obtained via various evaluation processes would be utilized to refine the system components. The system environment can have a major impact on CBE implementation. Potential deterrents to implementation must, therefore, be identified and dealt with. It is particularly important to account for factors at the local level that may work against educational change. Otherwise, the system environment may adversely affect the system itself.

Curriculum and Instructional Systems

Systems concepts apply most readily to curricular and instructional efforts. Systematic approaches to curriculum and instructional design can improve quality and, at the same time, provide a means of correcting

---

FIGURE 2–3. *A brief glossary of systems terms*

Environment. Context within which the system operates. May place constraints on system operation.

Feedback. Serves as a means of providing results of system output back into the system so it can be compared with desired output.

Input. That which enters the system from the environment.

Output. Product of the system that is returned to the environment.

Process. Subprocesses in the system that act on input and transfer it to output.

deficiencies in an organized manner. But how does one differentiate between curriculum and instructional systems? This question may be asked for several reasons—perhaps a need exists to develop a curriculum that has many implications for instruction, or a developer wants to be sure that curriculum functions are not emphasized in an instructional system. Regardless of the need, this is an extremely difficult question to answer. As discussed in Chapter 1, it may be noted that curriculum development and instructional development are distinctive in nature, yet share some common elements. The exact scope of their commonality is, at best, a gray area; elements may vary from one setting and situation to another.

As a starting point, it may be useful to examine some of the possible differences between curriculum and instructional systems. In terms of focus, the curriculum system largely emphasizes what is to be taught. The instructional system, on the other hand, places greater emphasis on how teaching and learning take place. Input for the curriculum system can range from philosophies, perceptions, and values held by curriculum participants to institution and community contexts, whereas input to the instructional system tends to have a more specific focus: a developed curriculum. Moving to the process aspect of systems, the curriculum system focuses primarily on planning for, selecting, and sequencing content. In the instructional system, emphasis during process is placed on instructional resource selection and development, instructional planning, instruction, and the evaluation of student progress. Output from the curriculum system is the developed curriculum, whereas the instructional system's output is student learning. Differences also exist between the two systems in terms of feedback. Feedback is used in the curriculum system for curriculum improvement and in the instructional system to enhance student learning.

Clearly, both systems are useful and some would say that one cannot function without the other. There are those who would argue that certain elements should be in a curriculum system rather than in an instructional system and vice versa. However, it must be recognized that the lack of absolute distinction between curriculum and instruction forces curriculum developers to make distinctions based upon professional judgment and the particular educational setting. Thus, there may be many creative and useful systems that cut across curricular and instructional domains.

Models

Curriculum and instructional developers may choose to communicate via models. A model may be defined as *a simplified yet communicable representation of a real-world setting or situation*. Of basic concern is how well the model communicates what is happening in the real world; if a model can convey realistically what is going on, it is said to be useful. Models communicate in several ways: systematically, procedurally, and conceptually. Thus, some models represent reality via systems whereas others communicate in a linear fashion or via an arrangement of concepts. It should be noted that some models may also be systems, and some systems may be models. In order to differentiate, one must keep in mind the previously mentioned definitions of a model and a system. A model that does not meet the standards set forth in this definition does not qualify as a system. Of course, the literature is replete with models that are called systems and vice versa. This discussion merely serves to heighten the curriculum developer's awareness of such conditions and, hopefully, clarify what a model is and is not.

Selected Designs

Moving beyond the basics of systems and models, it may be useful to examine some applications of systematic design to vocational and technical education. Unfortunately, fewer designs have been produced in this area than would be hoped. Although sound concepts are being used to develop most vocational curriculum and instructional programs, few developers have chosen to approach these tasks using systems concepts. There is, however, a trend in this direction, and it is predicted that future developmental efforts will utilize systems concepts to a much greater extent.

Designs chosen for inclusion in this chapter reflect the range of possibilities available to a developer. Each of the designs represents a somewhat different perspective. One can involve a cadre of professionals, whereas another may be more applicable to the individual developer/ teacher. One design may be most effective in a business or industrial training setting, whereas another utilizes computer interfacing to tie systems concepts to teaching and learning.

Training Technology System

First developed in 1978 by Richard Swanson and further refined in recent years, the Training Technology System (TTS) has as its purpose providing "an orderly means of separating training from non-training problems in industry and business" (Swanson, 1987). The TTS is based on theory and concepts prevalent in the fields of economics, psychology, management, and education. The economic/management foundation is tied to a premise that training can increase profits, whereas the psychological/ education foundation is based on the assumption that learning can be managed both efficiently and effectively.

The TTS has five major components or phases: analyze, design, develop, implement, and control, as shown in Figure 2–4. During the *analyze*

FIGURE 2–4. Training technology system

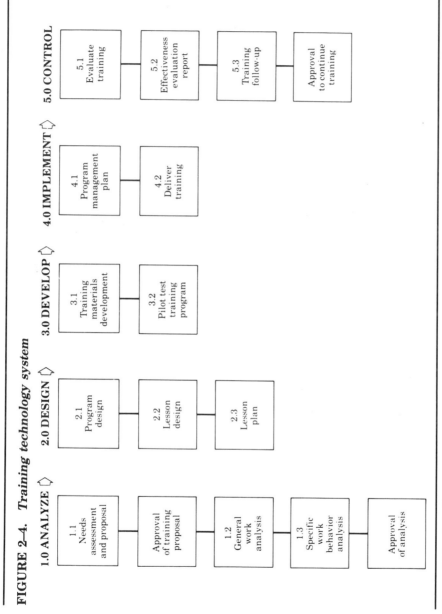

Source: Richard A. Swanson, "Training Technology System: A Method for Identifying and Solving Training Problems in Industry and Business," *Journal of Industrial Teacher Education* 24, No. 4 (Summer 1987). Reproduced with permission.

phase, an organization's training and nontraining problems are separated. Using needs assessment strategies, organizational needs are identified, causes of needs are determined, solutions are studied, and plans are proposed. Consideration is given to three aspects of organizational needs: types of needs assessment, causes of performance, and data collection methods. Each of these three dimensions must be explored in relation to the others as organization needs are being determined. A second aspect of this phase, called *work behavior analysis,* considers what people need to know and be able to perform at work. General work behavior analysis includes employee job description and task inventory efforts, whereas specific work behavior analysis may be conducted using procedure analysis, process and troubleshooting analysis, and subject matter analysis. The analysis of work behavior assists in confirming the needs assessment results and serves as a behavioral base for the design, development, and evaluation of a sound training program.

During the *design* phase, both program and lesson design are considered. Program design is concerned with matching a particular training program with organizational needs and constraints. This is where the economic/management foundations of training are considered. Included in the program design is a breakdown of individual lessons that constitute a particular program. Lesson design, on the other hand, is more closely associated with the psychology/education aspect of training. The eight variables considered as the lesson design process takes place include training readiness, objectives, content structure, instructional sequence, date of delivery, repetition and practice, reinforcement and rewards, and knowledge of results. Each lesson is initially prepared as a lesson flow based on work behavior analysis and the above eight variables. Ultimately, the lesson is refined in terms of content and method until it can be used by training personnel.

The *development* phase builds directly on previous phases. Revisions are made to lesson design as development occurs. It is at this point that instructor and media-based materials are prepared in support of lesson plans. This phase also includes peer review and pilot testing of materials to ensure they are satisfactory. Any deficiencies noted may serve as a basis for revisions to materials, lesson design, and program design.

Moving into the *implement* phase means it is time to deal with the management and delivery of training. A training management plan is prepared that includes course schedules, promotion, and management. Specific methods for organizing tasks necessary to implement a training program (e.g., media indexing methods and training materials storage) are utilized. Delivery of training includes the specification of thirty-one training methods, each of which may be used by instructors when appropriate to the particular audience, content, and setting. These methods aid the instructor in bridging the gap between what was identified in the analyze phase as the discrepancy between what people know and can perform and what they should know and be able to perform (Swanson, 1987).

The *control* phase focuses on three areas: evaluating and reporting training effectiveness, revising training, and maintaining trainees' proficiency once they are back on the job. This phase serves to "close the loop" between the other four phases by making provision for necessary adjustments and improvements in the training process. Four questions are asked of each training program with regard to its effectiveness.

1. Was the training delivered professionally?
2. Were the training objectives met?
3. Was the original training need met?
4. Was the training valuable? (Swanson, 1987)

Effectiveness evaluation also includes providing management personnel with training program results. This information is invaluable since it can serve as input for management decisions regarding further training and training program revision.

Although the TTS has been specifically designed for industry and business use, certain of its concepts have much application to public vocational and technical education programs. For example, public educators tend not to give sufficient thought to the economics of providing vocational programs. Applying the notion that training can increase profits to public education means that we should expect a reasonable return on our investments in vocational education programming. Although the exact definition of "reasonable return" may be somewhat more elusive than in business and industry, it is certainly of no less importance.

Front-End Analysis

Originally coined by Joe Harless, *front-end analysis* has become a key phrase in management and training technology circles. Simply stated, front-end analysis is a systematic means of seeking solutions to human performance problems while keeping in mind the problem's definition and characteristics as well as alternate courses of action. What is intriguing about front-end analysis lies in the precept that a performance problem may just as easily be caused by lack of motivation, poor environment, or lack of training.

In Figure 2–5, front-end analysis is represented by two models: a diagnostic model and a planning model. The diagnostic model focuses on describing and analyzing deficiencies for existing tasks, whereas the planning model focuses on preventing or avoiding problems in the future when new tasks are done by the individual. It may be noted that the

FIGURE 2–5. *Two models for front-end analysis*

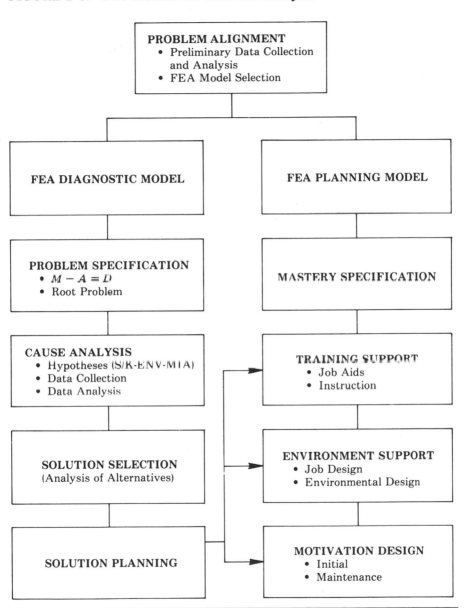

Source: From the J. H. Harless, *Performance Problem Solving Workshop* (Newnan, Ga.: Harless Performance Guild, 1977). Used with permission.

diagnostic model feeds into the planning model once diagnosis is complete. In either case, front-end analysis is initiated with a determination of problem alignment in order to select the appropriate model. If preliminary data analyses indicate that a general problem currently exists, the diagnostic model is appropriate. The future implementation of a new policy, service, program, or product would call for use of the planning model (Harless, 1979).

Diagnostic Model. The diagnostic model begins with problem specification. It is here that mastery (M) of tasks is clearly defined. Next, actual (A) performance is specified. When the two are compared, a deviation (D) will most likely appear. This is considered to be the root problem. Next, the various problem causes are hypothesized. Causes may be one or more of three types:

1. Lack of worker skills/knowledge (S/K)
2. Environmental deficiency (ENV)
3. Motivational-incentive deficiency (MIA)

Evidence is gathered for and against each of the hypotheses and the cause or combination of causes are described. Solution selection involves an analysis of each possible solution in terms of its cost effectiveness, feasibility, and so forth. Finally, solution planning occurs, which is the final aspect of the planning model.

Planning Model. As with the diagnostic model, the planning model begins with specifying mastery. Desired performance is detailed for the new program, policy, product, or service so there will be no question as to what is expected of workers. It is next appropriate to determine what training support is required. This includes the possibility of using instruction and/or job aids to enable individuals to reach mastery. Environmental support may, likewise, be needed. The job itself might be designed to ensure that desired performance will occur, or the environment might be reconfigured to achieve this end. Finally, a determination is made of needed motivational support, including plans for initial worker motivation as well as plans for maintaining that motivation at a sufficiently high level to ensure that desired performance is maintained.

Hopefully, this brief introduction to front-end analysis has provided an awareness of how systematic design can assist in the identification of alternative ways to achieve success in the work world. Too often, educators and trainers feel that instruction will solve a multitude of problems. In actuality, many of these problems or potential problems are tied to other factors: environment and motivation. The front-end analysis model enables us to move beyond the trainer/educator role and into the role of human resource developer.

Curriculum Pedagogy Assessment Model

Created by Daniel Vogler, a curriculum development authority, the Curriculum Pedagogy Assessment (CPA) Model embraces a number of futuristic concepts such as expert systems, artificial intelligence, and computer-based development processes. This comprehensive approach to curriculum development is built on eight basic concepts.

1. The knowledge, skills and affect required to exit a course are communicated in advance.
2. Course content drives the model. As a result, what is learned and what is taught are systematically identified.
3. The faculty member who delivers and evaluates the instruction is centrally involved in planning the instruction, thus maximizing the opportunities for successful curriculum implementation.
4. The student is the target for content planning, delivery, and evaluation of instruction.
5. Each content goal is analyzed by the instructor for domain, level, frequency, difficulty, purpose, and preferred sequence. This analysis creates a check-and-balance system to determine what, why, where, and when content is included or excluded from a course.
6. Content action verbs are carefully selected and manipulated to ensure that planning, delivery, and evaluation of instruction is aligned. As a result, what is planned is taught and what is taught is evaluated.
7. Each content goal requires approximately three hours of learning time invested by the student. This results in creation of (a) a direct match between content goals and performance objectives, (b) a direct match between the content goals and the lecture, lab, or clinical topics, and (c) a situation that facilitates sharing of instructional materials and evaluation items.
8. Micro-decisions made about course content create macro-based data that can be used to describe and prescribe the instructional system. Because these data can be aggregated by program, institution, and state, instructors are able to share instructional planning data, instructional materials, and test items (Vogler, 1990, 23–24).

These eight concepts are incorporated into the CPA Model presented in Figure 2–6. Planning, delivery, and evaluation aspects of the model utilize artificial intelligence (AI) application software programs that are employed by the instructor to build high-quality courses (PEAKSolutions, 1989A, 1989B, 1990). Additionally, a course information system is incorporated into the model so that information about each course may be aggregated by program, institution, and state with a purpose being to maximize benefits of investments in instructional development. The model and AI software have been used to create more than 15,000 differ-

FIGURE 2–6. *Curriculum Pedagogy Assessment (CPA) Model*

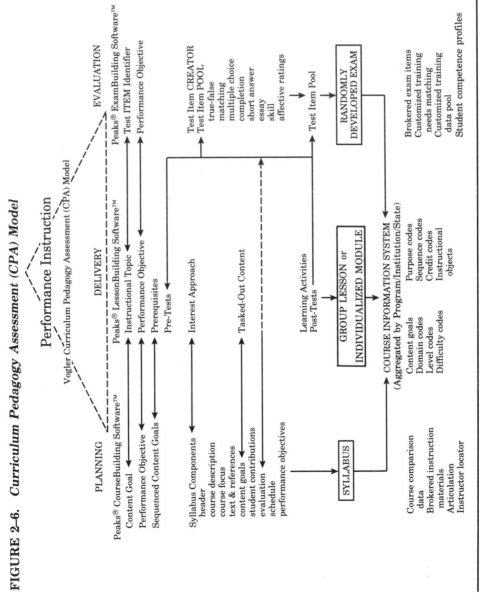

Source: Daniel E. Vogler. Used with permission.

ent courses that document in excess of 600,000 content goals and performance objectives. The software is especially sensitive to curriculum development needs of postsecondary vocational and technical education instructors.

Performance-Based Instructional Design System

The Performance-Based Instructional Design (PBID) System was created by David Pucel to provide a systematic means of developing instruction that would ensure the performance capability of learners. The PBID system can be utilized to develop instructional programs, courses, and individual instructional sequences (Pucel, 1989). The system includes seven major components: program description, content analysis, content selection, content sequencing, lesson structuring, lesson delivery formatting, and evaluation and feedback procedures development. Relationships among the seven components and how they form a system are shown in Figure 2–7. The system's output is an integrated plan of instruction, and each system component contributes to this output. Thus, the instructional developer must fully understand each system component and its relationships with other components in the system.

Instructional design begins with the preparation of a program description that includes program intent and context. This is followed by content analysis which focuses on the identification of specific content that might be used in the program. Content selection includes the determination of which content will actually be included in the program, whereas content sequencing involves arranging content in ways that will be most useful to learners. Lessons are then structured to facilitate the learning process and are formatted in ways they can be best utilized to deliver instruction (e.g., traditional, programmed, computer-assisted). And finally, the preparation of evaluation and feedback procedures ensure that learners are informed of their progress and that learning actually takes place (Pucel, 1989). Collectively, these components of the PBID System provide a meaningful framework for designing quality vocational and technical instruction.

Summary

This chapter has presented a brief overview of contemporary designs for curriculum development. The benefits of educational systems and models are quite obvious. These designs can show the relationships among education's various components and enable educators to provide high-quality vocational programs in an efficient manner.

FIGURE 2-7. *Performance-Based Instructional Design (PBID) System*

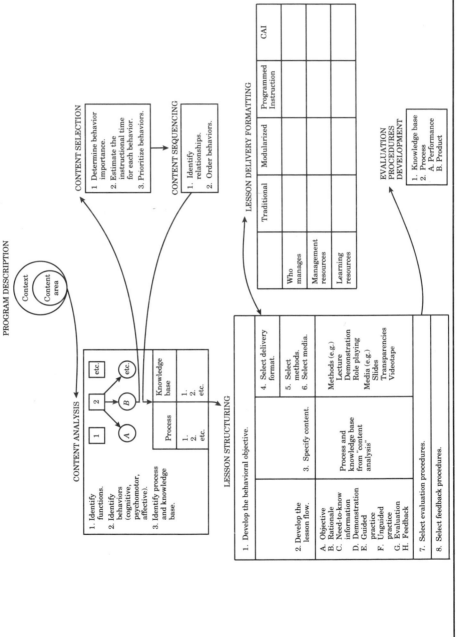

Source: David J. Pucel. *Performance-Based Instructional Design.* New York: McGraw-Hill (1989). Used with permission.

A basic educational system is comprised of input, process, output, feedback, and consideration for the system's environment. These elements are essential to efficient system operation. Whether the focus is on planning, instruction, implementation, curriculum, or evaluation, basic systems concepts should prevail. Although a distinction may be made between curriculum and instructional systems, this distinction is not always clear. The developer is thus obliged to keep each type in perspective and recognize that systems may cut across curricular and instructional domains.

The designs presented reflect the range of possibilities available to developers. The Training Technology System focuses on solving training problems in business and industry. This system consists of five components, each of which includes a distinctive business and industry focus.

Front-end analysis is so named because it emphasizes what is done before solutions are formulated for human performance problems. It acknowledges that a performance problem may just as easily be caused by a lack of motivation, poor environment, or lack of training. Front-end analysis is represented by two models: a diagnostic model and a planning model.

The Curriculum Pedagogy Assessment (CPA) Model is built on eight concepts, each of which focuses the developer on producing high-quality curricula. A highlight of the CPA Model is the availability of course-building, lesson-building, and exam-building computer software that utilize artificial intelligence principles. The software can assist instructors in creating curricula that will better meet students' needs and document curriculum information for use at the course, program, and institution level.

The Performance-Based Instructional Design (PBID) System includes seven components, each of which contributes to the development of meaningful instruction. One component's output becomes the input for the next component; thus, a cumulative benefit is derived that takes the form of improved learner capability.

Although some curriculum developers may not relish the thought of creating designs similar to those presented in this chapter, the extra effort involved should reap many rewards. Systems and models provide a means of better conceptualizing what will be taught, how it will be taught, and whether or not it will be successful. Additionally, contemporary designs can assist in keeping track of numerous curriculum and instructional components. These are but a few of the many benefits to be gained by utilizing systems and models.

Related References

Finch, Curtis R. "Instructional Systems Development in the Military." *Journal of Industrial Teacher Education* 24, no. 4 (Summer 1987): 18–26.

Hannum, Wallace H., and Briggs, Leslie J. "How Does Instructional Systems Design Differ from Traditional Instruction?" *Educational Technology* 22, no. 1 (January 1982): 9–14.

Harless, J. H. *Dialogue: Preview of Performance Problem Solving*. Newnan, Ga.: Harless Performance Guild, 1979.

——. *Guide to Front-End Analysis*. Newnan, Ga.: Harless Performance Guild, 1979.

Logan, Robert S. *Instructional Systems Development: An International View of Theory and Practice*. New York: Academic Press, 1982.

PEAKSolutions in collaboration with Daniel E. Vogler. *PEAKS Coursebuilding Software*. Minneapolis: PEAKSolutions, Inc., 1989A.

PEAKSolutions in collaboration with Daniel E. Vogler. *PEAKS Lesson Building Software*. Minneapolis: PEAKSolutions, Inc., 1989B.

PEAKSolutions in collaboration with Daniel E. Vogler. *PEAKS Exam Building Software*. Minneapolis: PEAKSolutions, Inc., 1990.

Pointer, R. "Minnesota's Quiet Revolution." *Vocational Education Journal* (March, 1989): 42–44.

Pucel, David E. *Performance-Based Instructional Design*. New York: McGraw-Hill, 1989.

Romiszowski, A. J. *Designing Instructional Systems*. New York: Nichols, 1981.

Swanson, Richard A. "Training Technology System: A Method for Identifying and Solving Training Problems in Industry and Business." *Journal of Industrial Teacher Education* 24, no. 4 (Summer 1987).

Vogler, Daniel E. "Evolution of an Expert System for Performance Instruction." *Journal of Interactive Instructional Development* (Spring, 1990): 21–25.

SECTION II

PLANNING THE CURRICULUM

Schools must assume the responsibility to develop, plan, and implement curricula that meet the needs of both students and society. Thus, the vocational and technical education curriculum development process must reflect the best thinking of educators and be carried out in a systematic and orderly fashion.

Section II concerns itself with beginning stages in the development of a curriculum or the revision of an existing curriculum. Topics in this section have application to vocational and technical education curriculum planning at any educational level. The three chapters in this section aid the curriculum developer in making decisions regarding whether or not a particular curriculum should be offered or continued.

Before any curriculum may be offered, a decision must be made to implement the curriculum, and there are many factors to be considered before that decision can be made. Chapter 3 treats the decision-making process in education and serves to introduce the curriculum developer to this process. Emphasis has been placed on sound decision making and how curriculum developers may work with others to achieve this end. The formulation of sound decision-making strategies as well as the development of standards for decision making and the identification of needed data provide curriculum developers with a basis for sound curriculum planning.

Chapters 4 and 5 focus on the kinds of data that are needed if one is to make sound decisions in the curriculum development process. Chapter 4 deals entirely with data related to the school. Data associated with the current status of vocational offerings, students' interests, parent input, followup of former students, future enrollments, and facilities are examples of information vital to sound curriculum decisions. Data related to the community are discussed in Chapter 5. These include sources of employment, labor supply and demand, and the identification of various resources.

It is recommended that all three chapters be read and application of planning information be made to the curriculum developer's local situation before decisions are made about vocational curriculum development. Meaningful vocational and technical education curricula will materialize only if the curriculum developer follows a systematic decision-making process based on accurate information about the school and the community.

3

Making Decisions in Planning the Curriculum

Introduction

The entire curriculum development process is interlaced with decision-making situations. Questions such as, "Should we take this approach or that approach?" "Should we offer Program A or Program B?" and "Which objectives reflect the goals of our program?" are typical of practical problems faced by the curriculum developer. At first glance, these problems appear to be relatively simple ones to solve. However, an examination of the decision-making process actually needed to find their solutions will readily show that few curriculum development problems can be properly attacked unless those involved are willing to make major time and resource commitments to this end, implying that strategic planning must precede any curriculum development efforts.

Curriculum development is an extremely complex and intricate process involving many decision situations. Decisions must be made about policy statements, procedures for setting priorities, educational program and course selections, standards, and many other aspects of the total curriculum. Although decisions are made at different levels in an educational system, decision making influences the total curriculum regardless of the level at which a decision is made. Thus, a strategic planning process should be applied to provide the necessary organizational framework needed for decisions that must be made affecting all segments of the educational institution.

This chapter deals directly with decision making as an integral part of curriculum planning. Special emphasis is placed on strategic planning, decision making, the value of systematic decision making, decision maker attributes, the establishment of standards for making decisions, and the types of data needed to make sound curriculum decisions.

Strategic Planning in Education

A planning concept recently adopted by educators is called strategic planning. Business and industry have been using this process since the 1960s, and schools have been implementing strategic planning with different degrees of success. Basically, strategic planning is a rational process or series of steps that move an educational organization through

1. understanding the external forces or changes relevant to it;
2. assessing its organizational capacity;
3. developing a vision (mission) of its preferred future as well as a strategic direction to follow to achieve that mission;
4. developing goals and plans that will move it from where it is to where it wants to be;
5. implementing the plans it has developed; and
6. reviewing progress, solving problems, and renewing plans. (McCune, 1986)

Strategic planning is somewhat different from long-range planning. Both planning processes involve looking at the future, but the underlying nature in which these processes are applied is different. Long-range planning has traditionally accepted the position that the organization will remain relatively stable and thus forms the mission, goals, and application of the mission and goals to the organization based on this stable premise. Strategic planning approaches the planning process by carefully examining the external environment that will influence the organization and, based on that information, develops guiding statements that will serve to guide the organization in the future. Strategic planning involves questioning the status quo, raising issues or questions relating to the purpose of the organization, and identifying new initiatives or thrusts that should be considered. In this sense, strategic planning is

a management process for changing and transforming organizations,
a management philosophy,

a way of thinking about and solving problems,

an educational experience and staff development activity,

an organizational development experience, and

a community education and involvement process. (McCune, 1986)

Although many schools have been incorporating some aspects of strategic planning into their traditional decision-making efforts, future decision makers and curriculum developers must become more systematic and future-oriented as they make crucial decisions relating to curricular programs and content in a rapidly changing technological society.

Site-Based Management

Another recent concept and practice in education that many times is discussed at the same time as strategic planning is called *site-based* or *school-based management*. This management concept is grounded on the premise that those who work in a local school system are the ones who can best provide the input to sound decision making and thus should be involved in the management role in that school system. Site-based management allows those individuals (principals and teachers) the opportunity to use their skills, abilities, and years of experience to arrive at the best solutions to curricular problems. For site-based management to be successful, the following key stages or concepts must be part of the overall process:

Involvement of stakeholders

Conduction of environmental scans

Identification of factors related to a program's success and failure

Development of vision and mission statements

Identification of current and future resources/restraints

Development of realistic goals and objectives

Formulation of plans of action

Monitor and follow up of activities

One of the important elements in an effective site-based management program is the principal. This individual is the key to the leadership needed to plan and implement a truly successful site-based management program.

Decision Making in Education

Any discussion about decision making cannot take place unless several basic factors are presented. First, consideration must be given to the distinction and relationship between decisions that must be made during the strategic planning process, decisions to be made during the program planning process, and, last, decisions related to the program delivery planning process. The interrelationships and impact that each of these decision-making points can have in the curriculum development process are shown in Figure 3–1.

Strategic Planning and Policy Decision Makers

Referring to Figure 3–1, policy decisions revolve around problem situations concerning the strategic plan, mission statement, goals, and decision points for achieving these goals. The final decision made in problem situations involving policy formulation rests with citizens or their representatives. Professional educators in this country cannot legally make policy due to the democratic nature of our society and of our school structure.

Policy decisions must rest with boards of education, boards of trustees, or other officially designated groups who represent the people.

FIGURE 3–1. *Levels of Planning in School Districts*

Type of Planning	Responsibility	Outcome	Questions to Answer
STRATEGIC PLANNING (Where are we going?)	Board and superintendent (with input from all groups)	Strategic plan, mission statement, goals, decision points	Are we going in the right direction? (relevance)
PROGRAM PLANNING (How do we get there?)	Central staff, principals (with input from teachers and staff)	Curriculum plan, personnel development plan, facilities plan, budget	Are we doing the right things to achieve our mission? (effectiveness)
PROGRAM DELIVERY PLANS (What do we do to get there?)	Teachers, counselors, staff (with input from parents, students, and the community)	Lesson plans, work plans	Are we doing things right? (efficiency)

Source: McCune, Shirley D. *Guide to Strategic Planning for Educators.* Alexandria, Va.: Association for Supervision and Curriculum Development, 1986, p. 36. Used with permission.

Members of these groups are spokespeople for the public and work toward the goal of providing the best possible educational program for their community. Although official policy decisions are made by these boards or others, the role that educators can and should assume during the process of decision making should not be underestimated or avoided. Membership on these boards may be comprised of individuals who are not accustomed or prepared for the full responsibility of decision making in education. This implies that professional educators must be involved in policy decision making by assisting these groups in the consideration of alternatives to problems, the impact of various alternatives, and assembling data needed for decisions, as well as a number of other vital activities. Although boards of education and similar groups are official policy-making bodies, input from others is needed and should be secured from professional educators (administrators and teachers), parents, students, voters, civic leaders, and business and industrial leaders.

Program Planning and Operational
Decision Makers

Decisions made at the operational level are the responsibility of administrators and/or teachers located throughout the educational organization. Once policy formation has occurred, then the policy must be applied in a professional manner to the educational organization. Policy-making groups depend on professional educators to take the lead in this task, and in fact, this is why professional educators are hired. Any operational decisions that need to be made must be handled by educators within the school organization. As with policy decision makers, operational decision makers may, in some instances, need input from parents, students, voters, civic leaders, business and industrial leaders, and policy-making groups when arriving at solutions to problems.

Program Delivery and Operational
Decision Making

Decisions at this level become very closely aligned with the application of content in everyday instructional settings. For the most part, individuals making the decisions at this level are the teachers who can personalize their plans, actions, and evaluations to the situations at hand.

Regardless of the level at which a decision is made, the results will affect all other segments of education and ultimately the curriculum. Policy decisions at the strategic planning level will affect future operational decisions at the program planning and program delivery planning levels. Operational decisions at the program planning and program delivery levels will support, define, modify, revise, or identify possible changes needed in policy statements as reflected in the current mission statement or overall goals of the educational institution.

Preparing to Make Decisions

Sound decisions are not made quickly, but require in-depth study by those persons involved. Before arriving at a decision-making stage, the problem to be solved must be stated in clear and concise terms. This is no easy task and one that may determine the degree to which a viable solution is found. Once the problem has been clearly stated and agreed upon by all parties involved, a plan of action or procedure should be outlined to serve as a guide for arriving at possible alternatives and ultimately the final decision. This procedure applies equally well to policy decisions or operational decisions.

In a later section of this chapter, possible models to follow in decision-making situations are presented and discussed in detail. In addition, later discussion will be devoted to the establishment of standards and collection of data needed for making decisions.

Irreversible Decisions

The decision-making process in curriculum development must not overlook the magnitude of each decision made. In fact, many decisions made today will affect the educational program tomorrow, next year, and even further into the future. Thus, each decision made must be considered in relation to its future impact on the curriculum. Few decisions are truly irreversible, but nevertheless some decisions may be easier to reverse or change than others.

The extent to which policy and operational decisions can be reversed depends upon the degree to which they have been implemented. For example, decisions can be reversed before money has been spent on equipment or buildings. However, after money or resources have been committed, or buildings constructed, decisions become more difficult to reverse. Money spent on equipment, supplies, or other parts of the curriculum is almost impossible to recover and certainly its recovery is beyond reason once goods or products have been delivered. This same situation may exist with buildings that are constructed. Reversible decisions regarding the use of buildings depend upon the flexibility that was included in the design of the facility. Laboratories and classrooms constructed with built-in features lower the probability of that space being easily redesigned in the future for other vocational and technical education programs.

Decision makers and curriculum planners must realize that the decision to construct and equip a twenty-million-dollar facility has a long-term effect. This type of decision will influence the curriculum for years to come and may come back to haunt school personnel if it is not made properly. Until technology advances to the point where buildings can be designed and built that will permit total freedom and flexibility for change, the magnitude and irreversibility of policy decisions will be a prime consideration. Furthermore, even operational decisions have a degree of irreversibility—especially decisions that tend to set precedents. For example, permission granted to one vocational department to take their students to a statewide youth organization convention will undoubtedly lead to similar requests from the other vocational departments.

Futuristic Decisions

Decisions made by curriculum planners are futuristic, with the true impact not being felt until the next year or even ten or twenty years from the time the decision is made. Making realistic and sound decisions today for the future is one of the most difficult dilemmas facing educational decision makers. Factors that are uncertain and unpredictable but which have a strong bearing upon curriculum development are many. Some of the more critical factors concern the economic situation of society, changes in technology that influence the nature of labor market needs, priorities of the local community, and other factors typically associated with curriculum development. Regardless of this dilemma, decision makers must think in futuristic terms. To do otherwise will only serve to stifle the growth and development of vocational and technical education.

Factors Affecting Decision Making

Decision making in education is quite different from decision making in a commercial organization. In commercial organizations, decisions are typically based upon economic returns of the different alternatives under consideration. In an educational organization, decisions must not only consider the economic aspects but must also take into consideration the philosophies possessed by those associated with the educational process. Unfortunately where philosophy is involved, there are no absolutes, only opinions based upon past experiences of each individual. Since each individual associated in one way or another with vocational education forms his or her own personal philosophy, this gives rise to differences of opinion—differences that must be resolved before meaningful educational decisions can be made.

Whose Philosophy Is Important?

Decision makers may well ask, "Whose philosophy is important to consider when decision-making situations arise?" The initial reaction to a question such as this would be to focus on those persons connected with an educational organization. Philosophies of students, parents, teachers, administrators, state and national educational agencies, and community members are certainly important. However, the philosophy least understood or considered by decision makers and yet the strongest factor affecting decisions is probably the philosophy held by the decision makers themselves. After all data have been carefully gathered and analyzed, conclusions drawn, and recommendations made, the decision maker ultimately faces the time when he or she must choose among alternatives. This responsibility cannot be delegated to anyone else. Thus, although all philosophies are important, the philosophy held by each decision maker must never be overlooked. If a decision maker gives no thought to the influence that his or her own philosophy is having, then decisions may unknowingly be made solely upon the feelings of the decision maker with little or no concern for others who will be affected by those decisions.

Personal Attributes of Decision Makers

All decision makers bring with them a set of personal attributes that influence the manner in which they approach thinking about decisions to be made and the ultimate decisions that they do make. Listed in Figure 3–2 are just a few of the attributes that each decision maker may possess. Each person's unique attributes will usually fall somewhere between the two extremes on the list. Curriculum planners must be aware of these attributes as related to decision makers, not with the intention of changing the decision maker's personality, but to be more effective in knowing how to collaborate with the decision maker individually or in a group setting.

FIGURE 3–2. *Personal Attributes of Decision Makers*

Leader	Follower
Prefers immediate action	Prefers reflection
Creative	Status quo
Emotional	Rational
Subjective	Objective
Idealist	Pragmatist

Influence of National and State Philosophy on the Local Level

As was discussed in Chapter 1, the influence of national and state philosophy on vocational education can be significant. It might be well to consider briefly the importance of such a force upon local educational programs and upon decision makers. The basic responsibility for education has been left up to the states, and the degree of latitude that local educational agencies have varies with each state. But it can be stated that each local community must be responsive to provide quality education for its youth and adults. Several observations are well worth making concerning relationships and influence between the federal and state level and the local level. On one hand, federal and state educational agencies can influence local decisions by developing statements reflecting national goals and program direction. In addition, incentives such as matching money, 100-percent reimbursement, national or state recognition, and other rewards can be offered to help speed up local adoption of ideas. On the other hand, creative programs that had their start in local programs have also served to keep national and state educational agencies from becoming stagnant and have provided fresh ideas for other states. The one point that must always be kept in mind is that as long as financial incentives are provided from either the national or state level, the philosophy held by the national or state agencies will have a significant role to play in decisions made at the local level concerning curriculum development.

In summary, a decision maker may be influenced by many internal and external forces. Several of these forces have been mentioned in the last few pages. In order to be effective, the curriculum planner must be aware of these forces and must plan to avoid situations where these forces become major blocks to effective decision making.

Decision-Making Strategies

Thus far, discussion has focused upon factors associated with the decision-making process. These factors may influence the identification of appropriate solutions to the problem. One aspect of the decision-making process not previously discussed deals with the various strategies used to expedite that process. Educators have several unique and well-accepted strategies from which to choose as they approach the business of decision making. Although each of the various strategies is useful in its own right, the creative decision maker should strive to develop and perfect a composite strategy that works for his or her educational organization. This strategy might include several of the various concepts to be described. Different decision-making strategies that may be considered include management by objectives (MBO), decision matrix, program evaluation and review technique (PERT), decision graph, and advocate team process.

Management by Objectives

The management by objectives (MBO) approach to decision making has been used by many educational organizations in recent years. Briefly, the MBO process in education may be described as the process where administrators and teachers jointly identify common goals of the organization and define each person's role in helping to fulfill those goals. Furthermore, those goals serve to measure the progress of each individual in accomplishing his or her responsibilities and the progress of the organization in fulfilling the goals.

At the heart of a MBO approach is the objective; thus, the objective must be carefully derived. A key element of the objective must be that percentages, ratios, numbers, averages, and other absolutes are specified so that all concerned know exactly what standard must be met. Once a decision has been made to use a particular standard, educators can then proceed to decide exactly what must be done to aid in meeting that standard. Five sequential steps are followed in developing an objective:

1. Finding the objective
2. Setting the objective
3. Validating the objective
4. Implementing the objective
5. Controlling and reporting status of the objective

Finding the Objective.   This initial phase in the MBO approach is critical, since later decisions rest upon the established objective. Individuals seeking out the objective must realize the immediate, short-, and long-range future of the organization. Trends, direction, scope, and other elements that may give rise to the current or future program must be taken into account.

Setting the Objective.   This phase serves to formulate and qualify the objective. For example, elements of the objective should point out time lines, should provide results to be achieved and not activities, should be written in positive terms, should be clear to others, and should incorporate facts (e.g., percentages, numbers, averages, and correlations).

Validating the Objective.   The need to establish each objective's worth and validity cannot be overlooked. Objectives must reflect the best efforts of those involved and should serve to describe current or future situations accurately.

Implementing the Objective.   Implementation of objectives is usually carried out by subordinates. This phase includes activities and events that permit each objective to be implemented within the organization. Congruent values of these objectives must be held by those in the organization.

Controlling and Reporting Status of the Objective.   Each objective must be controlled by indicating time, cost, quantity, and quality associated with that objective. If problems develop in achieving the objective, then corrective measures must be taken to avoid failure.

The real strength of the MBO process may be found within the organizational framework in the educational system. This approach delineates the roles and responsibilities of each member of the organization and what each member must do, by when, as activities of the organization are carried out in order to reach predetermined goals. Thus, if a goal of a vocational program within a school is to place 75 percent of all vocational graduates in jobs related to their educational experiences, decision makers must decide how this might be done. MBO also relates well to the establishment of standards. If a standard is set that at least twenty students must enroll in a particular class, then activities must be carried out to determine the actual number interested in enrolling and, finally, to ensure that a minimum of twenty actually show up the first day of class.

Decision Matrix

Ranking Option.   The decision matrix approach to decision making allows a group of individuals to reduce the alternatives available to a more manageable number for consideration and, hopefully, assist them in arriving at one single solution to a problem. This technique forces a group to discuss available alternatives or options and, at the end, each member must individually make a judgment on the value of each option. For example, assume a special task force of five individuals was considering the possibility of adding new programs to the curriculum. The group discussions thus far have highlighted that five new program options were feasible and that all five had merits worthy of consideration. However, the alternatives must be reduced to one or two, and the group must now arrive at some decision. The chairperson of the group asks each member of the task force individually to rank the alternatives from one to five, with one representing that individual's perception of the most worthy program. Figure 3–3 illustrates how the decision matrix works, and

FIGURE 3–3. *Decision Matrix (Ranking Options)*

Task Force Members	Ranking of Possible Programs				
	A	B	C	D	E
John Smith	3	5	4	1	2
Victor Hernandez	5	4	3	2	1
Sally Jones	4	3	5	2	1
Willie Ellis	3	4	5	1	2
John Camp	4	1	5	2	3
Ranking	19	17	22	8	9

through this process, the group narrows the alternatives to D or E. At this time the group could decide Alternative D is the best program to implement, or discussion could continue to consider further the merits of both D and E, then at a later time, the group could make its final decision.

Rating Options.   Another variation of using a decision matrix would be where a larger number of options, problems, issues, or situations are under discussion and the group wishes to end up with some indication of the merits of several ideas as perceived by members of the decision group. An example might be the situation where a group is identifying some problems (weaknesses) with the current educational program. Through a brainstorming session, twenty-five different problems were mentioned. Since these twenty-five problems came from five different individuals, the group discusses these problems to gain a better understanding of each, and they soon realize that some problems tend to be more serious than others.

The group then proceeds to reduce the list by half. This could be accomplished by requiring each individual (working alone) to make a decision as to which twelve problems are more critical. After all members have individually arrived at their twelve selections, the group leader takes the group's selections and the problem situations receiving the twelve highest number of votes will be discussed further. After ample time for discussion has occurred on the twelve problems, the group members are again asked individually (working alone) to reduce the number of problem statements by one half, identifying the most serious six problems that must be addressed.

This procedure will allow a group to arrive at a position where serious efforts can now be directed at improving an educational program through the correction of the six most important problem situations identified. However, one more step could be taken by the group to focus their efforts on the most serious problem. An alternative to the *ranking* contained in the decision matrix in Figure 3–3 would be a *rating* of the six problem situations as illustrated in Figure 3–4. In this exercise, each member of the group would be asked to *rate* the seriousness of the problems on a four-point scale, where one represents a very serious problem and four represents not a serious problem. Following this procedure, problem D surfaces as the problem perceived by the group as being the most serious.

In conclusion, the decision matrix technique is a process where a group can reach a consensus on a decision that must be made where various alternatives, solutions, problems, or situations exist. When handled properly, the technique forces group members to focus on the task at hand in a very efficient and effective manner while allowing each member's opinion to have impact on the final decision.

Program Evaluation and Review Technique

The program evaluation and review technique (PERT) focuses on identifying key events and activities leading to the accomplishment of a long-range goal or objective. The strength of this approach is that time lines, activities, and events can be illustrated graphically. Thus, the event and activity are depicted as follows:

Activity

Event   ⟶   Event

Events are either the start or end of a mental or physical task. Time is not consumed and the event cannot be accomplished until all activities

---

FIGURE 3–4. *Decision Matrix (Rating Options)*

| Task Force Members | Rating of Problem Situations* | | | | | |
	A	B	C	D	E	F
John Smith	3	4	1	2	2	3
Victor Hernandez	2	4	2	1	4	3
Sally Jones	4	3	1	1	2	4
Willie Ellis	2	2	4	2	3	1
Jim Camp	3	3	2	1	3	2
Mean Score	2.8	3.2	2.0	1.4	2.8	2.6

*Scale: 1—a very serious problem with the educational program
              2—a serious problem with the educational program
              3—a problem with the educational program
              4—not a serious problem with the educational program

leading to the event are completed. The *activity* describes the work required to accomplish an event. Time estimates for the events can be
hours, days, weeks, or whatever the planners choose, and time estimates
can be made for optimistic (earliest date possible), most likely, and
pessimistic forecasts (date likely for completion when unplanned problems arise). In addition, events are numbered sequentially so that they
may be easily identified. Figure 3–5 depicts a PERT chart that might
be used by decision makers in following a planned course of action to

---

FIGURE 3–5. *PERT network for feasibility study of vocational
program XYZ*

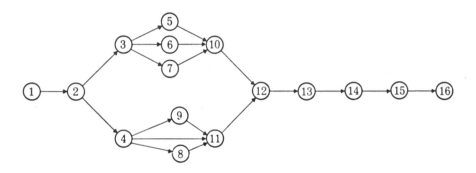

1.   Decision made to study
feasibility of establishing Program XYZ (1/5)

2.   Standards for Program
XYZ established (2/15)

3.   School-related data
identified (3/1)

4.   Community-related data
identified (3/1)

5.   Prospective enrollment
figures determined (5/1)

6.   Qualified instructors
available (5/1)

7.   Current facilities assessed (5/1)

8.   Current and future
budget support determined
(5/1)

9.   Current and projected
employment opportunities determined (6/1)

10.   School-related data analyzed (6/1)

11.   Community-related data
analyzed (6/1)

12.   Composite data analyzed
and final proposal prepared
(8/1)

13.   Report viewed by vocational education advisory
council (9/1)

14.   Proposal approved by vocational director and school
administration (10/1)

15.   Proposal presented to
school board (11/1)

16.   School board makes final
decision (12/1)

determine if a specific vocational program should be offered. Although this is a simplied version of a decision-making situation involving Program XYZ, the chart illustrates an overall plan of action and the dates when each event is to be accomplished. A supplemental activity assignment sheet might be developed to assign specific activities to certain individuals. The values of using a PERT strategy can be readily identified by reviewing Figure 3–5. First, key events can be identified for reaching a long-range goal. Second, these events can be placed sequentially on a continuum in the order in which the events must occur. Third, a time element can be assigned to each event to serve as a completion date for that event. Fourth, activities needed to complete each event are easier to describe once all events are identified. Fifth, the PERT chart permits an easy assessment of events completed to date and what still needs to be completed. Finally, the PERT strategy permits all who are involved in the decision-making process to be fully aware of the events, times, and the ultimate goal for which the activity is being conducted.

Decision Graph

The decision graph is another approach to help focus a group on problems that need attention. This process includes two steps. First, decision makers are asked to rate the importance of the problem on a ten-point scale, with 0 representing low importance and 10 as high importance. Second, they are asked to make a judgment as to the current level of activity the organization is directing toward that activity, with 0 indicating no activity and 10 as high activity. Figure 3–6 contains a form that can be used

FIGURE 3–6. Determining the Importance and Activity Level for Each Problem Identified

Problem	Smith I*	Smith A+	Hernandez I	Hernandez A	Jones I	Jones A	Ellis I	Ellis A	Camp I	Camp A
A	0	1	1	1	2	1	0	1	1	1
B	1	7	3	9	2	6	3	8	1	7
C	8	2	9	1	7	3	6	1	8	2
D	9	9	9	8	7	8	6	8	8	8
E	7	3	8	4	6	4	6	3	7	2

*Importance of the problem using a scale of 0–10, where 0 equals no importance and 10 equals high importance.
+Current activity directed at the problem using a scale of 0–10, where 0 equals no activity directed at the problem and 10 indicates a high level of activity.

for this purpose. Hypothetical values have been assigned for each of five problems.

After each group member has individually made a judgment for each of the five problems, the numerical values for the importance and level of activity directed at that problem can be transferred to the decision graph in Figure 3–7. This is done by finding the numbers that represent the values for the importance and activity on the correct axis and plotting the problem letter at the spot where the two lines intersect. After each person's viewpoint has been plotted and the intersecting points determined, the group can see which problems fall into which of the four quadrants: (I) Opportunity, (II) Appropriate High Level, (III) Appropriate Low Level, or (IV) Decision.

FIGURE 3–7. *Decision graph*

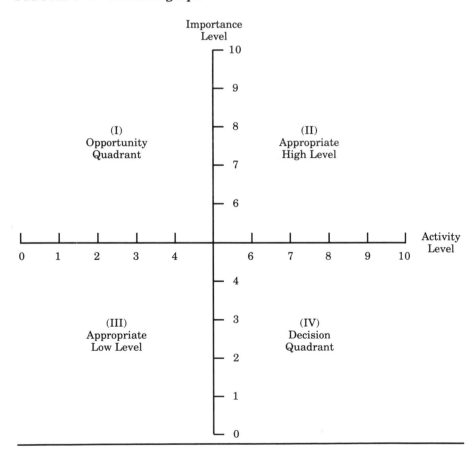

In the example given in Figure 3–8, where the input from the decision makers is taken from Figure 3–6, it can be seen that all group members viewed problem D as being important, and they also felt that a high degree of activity was currently being directed at that problem. Thus, this problem fell in quadrant II, Appropriate High Level. On the other hand, problems C and E both fell in quadrant I, Opportunity.

The value of the decision graph is that the group can visualize how different members view problem importance in relation to the level of activity currently being expended by the organization toward that problem. Furthermore, for any problem that falls in quadrant IV, as problem B did, the group could then ask if the resources currently being devoted to that problem represent the best decision and/or whether the resources should be redirected to problems C and/or E.

FIGURE 3–8. *Decision graph*

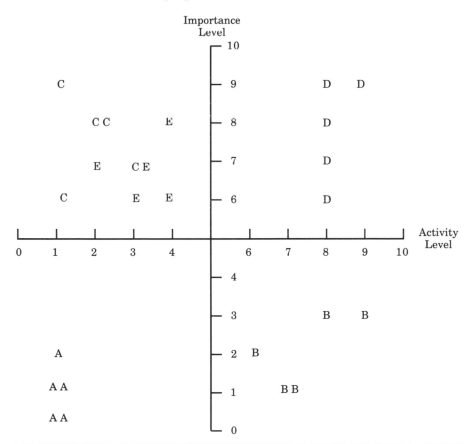

The Advocate Team Process

The basic procedure used for the advocate team process is that several teams of individuals work separately on the same problem to arrive at possible solutions or alternative suggestions. The recommendations from the individual teams are then used by decision makers in arriving at the one best solution to the problem at hand. The premise of this planning approach is that several teams working on the same problem will provide different approaches, solutions, or alternatives to a problem.

1. Identify the task for the teams, including objectives to be met.
2. Select at least two teams, composed of four to six members each. Individuals asked to serve should be knowledgeable on the subject, willing to express ideas, innovative, and able to work in a group setting.
3. Select a separate meeting location for each team and provide an adequate length of time for teams to discuss the topic thoroughly.
4. Prepare team members, through written materials and/or a joint orientation session, with appropriate background information that explains the task to the team, describes any constraints, details the format that the team's recommendations are to follow, and highlights how input from the teams will be utilized.
5. Hold separate team meetings, which first must include the selection of a chairperson for each team, then have the teams determine their own operating procedures, keeping in mind the deadline for completion of the team's final report.
6. Provide services to each team that will aid in effective and efficient work, e.g., technical writers, clerical staff, resource people, and copying equipment.

The final report submitted by each team could be presented in a meeting attended by all teams, or it could be submitted privately to the person or group requesting the information. The advocate team process has numerous applications in curriculum development in vocational and technical education or when a decision-making situation is at hand. Examples of uses for this planning technique are setting the goals of an organization, identifying strategies for reaching those goals, establishing new programs, developing components of a comprehensive plan, developing alternative education or training programs, or other situations where more than one alternative exists to a problem.

Summary of Approaches for Decision Making

In the last few pages, several approaches for decision making have been discussed. To bring this section of the chapter to a close, several general observations need to be made. First, regardless of the decision-making process used by an organization, all individuals must fully understand how the decisions are made and the proper procedures to follow when input is desired. An organization will never establish a procedure in which all individuals involved agree on the process, but if all understand the process, at least open lines of communications can be maintained. Second, once a procedure for making decisions has been agreed on, then the process of arriving at any future decisions must adhere to the established written guidelines. Deviation from established policy for decision making will result in a disruptive system and the development of distrust in others who must work with the organization. Third, educational administrators who work directly with the decision-making body must have realistic information and facts about their programs. Subordinates to administrators, teachers, and others who withhold information and present inaccurate pictures will not provide valid data to the decision makers on which to base their decisions. Fourth, all decision-making procedures must provide a system that assures multiple avenues for information to be fed into the decision-making environment. The use of advisory groups, consultants, and a proper atmosphere for individuals to volunteer information will assist in helping the decision-making process flow smoothly. Fifth, not discussed in this chapter but still a vital part of the decision-making process, there must be a followup of all decisions made. This would include the consequences observed, how the decision-making process could be improved, and the resulting effect decisions are having on program improvement. Sixth, all decision-making procedures must incorporate within their written policies the roles and responsibilities of all those involved either directly or indirectly with the process. Only in this way will individuals know what is expected of them and what they can expect of others. Finally, no approach is going to be perfect or will provide decision makers with direct answers to a problem under consideration. *Decision making ultimately focuses on human judgment, based on what is thought to be possible, desirable, and—once the decision is made—probable.*

Establishing Standards for Decision Making

The need for establishing standards before making decisions cannot be overemphasized. Yet, without a doubt, the establishment of standards before making decisions is usually avoided by curriculum planners and decision makers. For example, if a person were considering the purchase of an automobile, there would be certain minimum standards that automobile should meet before the person seriously considered making a purchase. These standards might be mileage of thirty miles per gallon, satisfactory handling qualities, adequate leg and head room, large enough capacity to transport five children, and so forth. The customer would consider these standards and collect the data that could assist him or her in determining which make of automobile would best serve the established purposes. If a particular car did not meet any of these standards, the customer would then eliminate that make of automobile or reconsider the standard in light of the importance of that standard to the overall satisfaction or degree of dissatisfaction if that automobile was purchased. Establishing standards would then assist this individual in making a sound personal investment in an automobile.

A similar case could be made with regard to standards for educational programs. If standards are not established before program decisions are made, programs might exist where unqualified teachers would be teaching, thirty students might be working in laboratories designed for twenty, programs might be developed and implemented on the personal bias of decision makers, or eventually quality programs in vocational education would not exist.

Who Establishes Standards?

The determination of the ultimate standards to be used in deciding whether or not a program or curriculum is developed rests with the decision-making body. This body might be a school board, board of trustees, or similarly designated group. However, the underlying force that has a major impact on the type of standards recommended to this body consists of teachers or representatives of business or industry related to the occupational area under consideration. In most cases, the decision-making body will not have the expertise needed within a specific vocational area to make decisions concerning that area. Thus, the group will rely heavily on school administrators or others to provide standards for them to use in arriving at decisions.

How Are Standards Established?

Standards should be established by those who are best able to develop criteria for quality vocational programs. Individuals who might assume a key role in the establishment of standards include vocational teachers, students, employers, employees in occupations associated with the vocational area under discussion, vocational directors and supervisors, and curriculum planners. In some cases, certain standards could be developed nationally and applied to all state and local programs. Additionally, certain standards might need to be established by state educational agencies, with local agencies needing to use these state standards in developing standards relevant to their locality.

When Are Standards Established?

Once a problem or opportunity has been identified and the decision-making body defines it and agrees to focus on this area, standards must then be established to guide the decision-making process further. Data needed by decision makers to help provide a basis on which to arrive at decisions cannot be collected until the data collectors know what is needed for the decision. Otherwise, useless data might be collected.

What Standards Need to Be Established?

Standards must be established that will provide a framework for quality vocational programs. Although the number of standards may vary with different vocational programs, there are several common standards that should be established regardless of the vocational area. General categories of standards are

1. Prospective enrollment
2. Availability of qualified instructors
3. Available facilities
4. Available equipment
5. Available funding
6. Employment opportunities
7. Availability of other similar vocational programs
8. Extent to which the vocational programs under consideration support the goals and philosophy of the school
9. Extent to which delivery of the programs uphold established guidelines
10. Opportunities for cooperative vocational education programs

For example, if a course in word processing were under consideration, a standard referring to equipment might be "Fifteen computers must be available." Or a standard for masonry might be "At least twelve students per year must express an interest and enroll in the class." An example of a standard for marketing education might be "A cooperative training station must be available for each eleventh and twelfth grade student." In each of these examples, standards are stated that relate specifically to program quality. Detailed standards that focus directly on program quality greatly assist decision makers in arriving at sound decisions concerning curriculum development.

Identifying Types of Data to Be Collected

Once standards have been established, the various types of data needed to assist decision makers may be identified. Using the word processing example, if one standard indicates that a minimum of fifteen computers are needed to offer a course, a check of current inventory would immediately show whether fifteen units were on hand. If the computers were there, then this standard would be met. If they were not on hand, then the cost of securing fifteen units would need to be reflected in the proposed budget, and later it would have to be determined if funding resources were adequate to provide for their purchase. In addition, other alternatives might be investigated. Donations of equipment from a company or equipment loans from local businesses are just two examples of ways that equipment might be obtained. The key factor to keep in mind would be that if the minimum standard for a quality program was established as fifteen units, anything less than this might seriously reduce program effectiveness. Thus, not only must program standards exist, but data must be available to support these standards.

Aligning Standards and Sources of Data

Once standards are established, data collection may begin. There are two major areas from which data will be needed. The first might be referred to as school-related data, and the second as community-related data. School-related data basically consist of any type of information directly associated with the school. Several examples might be current facilities available, enrollment trends, and funds available. Community-related data assist in examining the geographical area served by the school. Examples of community-related data might be population trends, labor market demands, and the possibilities for cooperative training centers. In some cases, data from several nearby counties would be needed. These might include federal, regional, or state data related to the standard under consideration. For example, a state may have a printing program at a community college to serve the regional needs of that state. Figure 3–9 provides a list of data sources that might be used to determine if, in fact, previously established standards could or could not be met. These data sources will be discussed in detail in later chapters; however, the curriculum planner must understand how various kinds of data sources align with basic program standards.

Making Decisions in Curriculum Planning

From the standpoint of curriculum planning, the decision-making process may be viewed as consisting of several stages, each of which builds

FIGURE 3–9. *Possible sources of data needed to determine if vocational program standards may be met*

General Standard	School-related Data	Community-related Data
Prospective enrollment	Student interest Student ability Enrollment trends Dropout rates Reasons for dropouts Parents' concerns and expectations	Population trends Community goals Industry movement Other vocational education programs available
Availability of qualified instructor	Background of current instructors	Qualifications of local businesspersons and laypeople College graduates
Available facilities	Current facilities Potential for expansion or remodeling Funds available	Local facilities available
Available equipment	Current equipment Funds available	Equipment available in the local area
Available funding	Current and future budget	Current and future budget support Special funding categories from state and/or federal sources Private sources
Employment opportunities	Followup of graduates Followup of adults enrolled in continuing education programs	Population trends Current and projected employment opportunities Current and projected supply and demand of labor Community goals Other vocational education programs available

---

FIGURE 3–9. *(Continued)*

General Standard	School-related Data	Community-related Data
Other similar vocational programs available	Current and planned vocational programs	Other vocational education programs available
Vocational program being considered that supports goals and philosophy of	Goals and philosophy of the school	Goals of the community
Delivery of program that upholds established guidelines	Current class schedules	
Opportunities for cooperative vocational programs	Possibility of school-related stations	Number of businesses willing to participate and number of stations Business and industry movement in and out of the community

---

on the others and progressively involves the curriculum specialist in data-gathering and decision-making activities. The entire process is represented graphically in Figure 3–10. Note that the stages parallel discussions dealing with areas such as establishing standards, gathering data, and examining the alignment of standards and data. A discussion of each of the five stages follows.

Stage 1—Define Problem or Opportunity and Clarify Alternatives

In this stage, a critical step is defining the problem or opportunity at hand. Once the problem or opportunity has been defined and agreed on, then possible alternative solutions can be identified and clarified. For example, a community college may be considering offering four different vocational and technical programs. Data concerning each of these four programs could be collected and analyzed simultaneously to decide which, if not all four, should be implemented.

FIGURE 3–10. *Making decisions in curriculum planning*

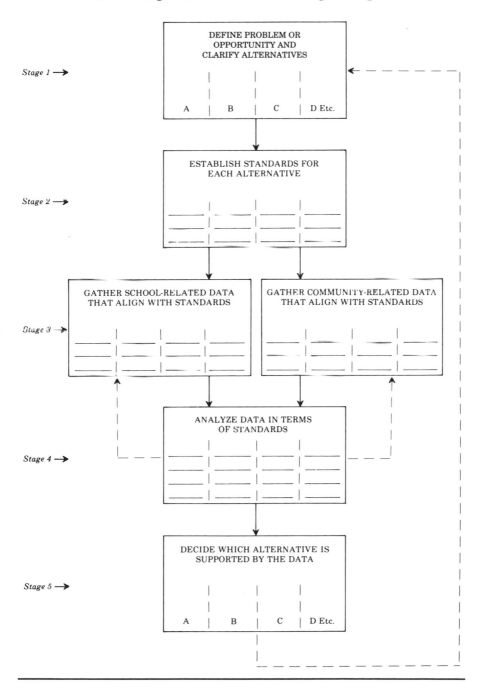

Stage 2—Establish Standards for Each Alternative

Once alternatives are clarified, Stage 2 allows for the establishment of standards for each of the alternatives. Standards help the decision maker to determine if the alternative under consideration should be offered and if the necessary resources are available. Standards also assist curriculum planners in the establishment and operation of quality vocational and technical education programs.

Stage 3—Gather School-Related and Community-Related Data That Align with Standards

With the establishment of standards in Stage 2, data can now be identified and collected for each alternative in Stage 3. Data will need to be collected from both the school and community.

Stage 4—Analyze Data

In Stage 4, the curriculum planner must objectively analyze all data in terms of the established standards. This stage involves assembling, summarizing, analyzing, and preparing the data in a form that can be used when the decision-making time arrives. The situation may occur during this stage that additional data are needed that were not collected; thus, provision must be made for collecting data before all the data can be fully and accurately analyzed. This process is indicated by the dashed lines from Stage 4 to Stage 3.

Stage 5—Decide Which Alternative Is Supported by the Data

Stage 5 represents the final step in the decision-making process. At this stage, alternatives are ruled out as unfeasible or accepted as feasible approaches to curriculum development. In some cases, only one alternative may be selected from many possibilities, or all alternatives may be deemed inappropriate. In other cases, all alternatives may be feasible. Decision makers also identify other alternatives not previously considered, and thus the process would be repeated for each new alternative. Repetition of the process is repeated by the dashed line from Stage 5 to Stage 1.

Summary

The importance of strategic planning and decision making in educational curriculum planning cannot be overemphasized. Of all the activities and elements associated with an educational organization, the instant that a decision is made is one that will have lasting effect on the future of the curriculum. Hopefully, that effect will be desirable.

Decision making in the educational arena usually involves two major areas: policy decisions and operational decisions. Operational decisions involve day-to-day activities of the curriculum and serve to move the curriculum smoothly ahead. Policy decisions deal with goals, objectives, and some basic structure for achieving these goals and objectives. Curriculum planners must be involved at both levels of decisions. Whereas policy decisions serve to establish the type of curriculum a school will or will not follow, operational decisions deal with the management of the approved curriculum. Both of these areas have a direct influence on whether the curriculum will be successful.

The value of strategic planning must be recognized by all who deal with the curriculum. Vocational education curricula must be planned and implemented in such a way to assure that students and societal needs are served. Nothing less than this should be attempted or accepted.

Curriculum planners should be aware of the effect that philosophy and personal attributes have on those who are in decision-making positions. An understanding of these important elements as they relate to decision making aids curriculum planners as they provide data needed by decision makers to arrive at sound decisions, and also provides input as to how curriculum planners can work effectively with those who are in key decision-making roles.

Although many approaches can be useful in guiding the decision-making process, each educational organization must establish a system that is compatible with its particular structure. This procedure should be written and shared with all to ensure a complete understanding of how decisions will be made. Once the procedure is established, a continual review and evaluation should be made to determine how the process can be improved.

Decision makers cannot be expected to reach decisions unless standards are established to help determine whether a program should or should not be offered. Curriculum planners must take the initiative to see that realistic standards are established that support quality programs. Once standards have been established, data can then be identified and collected to determine if the program should be offered. These data can basically be thought of as either school-related or community-related.

Although much has been said about sophistication associated with decision making in education, the final decision rests upon human judgment. This judgment must be made by responsible members of society, who are representatives of the community in which a school is located. As society and technology advance, hopefully the data provided to these decision makers will become more sophisticated and accurate, and the decisions will represent a higher level of objectivity.

Related References

Finch, Curtis R., and McGough, Robert L. *Administering and Supervising Occupational Education.* Englewood Cliffs, N.J.: Prentice-Hall, 1982.

Hansen, J. Merrell. "Site-Based Management and Quality Circles: A Natural Combination." *NASSP Bulletin* 74, no. 528 (1990): 100–103.

Herman, Jerry J. "A Vision for the Future: Site-Based Strategic Planning." *NASSP Bulletin* 73, no. 518 (September 1989): 23–27.

———. "External and Internal Scanning: Identifying Variables that Affect Your School." *NASSP Bulletin* 73, no. 520 (November 1989): 48–52.

Kaufman, Roger. "Strategic Planning and Thinking: Alternative Views." *Performance & Instruction* 29, no. 8 (September 1990): 1–7.

Kirst, Michael W. "The Changing Balance in State and Local Power to Control Education." *KAPPAN* 66, no. 3 (November 1984).

McConkey, Dale D. *How to Manage by Results, 4th ed.* New York: American Management Association, 1983.

McCune, Shirley D. *Guide to Strategic Planning for Educators.* Alexandria, Va.: Association for Supervision and Curriculum Development, 1986.

Migliore, R. Henry. *An MBO Approach to Long-Range Planning.* Englewood Cliffs, N.J.: Prentice-Hall, 1983.

Summers, Susan R. "Effectiveness in Continuing Education: A Model for Planning and Evaluation." *Catalyst* 21, no 1 (Winter 1991): 28–31.

Swap, Walter C., and Associates. *Group Decision Making.* Beverly Hills: Sage Publications, 1984.

Wales, Charles E., and Nardi, Anne. *Successful Decision Making.* Morgantown: West Virginia University, Center for Guided Design, 1984.

4

Collecting and Assessing School-Related Data

Introduction

As discussed in the previous chapter, decision making in educational curriculum planning must take many factors into consideration. One factor that must be considered in the curriculum-planning process and yet is often found to be lacking consists of conditions surrounding the school setting. The major goal of vocational instruction is to prepare students for successful employment in the labor market. Many curriculum planners casually mention the student as one factor to consider in the planning processes, but few actually deal with student needs in a comprehensive manner. As a result, curricula may be developed with little or no student input and little consideration given to the current situation existing in a school system.

This chapter focuses on the collection of data relating to a school system or technical or community college under study by the curriculum planner, or, as some may call it, "internal scanning" of the environment. Major points to consider in this regard are the status of current vocational and technical education programs, the current dropout rate and the reasons for it, occupational interests of students, parents' interests and concerns, followup of former students, projection of future enrollments, and assessment of facilities currently available. While financial resources could be discussed in this chapter, this topic is treated in Chapter 5 since finances are closely linked to community resources.

The goal of this chapter is to provide the curriculum planner with the capability to conduct an internal scan of what is really happening in the school system or technical or community college as it now exists and to identify data for use in either establishing program standards or determining if established standards can be met. One of the first steps in curriculum development is to study the current program.

Assessing the Current Status of Vocational and Technical Education Programs

Before any curriculum-planning decisions can be made, consideration must be given to assessing current programs and developing a basic understanding about them. Whereas some curriculum planners are able to build a vocational and technical education program where none exists, most will be faced with making decisions related to the improvement, redirection, and/or expansion of ongoing programs. Thus, it is imperative that full consideration be given to the current vocational and technical education program.

Current Vocational and Technical Programs, Enrollments, and Capacity

The assessment of current programs begins with identifying and listing individual courses that are presently being offered. This may seem a trite step to some, but the listing will help to eliminate some future problems and misunderstandings, especially with those involved in curriculum planning who do not have vocational education backgrounds.

The use of a form, such as that in Figure 4–1, enables the curriculum planner to produce a clear, concise picture of current vocational and technical education programs. Column 1 is used to list specialty program areas and the courses offered under each program area. Titles approved by the state department of education should be used in listing program areas or courses. The use of abbreviated names or nicknames will often lead to confusion and misunderstanding in communications between curriculum planners and noneducational decision makers. If the state department of education has assigned code numbers to approved courses, these could also be used and placed in parentheses after each course offering. The second column is designed to help identify the location in which a course is currently being offered. This would be of special value

FIGURE 4-1. Current vocational and technical programs, enrollments, and capacity for school district, community college, etc.

Vocational and Technical Programs and Courses (1)	Room Number or Name & Facility (2)	Enrollment			Number Over- or Under-enrolled (6)	Number of Students by Grade Level (7)									Remarks (8)
		Capacity (3)	Current (4)	Percent of Capacity (5)		6	7	8	9	10	11	12	13	14	

73

when vocational courses are offered in different buildings or when students are bused to different locations for their vocational and technical courses.

Columns 3, 4, 5, 6, and 7 deal with the course enrollment status. In planning any educational program, planners must be aware of the current capacity of courses in the school system. Capacity could be interpreted as either state-established levels or maximums set for the current facility used. Columns 4, 5, and 6 help the curriculum planner to determine whether current program offerings are operating at maximum capacity. Listing the grade level of students enrolled in each course in Column 7 assists planners in assessing whether students are enrolled in vocational and technical courses designed for their grade level. Thus, a standard may be established that in order for course X to be offered, a facility must be of sufficient size to permit twenty-two students to enroll. Information collected on the form in Figure 4–1 can assist a curriculum planner in determining if that program standard will be met.

An example of how the form can be of assistance to vocational teachers and administrators in understanding the current status of a total vocational program is illustrated by the data in Figure 4–2. Let's assume the data represent the current status at East Central High School in December of a school year. The following observations of the data could be made. The letter for each statement appears in Figure 4–2 near the data from which the observation has been made.

Marketing Education

A. Classes are operating at about 80 percent of capacity.
B. Courses tend to have a high degree of holding power as students advance.

Home Economics

C. Low enrollment exists with Food Occupations II.
D. Overenrollment exists with Introduction to Foods and Cuisine Foods.
E. Number of seniors enrolled is substantially lower than the number of juniors.
F. The program may be operating at near capacity with only one teacher.

ICT

G. Program could serve twice as many students.
H. Do scheduling problems exist since a high number of seniors are enrolled in ICT I?
I. One teacher could be reassigned.

FIGURE 4–2. Current vocational and technical programs, enrollments, and capacity for East Central High School

Vocational and Technical Programs and Courses (1)	Room Number or Name & Facility (2)	Enrollment			Number Over- or Under-enrolled (6)	Number of Students by Grade Level (7)									Remarks (8)
		Capacity (3)	Current (4)	Percent of Capacity (5)		6	7	8	9	10	11	12	13	14	
Marketing Education															
Fash. Merch.	Room 126	20	16		– 4					16					
ME I	Room 124	20	16		– 4						7	9			2 teachers
ME I	Room 116	20	20		—					20					
ME II	Room 126	20	13		– 7						8	5			
ME II	Room 128	20	22		+ 2						10	12			
ME II	Room 124	20	15		– 5						13	2			
ME III	Room 121	15	10		– 5							10			
ME III	Room 121	15	8		– 7							8			
Sub total		150	120	(A) 80						36	38	(B) 46			
Home Economics															
Food Occup. I	Room 164	20	14		– 6						10	4			1 teacher
Food Occup. II	Room 164	20	(C) 6		–14						2	4			(F)
Marriage/Family Living	Room 162	24	19		– 5						14	5			
Introd. Foods	Room 162	20	26		+ 6 (D)				6	20	10				
Cuisine Foods	Room 162	20	25		+ 5					15	10				
Clothing	Room 162	24	24		—						8	16			
Sub total		128	114	89					6	35	44 (E)	29			

75

FIGURE 4-2. (Continued)

Vocational and Technical Programs and Courses (1)	Room Number or Name & Facility (2)	Enrollment Capacity (3)	Enrollment Current (4)	Percent of Capacity (5)	Number Over- or Under-enrolled (6)	6	7	8	9	10	11	12	13	14	Remarks (8)
ICT Courses															
ICT I	Annex Room 247	20	9		−11							9			
ICT I	Annex Room 249	20	11		−9							3	8 (H)		2 teachers (I)
ICT II	Annex 247	20	11		−9								11		
Sub total		60	31	52 (G)								12	19		
Technology Ed.															
Eng. Drawing	Annex 114	23	25		+ 2					6	14	5			4 teachers
Eng. Drawing	Annex 116	23	26		+ 3					11	9	6			all double
Comm. Tech.	Annex 110	27	20		− 7					17	1	2			periods
Woods Tech.	Annex 123	27	15		−12					12	2	1			except
Woods Tech.	Annex 123	27	19		(K) − 8					15	3	1			Comm.
Metals Tech.	Annex 123	27	8		−19						4	4			Tech.
Energy & Power	Annex 125	20	21		+ 1					15	4	2			
Construction	Annex 125	20	8		(K) −12						2	6			
Sub total		194	142	73 (L)						76	39	27			
Total for Vocational Program		532	407	77 (N)					6	147 (M)	133 (M)	121 (O)			9 teachers

Technology Education

J. Could the large number of 11th and 12th graders in Engineering Drawing be prohibiting 10th graders from taking the course?
K. Woods Technology, Metals Technology, and Construction are underenrolled to a high degree.
L. Program could serve more students.
M. There may be a high attrition of students when comparing enrollment of 10th graders to enrollment of 12th graders.

Overall Vocational Program

N. Program is operating at 77 percent capacity.
O. Can the program do a better job of holding students?

As with these observations for East Central High School, it is evident that the use of the form and type of data in Figure 4–2 would be very valuable to the teacher, administrator, and curriculum specialist in gaining a perspective of the current status of the vocational program. The data collected by use of the form would become even more valuable as data are collected over time and trends are identified. For example, someone could raise the following questions:

Is the enrollment of 120 students in Marketing Education (80 percent of capacity) good or bad?
Is the number of seniors (27) enrolled in Technology Education high or low?
Is the percentage of the student body at East Central High School who are enrolled in vocational education increasing or decreasing?

The answer to each of these questions is "That depends." If the enrollment in Marketing Education for the previous two years was 140 and 130, then a current enrollment of 120 could imply that problems exist. If the number of seniors enrolled in Technology Education has decreased in the last few years, then someone needs to take a close look at the program and/or the scheduling to pinpoint what may be causing this decrease. If the percentage of the student body at East Central High School enrolling in vocational courses for the last three years has increased from 50 to 52, and now to 56 percent, then one may conclude that the program is gaining in quality, serving more students, and operating at an increased efficiency.

It must be remembered that the data collected for any one point in time will limit the analysis that can be made. Data collected over time where trends can be identified will enhance the abilities of teachers, administrators, and curriculum planners to make the right decisions for strengthening current programs.

Determining Student Occupational Interest

The story is told of how a new vocational program was added to a school's curriculum and the most up-to-date facility was constructed for it, but when it came to enrolling students, no one wanted to take the program. Although this story may be more fiction than fact, administrators and teachers have no doubt wondered from time to time if students were really interested in the courses being offered. Planners must take into account the occupational interests of students when measuring program standards.

Standardized Tests

One approach to assessing the occupational interests of a large group of students is through the use of standardized tests. This is especially helpful if several different grade levels are to be surveyed. Such tests are available to educators and can be an effective tool in curriculum planning. But it must be kept in mind that no test is available that specifically identifies into which occupation a person should go. Vocational interest tests are intended to point out general vocational interests of students and should not be interpreted beyond this point.

Interest Inventories.   Students will be more highly motivated to investigate occupations and firm up career decisions if they have a good understanding of themselves. Interest inventories not only help students to learn more about themselves but also aid curriculum planners in making generalizations about future program direction.

The following factors should be kept in mind by students and curriculum planners when using standardized interest inventories:

1. Interest inventories do not indicate ability. A student may be interested in an occupation but not have the ability to succeed in it.
2. Interest inventories may help students recognize interest in occupations that they did not know existed.
3. Interest inventories may help students confirm what they thought were their interests.
4. Interest inventories should never be used as the only method of assessing student occupational interests. Other factors to con-

sider are stated interests, individual observations, and activities in which the student has participated.

Several interest inventories are currently available. Four of the more common tests are the Kuder Occupational Interest Survey Form DD (KOIS), the Ohio Vocational Interest Survey (OVIS), the Differential Aptitude Test (DAT) Career Planning Program, and the Self-Directed Search (SDS).

The KOIS takes about thirty minutes to administer and can be given to tenth graders or above. A unique feature of the third edition of KOIS is that scales are included that focus upon occupational interests as well as college majors. The inventory cannot be scored by hand.

The OVIS is designed for grades eight through twelve and requires sixty to ninety minutes to administer. This survey measures an individual's preferences on the following twenty-five interest scales: manual work, machine work, personal services, caring for people or animals, clinical work, inspecting and testing, crafts and precise operations, customer services, nursing and related technical services, skilled personal service, training, literary, numerical, appraisal, agriculture, applied technology, promotion and communication, management and supervision, artistic, sales representative, music, entertainment and performing arts, teaching, counseling and social work, and medical. This survey must be machine-scored.

The SDS is a recently developed interest test that is a reasonably short, self-administered, self-scored, and self-interpreted inventory. It reflects a person's interests and relates them to appropriate occupational groups. The SDS can be completed in forty to fifty minutes and is suitable for students age fifteen and older.

Standardized Aptitude Tests

Scholastic aptitude tests are also available and can give a rough estimate of a student's ability to learn from books or from tasks required in school. Several aptitude tests that may be administered are California Test of Mental Maturity, Otis-Lennon Mental Ability Test, SRA Primary Mental Abilities Test, and the Lorge-Thorndike Intelligence Test. To prevent "branding" or labeling of students, educators should refrain from using specific test scores or IQ scores. The recommended practice is to use test scores in general terms.

Another aptitude test is the General Aptitude Test Battery (GATB), which is administered by the branches of the state employment service. The nine factors included in this test are general reasoning ability, verbal aptitude, numerical aptitude, spatial aptitude, form perception, clerical perception, motor coordination, figure dexterity, and normal dexterity.

Standardized Achievement Tests

Tests such as the Stanford Achievement Test and the California Achievement Test are also used by many school systems. Achievement tests measure what a student has already learned, whereas aptitude tests are used more for predicting future performances.

Selecting Standardized Tests

With the multitude of tests on the market, the curriculum planner may wish to review current listings in the Education Index. However, he or she must eventually decide which test to administer to students. A review of the different types of standardized tests may lead the planner to eliminate some tests immediately, since the purpose for which a particular test is to be administered may not be appropriate for curriculum planning.

In addition to the purpose for which a test is to be used, several other factors should be considered regardless of the type of test desired. Information regarding the following factors is usually found in the booklet describing each test: *reliability* refers to the ability of the test to give the same results if administered to the same student at a later time; *validity* refers to the ability of the test to measure what it purports to measure. Several other items should be considered to determine if the test is practical to administer. One factor to consider is the time required to administer the test. The time should be reasonable; it is helpful if the test can be administered within a single class period. Another factor is the cost. Although curriculum planners would not want to select a test solely because it is the least expensive one available, tests that entail a higher cost per student could run into a sizeable figure if administered to a large group of students. The last factor to consider deals with the ease of administering, scoring, and interpreting the results. A test should be selected only if it gives understandable and usable results.

Specialized Interest Scales for Specific Vocational and Technical Program Areas

Although some research and development on special-interest tests have been initiated, curriculum planners will not, in general, for the foreseeable future, be able to use standardized tests to any great degree for determining occupational interests of students within specific program areas. Further research and development need to be carried out in each of the vocational program areas before interest tests can be used with any degree of accuracy for program planning.

Teacher-Made Surveys

Many planners have relied on teacher-made surveys for use in specific program areas. Although these surveys are not as sophisticated as standardized tests, teacher-made surveys can prove valuable to curriculum planners. Each survey must be developed with a purpose in mind. If the need arises for determining the occupational interests of students in the area of marketing education, then occupations or situations that lend themselves to occupations found in this area must be identified and incorporated into the survey.

The format and length of such surveys can vary widely, depending on the degree to which a curriculum planner desires to pinpoint occupational interests. The survey should be relatively short and easy for the students to complete. Short answers or questions that students can check or circle will aid in maintaining student interest throughout the survey. A section of a teacher-made survey is included in Figure 4–3.

Although teacher surveys are usually developed for specific vocational program areas and are used with students already enrolled in those areas, administration of the survey to other students has some merit. The standardized instruments discussed earlier indicate student interest in occupational groups. Teacher-made surveys, however, assist students in

FIGURE 4–3. *Agricultural student interest survey*

1. Do you think you might be interested in any of the following occupations after graduation from high school? Check (✓) all that might interest you. Place an (X) on the line if you would like more information about that occupation.

_____ Agricultural advisor to bank and other lending agencies

_____ Small engine mechanic

_____ Florist

_____ Field representative for buying and selling activities in farm organizations

_____ Selling feed, seed, fertilizer, machinery, and spray materials

_____ Landscape consultant

_____ Lawn caretaker

_____ Buying agricultural products

_____ Servicing machinery and equipment

_____ Artificial breeding technician

_____ Crop-dusting or spraying (aerial and otherwise)

_____ Conservation service employee

_____ Forestry technician

_____ Agricultural missionary

_____ Poultry specialist

identifying specific interests within a certain area. To administer any interest survey or test to a certain group of students and not to others assumes that the students not provided the opportunity to express their interests do not possess occupational interests in that area. This is often a false assumption and one that curriculum planners cannot afford to make.

Administering Tests and Surveys

One important factor to determine is when a test should be administered. Typically, standardized tests are administered to all students in a school system to assess their current occupational interests. If a program is being planned that will go into effect two years from the time a survey is administered, instruments should be administered to students in the lower grades who will be able to select vocational and technical courses two years hence.

Obtaining Assistance

Curriculum planners who are unfamiliar with the administration and interpretation of test results may want to seek professional assistance. Most colleges and universities with vocational and technical teacher education programs have personnel who can provide assistance to local schools in collecting and interpreting data related to educational decision making. Specialists in state departments of education also have expertise in this area. Furthermore, private consultants are available to local school systems on a fee basis; however, the cost for this type of service may prove to be prohibitive.

Interpreting Test Results

Once the tests have been administered and the data summarized, the task becomes one of interpreting or analyzing the data in light of established program standards. As mentioned earlier, test scores should never be the only source of information to the curriculum planner. Data received through the administration of tests or interest surveys should be one of a number of factors to consider.

Standardized tests come with booklets or other aids for use in interpreting test results. However, curriculum planners must realize that the final decision regarding a priority listing of courses to be offered must come from them. In addition to data collected from either standardized or teacher-made tests, curriculum planners should conduct personal interviews with as many students as possible. This not only helps to refine data further to be used in the decision-making process, but also provides a source of input from students which cannot be readily collected during the administration of standardized tests.

Following Up Former Students

Followup studies are designed to evaluate the "product" of career programs—the graduate. The primary goal of such education—the preparation of individuals for employment—can best be assessed by examining the placement records of graduates and gathering job performance data from employers. Furthermore, former students can be an excellent source to gather information about program strengths and weaknesses.

Identifying and Locating Former Students

The identification of students should pose no special problems to curriculum planners. Most schools maintain files of former graduates and students and these can serve as a basis for composing a followup list. Locating former high school or community college students may be more of a problem. This emphasizes the need for placement coordinators to provide leadership in the placement of students and maintenance of files to keep abreast of students for followup situations. If no records have been maintained, usually parents, relatives, or teachers can provide addresses of students.

Contacting Former Students

The best practice to follow in order to assure a high response rate from students is personal contact. Again, selected mature students, retired individuals, PTA members, or other interested individuals can greatly assist in the collection of data. Telephone calls could be made to those living out of the community. Another approach would be through a mailed questionnaire; however, the rate of return would not be as high as from personal contact.

Regardless of the approach used, curriculum planners must demand a high rate of return from former students. Otherwise, the validity of the study may be seriously questioned.

Information to Gather from Former Students

The type of information to gather from former students depends on what the student has done or is currently doing since leaving school. Activities

84   Planning the Curriculum

can usually be separated into two categories: employment or continuing education.

Students Employed or Continuing Their Education. The form found in Figure 4–4 serves the purpose of soliciting information valuable to curriculum planners. It is designed for use with former students who may be currently employed or continuing their education. For those students who are currently employed, the information collected will indicate employment status, job titles, and job stability. Provision is made for those students continuing their education to indicate reasons why they selected their particular courses of study.

Individuals Enrolled in Adult Classes. If valuable information can be obtained by following up former high school or community college students, then the assumption can be made that a followup of adult students would also prove to be valuable. Figure 4–5 is an example of a form that can collect information as to why adults enrolled in courses and whether they were able to accomplish their goals after completing them.

The information discussed in the last few pages can provide valuable data for curriculum planners. For example, discussion may be underway as to whether a vocational program should be continued. A standard may be thus established that at least 75 percent of the graduates from a particular vocational service area either must be employed in a job related to their training or must be continuing their education. Data collected by use of the forms in Figures 4–4 and 4–5 will provide this information.

Projecting Future Enrollments

The need to project into the future is vital to the effectiveness of any educational program and is basic to any curriculum planning. Many times programs developed will not be available to students until two, three, four, or more years in the future. Therefore curriculum planners need to establish standards concerning potential enrollments for an educational program in order to balance the program with the number of students in the school system or attendance area.

Community Data

Most projections begin by considering only those students currently enrolled in school, although it would not be too premature to look even further. Securing data about the current birth rates in any one county or school district may give curriculum planners leads as to trends that

---

FIGURE 4-4. *Followup of former students*

I. Name _____ Year Graduated _____
   Address _____

II. What is your current employment status?
   Employed full-time _____ or part-time _____ Unemployed _____ (Check one)
   Current job title _____ Employer _____

III. Did you continue your education after high school? Yes _____ No _____ If
    yes, answer the following:

Type of School	Currently Enrolled	Completed Program	Major Field of Study
Community college	_____	_____	_____
Technical school	_____	_____	_____
Four-year college	_____	_____	_____

IV. Why did you continue your education? (Check all that apply)
   Preparation for job _____
   Upgrading in present job _____
   Maintaining competency for present job _____
   No occupational objective _____
   Other reason (specify) _____

V. Information about the vocational program taken
   1. In what program were you enrolled? _____
   2. What specific courses did you take? _____
      _____

   3. If you took no more than one course, what were the reasons that
      made you decide not to reenroll? _____
      _____

   4. Have you used the knowledge and skills learned in the vocational
      courses? _____ Yes _____ No
      If yes, please describe. _____
      _____
      _____

   5. Would you say that the training received in your vocational course
      was important in securing your first job? _____ Yes _____ No

VI. List all jobs held since graduation for high school.

Dates	Job Title	Employer
_____	_____	_____
_____	_____	_____
_____	_____	_____
_____	_____	_____

FIGURE 4–5. Followup of adult students

Name _____ Date _____

Address _____ Telephone _____

Highest grade completed: (circle) Under 7, 7, 8, 9, 10, 11, 12, 13, 14, 15, 16, over 16

Present occupation or job title _____

Adult courses in which enrolled	Year[a]	*Purposes for which enrolled*				Evidence of accomplishment of purpose—record any evidence available[b]	Location of course
		Improve in present occupation	Prepare for new occupation	Personal growth	Other reasons [specify]		

Would you recommend this course to others? _____ Yes _____ No

What suggestions would you have for future courses/programs? _____

_____

_____

[a]For the year or years offered by School Division.

[b]Evidence such as job or salary promotions, employment in new occupation, recognition for work performed, comments regarding increased job satisfaction, or increase in net income and net worth.

might occur in the future. Tentative answers can be found for such questions as: "Will school enrollments increase or decrease in the future?" "What will be the sex ratio?" "Will the educational programs and facilities be adequate to meet future needs?" Seeking answers or at least tentative answers to questions such as these through the use of census data might have prevented some of the critical enrollment situations that some schools find themselves involved in today.

Projecting School Enrollments

Once students begin to attend school, more accurate data can be secured for use in projecting trends. A format such as the one presented in Figure 4–6 will provide curriculum planners with a quick and concise look at

---

FIGURE 4–6. *Description of school population—Current grade level*

Information	Current Year 19 _____	Projected Enrollment Year _____	Year _____	Year _____
Gender				
1. Male	_____	_____	_____	_____
2. Female	_____	_____	_____	_____
Ethnic Groups				
1. African American	_____	_____	_____	_____
2. White	_____	_____	_____	_____
3. Native American	_____	_____	_____	_____
4. Asian	_____	_____	_____	_____
5. Hispanic	_____	_____	_____	_____
Disadvantaged				
1. Academic	_____	_____	_____	_____
2. Economic	_____	_____	_____	_____
3. Social	_____	_____	_____	_____
4. Cultural	_____	_____	_____	_____
Special Needs				
1. Deaf/Hard of hearing	_____	_____	_____	_____
2. Blind/Visually impaired	_____	_____	_____	_____
3. Speech defect	_____	_____	_____	_____
4. Orthopedically impaired	_____	_____	_____	_____
5. Learning disabled	_____	_____	_____	_____
6. Mentally retarded	_____	_____	_____	_____
7. Emotionally disturbed	_____	_____	_____	_____
8. Other health impaired	_____	_____	_____	_____
9. Gifted	_____	_____	_____	_____
10. Talented	_____	_____	_____	_____

what they might expect as far as enrollments in the future and the composition of the student body are concerned. This form could be used for any class for which curriculum planners may wish to collect information. In addition, the projected-year column can be readjusted to reflect the future years under discussion. The one point that needs to be remembered is that curriculum planners must continually keep abreast of population shifts in the community, industry movement, unemployment rates, or other factors that could greatly affect the size of the community and the number of students. For example, if a state or city is located in the sunbelt, in one of the mega-states, or in a major growing urban corridor, conditions in these areas can have a serious impact on future educational programs.

Assessing Facilities

In an earlier section of this chapter, a form was suggested that would help indicate to planners the use made of current facilities by the vocational and technical program. Although this form can provide some data about the use of facilities, several other points also need to be made.

School Facilities

Curriculum planners must always be working toward a more efficient use of current facilities. With the increased cost of building construction and the reluctance of taxpayers to spend more money on education, decision makers in the future must spend more time identifying alternative ways of using current facilities. Remodeling schools and adding new sections to existing ones are becoming more common.

Seeking Input from the Community Through Partnerships and Other Collaborative Efforts

Chapter 5 provides an in-depth look at the community and its relationship to planning quality vocational programs. It would be a serious mistake for curriculum planners to avoid seeking input from the community as they assess and evaluate current educational programs of the school. The involvement of parents, business, industry, and public through meaningful partnerships will help create an educational program that will not only serve the students, but also the community in which the school is located.

Various strategies can be used by curriculum planners to involve the community in local school planning activity. Parent-teacher associations, craft advisory committees, advisory boards, parents, employers of students who have been placed for cooperative programs, retired tradespersons, and skilled craftspersons are just a few of the examples of groups who can become involved in partnerships and assist in assessing a school's situation, whether it be a comprehensive high school, vocational center, or community college.

Input from community groups can focus on their recommendations concerning facilities, tools or equipment, curriculum content, program emphasis, instructional materials, and other elements associated with quality vocational programs. The important thing for curriculum planners to keep in mind is that each community includes unique resources that can be tapped when assessing a local program.

Summary

The importance of understanding the school system and related data cannot be underestimated when vocational and technical education curricula are being planned. Many curriculum planners will not be developing programs from scratch; thus, the current school situation and existing programs may have a great impact on decisions that must be made in the future.

One of the first factors that must be assessed is the status of the current program. This includes the listing of all vocational and technical courses as well as an understanding of all courses offered. Course capacity, current enrollment, and especially trends must be studied. Obtaining input of students is vital to sound educational planning. Students can provide valuable ideas and suggestions if provided the opportunity. The community also has a right to express its feelings, and planners must assure that input from parents is secured in order to promote acceptance of new and different programs.

Without a doubt, the followup of former students is a must if planners and decision makers are to have sound and realistic data on what is happening to former students of their school system. Distinct trends can be identified that have strong implications for planners. The projection of future enrollments and the assessment of facilities will serve to provide planners with input to help avoid critical problems in the future.

Related References

Beane, James A., Toepfer, Conrad F., Jr., and Alessi, Samuel J., Jr. *Curriculum Planning and Development*. Boston, Ma.: Allyn and Bacon, Inc., 1986.

Borden, Robert B. "A State Advisory Council Looks at Curriculum." *VocEd* (March 1985): 33–35.

Copa, George H., and Moss, Jerome, Jr., eds. *Planning and Vocational Education.* New York: Greg Division, McGraw-Hill, 1983.

DAT Career Planning Program. New York: The Psychological Corporation, 1973.

Develop Local Plans for Vocational Education: Part II, Module L T-A-2. The National Center for Research in Vocational Education, The Ohio State University, 1980.

Dyer, Joanne, and McCauley, Jan. "How We Redesigned Our Curriculum." *VocEd* (March 1985): 38–39.

Ebel, Robert L. "Three Radical Proposals for Strengthening Education." *Phi Delta Kappan* 63, no. 6 (February 1982).

Elson, Donald E., and Strickland, Deborah C. *Vocational Education Evaluation in Virginia.* Richmond, Va.: Virginia Polytechnic and State University, Division of Vocational and Technical Education and the Division of Vocational Education, State Department of Education, 1987.

Fenstermacher, Gary D. "Three Nonradical Proposals for Strengthening Ebel's Argument." *Phi Delta Kappan* 63, no. 6 (February 1982).

Finch, Curtis R. "Futures-Oriented Methodologies: Implications for Applied Research." *Journal of Vocational and Technical Education* 1, no. 2 (Spring 1985): 3–10.

Handbook for Conducting Future Studies in Education. Bloomington, Ind.: Phi Delta Kappan, 1984.

Haub, Carl. "Demographics: What Lies Ahead? Shifts, Growth and Change." *VocEd* (May 1984).

Herman, Jerry J. "External and Internal Scanning: Identifying Variables that Affect Your School." *NASSP Bulletin* 73, no. 520 (November 1989): 48–52.

Hintzen, Neil. "An Approach to Conducting Follow Up on Vocational Students: Implications for Educational Planning." *Performance & Instruction* 29, no. 9 (September 1990): 33–40.

Kuder (KOIS) Form DD—General Interest Survey. Chicago: Science Research Associates, 1985.

Long, James P. "Vocational Education in the Community Colleges." *VocEd* (March 1985): 47–50.

McCune, Shirley D. *Guide to Strategic Planning for Educators.* Alexandria, Va.: Association for Supervision and Curriculum Development, 1986.

McKee, William L., and Froeschle, Richard C. *Where the Jobs Are.* Kalamazoo, Mich.: W. E. Upjohn Institute for Employment Research, 1985.

McKenzie, Floretta D. "City Schools with Corporate Partners." *VocEd* (November/December 1985): 40–42.

Ohio Vocational Interest Survey (OVIS). New York: Harcourt Brace Jovanovich, 1981.

Sanders, Donald, and Chism, Nancy. "Updating Curriculum: A Process that Never Ends." *VocEd* (March 1985): 28–30.

Sawyer, David E. "Hands-on-Labs in an Academic High School." *Vocational Education Journal* (May 1986): 50–52.

Walsh, W. Bruce, and Betz, Nancy F. *Tests and Measurements.* Englewood Cliffs, N.J.: Prentice-Hall, 1985.

5

Collecting and Assessing Community-Related Data

Introduction

The development of vocational education curricula cannot be discussed without giving some consideration to the community in which a school is located. Some may refer to this as "external scanning" of the environment. The community surrounding a school has a major influence on the type of curriculum offerings, since local labor supply and demand, program resources, and existing educational programs will aid curriculum planners in determining if established quality program standards can be met.

Labor supply and demand data reflect the current employment situation in a community; resources aid in determining the level of funding available, personnel on hand, and facilities and equipment feasible; and existing educational programs point to voids in current curricula offerings. Thus, the following discussion focuses on various aspects of the community and how they affect the curriculum planner.

The Community

Curriculum planners cannot develop realistic educational programs if they do not first obtain a valid picture of the community in which a school is located; familiarity with the community is an important aspect of curriculum planning. If an understanding of the community is lacking, the planner must devote sufficient professional energy to bringing himself or herself up to date. Only then is one able to speak and react knowledgeably about the community during curriculum development activities.

Community Boundaries

A major question that the curriculum planner must answer (if it has not already been defined) is "What are the geographical boundaries of the community?" To solve this problem accurately, he or she must take into account several considerations. For example, in one situation, the community might represent the same geographical area contained in the established school district's lines. In another situation, the word *community* must take on a broader concept, especially if graduating students tend to migrate out of a local area into surrounding areas for employment. Thus, the community might include two or more counties or sections of counties surrounding the school. However, it may be appropriate and necessary in special situations to think in terms of regional and statewide areas. An example of this might be a postsecondary institution that offers a program for farriers with graduates being prepared to fill the labor needs within a particular region of the state.

The curriculum planner must use established standards as a focal point in determining the geographical lines of a community. In fact, one may need to readjust community boundaries for different types of data collection. For example, in assessing occupational programs currently available to students, a planner might need to consider a smaller geographical area than if he or she were attempting to assess labor demands that might influence the type of curricula offered within a local school.

Population Trends

The number of people within a community will vary over the years, and the curriculum planner must be aware of any shifts in population. One shift that may occur would be immigration or emigration. Either population shift has major implications for developing vocational curricula. An emigration of people would cause curriculum planners to look outside their traditional community lines to discover the types of jobs taken by graduates. An immigration could result in increased school enrollments and thus in a demand for greater diversity of vocational education offerings. One of the most popular methods of determining population trends is the use of census data. A curriculum planner could also study other indicators of population trends, such as school enrollments, housing starts, and new businesses or factories coming into the area.

Another aspect of the population would be its makeup. For example, number of people by age groups, number of students reaching high school age (ninth grade), or number of graduating seniors. Statistics such as the number of citizens reaching retirement age each year will give some indication of openings each year and type of occupational openings. Some national statistics now indicate that the increase in number of students in the lower grades is beginning to level off or even decrease. This implies that in the future curriculum planners will need to determine how the shift in elementary school enrollments will affect the vocational education student's needs.

Furthermore, the impact of international situations can influence local educational planners. Unemployment is no longer just a concern to developing countries; technological change affects the workforce in every country. This means that countries are obliged to come to grips with the problem of how to prepare young people for employment and how to offer adult workers the means to adapt to structural or technological change and to advance in their careers (*Policy, Planning, and Management in Technical and Vocational Education*, 1984).

Community Goals

A discussion in Chapter 3 concerned the philosophy held by members of the decision-making groups and the effect that their philosophy might have on decisions. Associated with this philosophy are community goals. Whether the goals are for an entire community or individual members of that community, they are nonetheless an important source of community-related data.

The logical place to begin the formulation of community goals would be the development of a workforce or labor policy, or as some individuals would state it, a written set of priorities for a particular community based upon political, social, and moral values. Examples of local situations that might give rise to community goals are (1) reduce unemployment; (2) reduce unemployment in target groups (i.e., teenagers, the twenty-to-thirty-year age group); (3) provide qualified labor for new and expanding businesses; (4) retrain the underemployed; or (5) provide more educational opportunities for females and minorities. These five examples are not intended to be all-inclusive; any particular community may identify similar or different goals. For example, one community might place a higher priority on helping disadvantaged students to obtain employment rather than helping those who are unemployed.

If the curriculum planner discovers that goals do not exist for a community, steps must be taken to ensure that decision-making groups (e.g., school boards) take the lead and, in cooperation with lay people in the community, develop these goals. The important point to keep in mind is that before any decision is made to establish a vocational program, standards should be established which, when met, indicate that the program will indeed serve to meet a community's priority in vocational education. (Chapter 8 treats goal development in greater depth.)

Obtaining Assistance in Data Collection

Identifying the data needed to make effective decisions is only the beginning in data collecting. A necessary next step is the actual collection of data. The curriculum planner will not usually have time to travel about a community collecting needed data. Alternate methods of either collecting or identifying current information about the community must be considered. In fact, many times the data may already exist; the problem will be finding out which individual, agency, company, or other group has this data.

Referring to Figure 3–9 in Chapter 3, much community data may be found in one central location. For example, census data would be a source to utilize when assessing population trends, characteristics of the population, educational level of the community, and other related information. State employment commissions or agencies would have current information available about industry movement, current job openings, projected employment opportunities, and types of businesses and companies in the community. Many times the Chamber of Commerce, Better Business Bureau, and similar organizations conduct surveys in the local community and collect data that may prove useful to the curriculum planner. State, regional, or local planning commissions may also provide valuable data about the community.

However, from time to time, the curriculum planner may discover that needed data have not been collected and thus must proceed to gather the data from sources in the community. When this situation occurs, assistance may be obtained from students, retired individuals, or other community members who want to volunteer their time to a worthy cause. In some cases, schools might consider hiring individuals who, for a reasonable cost, may be able to collect ample data to aid in the decision-making process.

Current and Projected Sources of Employment

Before an assessment can be made of the projected supply and demand for labor, sources of employment must be identified. Some curriculum planners may see this as a minor item, but the identification of every possible source of employment within a community is critical to the development of relevant vocational education curricula. Therefore, curriculum planners must be sure that all areas of employment are identified.

Identifying Current Sources of Employment

Several approaches to identifying current sources of employment may be utilized by curriculum planners. These approaches may be used individually; however, alert planners will use several approaches to ensure that all areas are identified. A brief discussion of each approach follows.

State Employment Commissions.   The two basic roles of employment commissions are to assist employers in finding employees and to help those seeking jobs to find openings. Thus, employment commissions are an important resource in identifying sources of employment. However, curriculum planners should not rely only on them, since only those businesses and industries who seek help from employment commissions may be identified by the planners. Larger businesses tend to hire their own personnel managers to recruit new employees, and small businesses may choose to seek and hire their own employees directly. Thus, some businesses will not be identified if a planner relies only on employment commissions for information.

Chamber of Commerce.   The Chamber of Commerce, as well as similar civic organizations, will usually be knowledgeable about businesses and industries within a community. Many times, these organizations prepare fact sheets or brochures that highlight local firms.

Planning Commissions.   Planning commissions may exist at the state, regional, or local level. In some instances, electric power companies have planning commissions in certain geographical areas to plan and project population growth and business expansion in order to meet electrical demands.

Yellow Pages in Telephone Books.   A telephone book may yield valuable data that might otherwise have been missed. For example, students in a class were surprised to learn that by checking the Yellow Pages, seventy-three service stations, fifty-five retail groceries, and fifty-four restaurants existed within a small community under study. When all businesses such as these are added together, a sizeable number of occupations can be identified in any community.

Products Produced in the Area.   Another approach to identifying employment sources in a community is to list the products or types of materials and goods produced in the community. The end product of any business or industry will give strong indication to types of employment. For example, the following items might be identified:

Clothing	Concrete products	Microcomputers
Furniture	Campers	Aluminum bearings
Animal food	Powder	Automobiles
Torque motors	Processed cheese	Modular homes

These items would indicate that sewing machine operators, electricians, technicians, and dairy farmers are among the occupations existing in the area.

Students Enrolled in School.   A teacher once remarked that the best assistance received in the identification of employment sources was through his own students. In fact, businesses were identified that the teacher did not realize existed. Within two short class periods, the entire class had constructed a valuable list of employment sources. Furthermore, this exercise proved to be a beneficial learning experience for the students.

Identifying Emerging Areas of Employment

The curriculum planner must be able to project into the future regarding employment trends. Although any long-range projections run the risk of being inaccurate, efforts must still be devoted to identifying emerging occupations. Furthermore, the development of vocational programs should not be based solely on today's labor market, since the time span between the original program concept and the first student graduate may be five years or more.

Even with future uncertainties, selected elements of a community can be studied to help predict employment sources. For example, if population is on the increase, certain services must be expanded. Hospitals, utilities, food services, and housing contractors are just a few areas in which increased employment might occur. Close contact should be made and maintained with Chamber of Commerce organizations, since one of their efforts focuses on attracting new businesses to the community. Other people to maintain contact with would be key political figures, business leaders, and those individuals holding leadership positions.

In addition to identifying emerging areas of employment, one must also be alert to areas that are tending to experience a decrease in employment. Some communities may find that as inflation and/or recession affects our society, certain businesses may relocate or reduce the number of employees. Very few communities are stable in the size of their workforce and employment sources; thus, curriculum planners must continually reassess local sources of employment.

Finally, curriculum developers should look beyond their own communities when identifying emerging jobs. Sources to review on a regular basis are publications and reports published by the U.S. Department of Labor, the Bureau of Labor Statistics. These not only reflect trends in employment, population demographics, and demands for various jobs, but also reflect the impact that a global economy is having on the U.S. economy and labor market. This latter situation implies that curriculum developers of the future will need to become more skilled at assessing the global environment and what impact these ever-increasing forces will have on future labor demand and supply.

Projecting Labor Supply and Demand

One of the crucial stages in the development of relevant vocational programs deals with labor supply and demand. The major thrust of vocational education is to prepare individuals for employment and certainly for opportunities that actually exist. To be an effective curriculum planner, one must be knowledgeable as to the different vocational education service areas and the occupations most closely related to those areas. For example, when marketing education is mentioned, people immediately think of salespersons, agricultural education such as farming, and so forth. However, a close search of the literature will point up many other occupations. The point is that a curriculum planner must be open-minded as he or she goes about the job of assessing labor supply and demand.

Assessing Current and Future Labor Demands

The Vocational Education Acts of 1963 and 1968 and their subsequent amendments, as well as the Perkins Act, were explicit in pointing out that vocational education must focus upon education that is realistic in terms of opportunities for gainful employment. These legislative actions imply that the curriculum planner must develop vocational education programs based on employment opportunities. Fundamental to this implication is that planners must assess current and future labor demands in their communities if they expect to develop relevant programs.

The first problem faced by curriculum planners is that accurate and guaranteed approaches to use in projecting precise labor demands do not exist. Labor demands projected beyond four years are often inaccurate and could lead decision makers in the development of inappropriate curricula. However, this situation should not stop curriculum planners from assessing future labor demands as best as they can with the information that is available.

Types of Labor Forecasts. Curriculum planners have several different approaches to choose from when preparing to assess labor demand. Realistically, several of the following approaches may be used rather than relying on data collected by a single approach. The four approaches consist of employer surveys, extrapolation, the econometric approach, and job vacancy.

Employer Surveys. Probably the most widely used approach in assessing labor demand data is through what many educators refer to as employer surveys. This approach basically involves contacting the employer in order to assess current and projected labor demands. The strength of such an approach is that meaningful data can be obtained at a relatively low cost. Employer surveys are easy to administer and can provide labor demand data in a reasonably short time. In addition, employers' short-range plans can be assessed as to their influence on possible emerging employment opportunities. Finally, educators may feel the direct contact between employers and the school will lead to further cooperation between the two.

Curriculum planners using the employer survey approach must also be aware of certain limitations. First, employers may be reluctant to share employment data with strangers who come to their business (sometimes they may not even share information with individuals they know). Thus, when using this approach, it is helpful to contact employers before the actual personal interview to make them aware of why information is needed and how it will be used. Another limitation in using this approach is that businesses moving into the area may not be reflected in the final data. The best that planners can do in this situation is to stay alert to business and industry movement and through a brief reassessment of the community be able to identify areas of key employment opportunities or possibly of a decrease in opportunities.

If the curriculum planners intend to use employer surveys, a data-collecting instrument must be developed that will assist in determining if established program standards in the area of labor demands can be met. Data should be collected regarding current and projected labor demands, and the instrument used should accomplish both purposes. The form illustrated in Figure 5–1 is designed to accomplish that task. Figure 5–2 provides an example of how this form will appear once it has been completed. Using this example, the curriculum planner can readily see that here is a business currently employing twenty-two full-time and five part-time workers, with the projection of thirty-three employees three years hence and, in six years, forty-four. Furthermore, the projected

FIGURE 5–1. *Employer survey*

Telephone _____ Date _____

1. Company name _____

2. Company address _____

3. Person interviewed and title _____

4. Number of workers by job titles and expected turnover:

Job Titles	Number Employed Full	Part	Percent of Expected Annual Replacement (full time)	No. of New Workers Needed 1 9 ___ 1 9 ___
_____	_____	_____	_____	_____ _____
_____	_____	_____	_____	_____ _____
_____	_____	_____	_____	_____ _____
_____	_____	_____	_____	_____ _____
_____	_____	_____	_____	_____ _____
_____	_____	_____	_____	_____ _____

5. If you have seasonal demand for labor, please indicate job titles and the number needed in
   a high demand time.

Job Title	Number Extra Employees Needed	Months
_____	_____	_____
_____	_____	_____
_____	_____	_____

6. Is your business available as a training station for occupational experience programs?

  ☐ Now being used   ☐ Need more information
  ☐ Interested in possibilities   ☐ Not interested

_____
Signature of Interviewer

demand for each job title can be assessed as well as the number of extra
people needed at high demand times.

Once data have been collected from businesses and companies in the
community, information can then be summarized using the form shown in
Figure 5–3. Sample data have been included to illustrate how this form

---

FIGURE 5–2.　*Employer survey*

Telephone ___555-3322___　　　　　　　　　　　　　　　　　　　Date __3/2/x0__

1. Company name ___AJAX COMPANY___

2. Company address ___1234 DELAWARE STREET, ANYWHERE, USA 12345___

3. Person interviewed and title ___JOE BROWN, SUPERVISOR___

---

4. Number of workers by job titles and expected turnover:

Job Titles	Number Employed		Percent of Expected Annual Replacement (full time)	No. of New Workers Needed	
	Full	Part		19 _X3_	19 _X6_
ELECTRICIANS	4	0	0	2	4
ELECTRICIAN HELPER	1	1	100	1	3
CARPENTERS	10	0	10	5	10
BULLDOZER OPERATOR	2	1	0	1	1
POWER SHOVEL OPERATOR	2	1	0	1	1
PLUMBERS	2	2	0	1	2
SUPERVISOR	1	0	0	0	1

5. If you have seasonal demand for labor, please indicate job titles and the number needed in a high demand time.

Job Title	Number Extra Employees Needed	Months
BULLDOZER OPERATOR	1	MAY-OCTOBER
CARPENTERS	2	APRIL-NOVEMBER

6. Is your business available as a training station for occupational experience programs?

☐ Now being used　　　　　　　　☐ Need more information
☑ Interested in possibilities　　　☐ Not interested

_____
Signature of Interviewer

FIGURE 5–3. *Number of workers and projected demand by job title*

Plumbers
Job Title

Name of Company	Number Employed	Percent[1] Annual Replacement Demand	Number of New Workers Needed in	
			3 Years	6 Years
Ajax Company	2	0	1	2
Brown's Hardware	2	0	0	1
Harry's Plumbing	4	25(1)	2	2
Hale's Enterprises	10	10(1)	2	3
Smith's Home Builders	3	0	1	3
Joe's Hardware	1	0	0	0
Total	22	9(2)	6	**11**

[1]Numbers in parentheses indicate numbers of workers needed per year based on current replacement data.

could be used by the curriculum developer. Using the forms provided in Figure 5 1 and Figure 5 3, the planner can begin to determine if established standards may be met regarding labor demand and occupational-experience training program stations. In addition to the information collected by use of the form depicted in Figure 5–1, the planner may identify other relevant data needed for a particular school and provide for the collection of these data. It should be kept in mind that data collection instruments must be as short as possible in order to help ensure an employer's cooperation and assistance.

Several approaches may be used in the collection of data from employers. Mailed questionnaires, personal interviews, and telephone calls constitute the most common approaches. The personal interview approach is by far the best to use, since a high rate of response may be obtained. If the telephone approach is to be used, a letter and sample form should be sent to the employer in advance in order to ensure cooperation and to assist in collecting data during the conversation.

Extrapolation. This approach to projecting future labor demands is based on the assumption that past and current trends will give an indication as to what will happen in the future. The strength of this approach is that it is relatively easy to perform and can be done in a short time. Additionally, the cost of extrapolating is quite low. An example of this procedure, as applied to the occupation of child care assistant, follows.

1980	1985	1990	1995	2000	2005
5	8	13	21	34	54

In this situation, a community might have had five individuals employed as child care assistants in 1980, and by 1985, the number had increased to eight. By 1995, the number employed had reached twenty-one, or about a 160-percent increase every five years. Extrapolating into the future, and making the assumption that the number of child care assistants will continue to increase at approximately the same rate, the curriculum planner may project that by 2005, fifty-four child care assistants will be needed within that community. Further analysis of the data for 1995–2005 indicates that about three to four new positions of child care assistant would occur each year, thus giving the curriculum planner a basis for determining if this type of vocational education program should be initiated. However, the planner must realize that the further into the future projections are made, the greater likelihood that projections will be inaccurate.

The Econometric Approach. The econometric approach to labor forecasting appears to be the most sophisticated labor forecasting in use today. This approach is utilized by the Bureau of Labor Statistics (BLS) of the U.S. Department of Labor.

The BLS projections are developed in a series of six steps, each of which is based on a separate model. They are as follows:

1. Labor force projections—based on future age, sex, racial composition, and percent of a specified population who will be working.
2. Aggregate economic performance—projects the Gross National Product (GNP) and major categories of demand and income.
3. Industry final demand—U.S. economy is disaggregated into 226 producing sectors that cover the U.S. industrial structure, both public and private. Industry output projections are estimated using input-output data associated with the industrial activities needed to produce the expected GNP.
4. Input-output—given the final output expected from the 226 industrial sectors, estimates are then made of the occupational structures needed to produce that output.
5. Industry employment—a regression model containing an equation for each industry to estimate worker hours as a function of the industry's output and the relative cost of labor compared to the costs of other inputs.
6. Occupational employment—an industry-occupational matrix is developed showing the distribution of employment for the 258 industries and for the more than 491 detailed occupations in those industries (*Outlook 2000,* 1990).

Although the econometric approach as used by the Bureau of Labor Statistics yields data that are more relevant at the state and regional levels, curriculum planners may find implications for using this approach at the local level. For example, data concerning a population's age, sex, race, and geographical distribution could be easily obtained for a community. Furthermore, workforce projections by age, sex, race, and educational level are available by regions or counties within a state. As with other labor demand forecasts, the econometric technique has several limitations. Among the major drawbacks is that economic activity in our society fluctuates widely and international situations can greatly influence our labor needs; thus, projections may be inaccurate. Other limitations center around the unpredictable rate of technological advances and the attempt to predict the educational requirements for occupations that now are few in number but which in the future may represent a sizeable share of the workforce.

Job Vacancy. This approach to labor demand forecasting is based on current job vacancies existing for thirty days or more within a community. The job vacancy approach depends heavily on information obtained and compiled by state employment agencies. The strength of this approach is that immediate needs of an area can be quickly ascertained. Furthermore, curriculum planners can easily rank job vacancies by priority of importance of number of vacancies. If any ranking occurs, reasons as to why these openings continue to appear must be considered. For example, do the openings exist because of the lack of qualified people, low wages, or poor working conditions, or are qualified people available but reluctant to go into the occupation? Job vacancy as a means of labor demand forecasting does have some limitations. First, are the jobs listed by this approach permanent jobs or seasonal jobs? Answers to this question must be provided before job vacancy information becomes of value to curriculum planners. The second consideration when vacancies continue to appear for the same job, would be to ascertain whether the actual job entry qualifications are similar to traditional competencies required for that specific occupation. For example, employers may actually have a higher standard of employment for a particular occupation than may be the established standard, due to other internal factors (say, promotional opportunity) within their organization. A third limitation to the job vacancy approach is that if one vacancy was filled, it might lead to three other vacancies or jobs becoming available that complement the original vacancy. An example would be the hiring of a carpenter, which would lead to a need for a carpenter's helper. Finally, vacancies related to contract or government work may be duplicated, especially where companies or businesses within a community are competing for the same labor. Another way to look at this last limitation is that the number of vacancies identified is not the same as the total number of individuals who could be hired.

Summary of Labor Demand Forecasting

The four labor demand approaches treated in this section are just several of those curriculum planners may choose from to collect labor information. The selection of an approach depends on the resources and time available to the planner. Furthermore, selection of approaches depends on whether the planner needs information about the current labor demand or about future labor demands. For example, the employer survey can provide data on both current and projected labor demands. The collection of data by this method may take longer, and the cost would depend on the manner in which information was obtained. Extrapolation procedures would be faster; however, past and current data are needed in order to project into the future. Thus, an employer survey or a job vacancy approach would need to be used if current information about vacancies were not available. The econometric technique is based on detailed information concerning characteristics of the population and workforce. Although this information may be available, curriculum planners may be reluctant to use it due to lack of specific information about a local school district or community in which a school is located. The job vacancy approach is relatively fast, easy, and reflects more of the current situation rather than what might be the situation in the future. All four approaches have distinct advantages and limitations, and the relative accuracy of information obtained by each approach has not been determined or agreed on by economists or educators. Thus, the final selection a planner makes in determining the labor demand for his or her school district must be based upon the established standard to be met. Another way to view the situation is "What data collection approach will yield the type of information needed to determine if the standard can be met?"

Assessing Current and Projected Labor Supply

Projecting labor demand is not complete unless an effort is made to assess the current labor supply. By projecting labor demand in conjunction with the assessment of current labor supply, the planner is able to estimate fairly accurate labor needs within the community. Assessment of the real labor supply in any community is illustrated in Figure 5–4, and a discussion follows related to various segments of this supply.

FIGURE 5-4. *Assessing real labor supply*

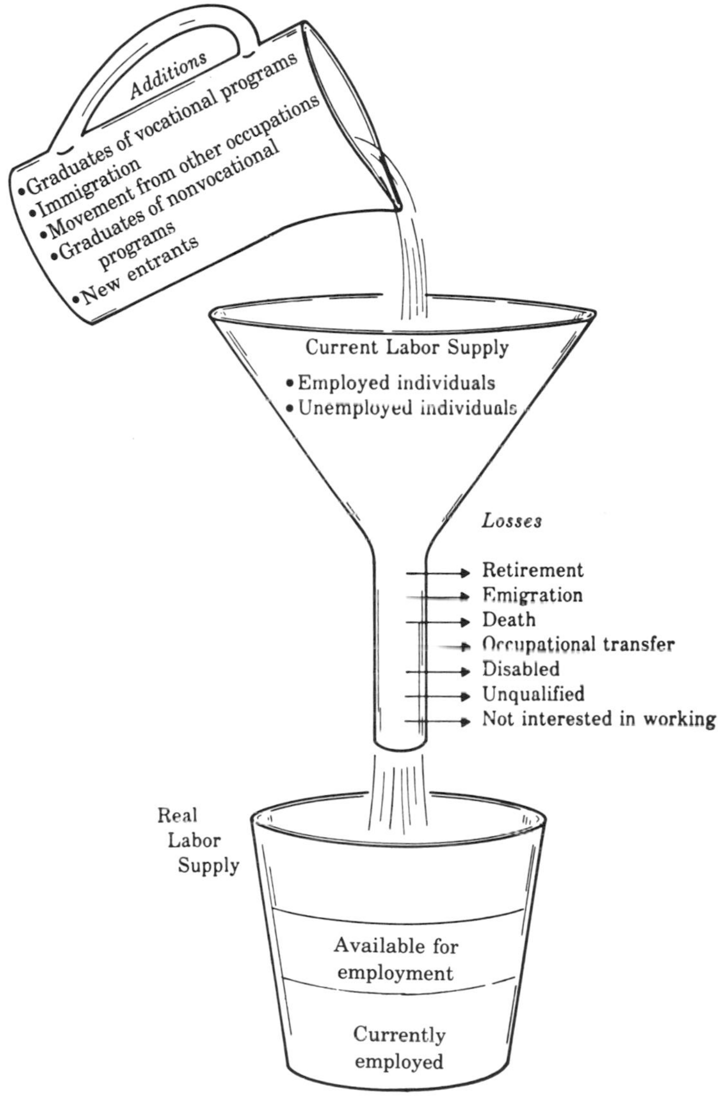

Additions to the Current Labor Supply

Additions to the current labor supply in any community occur continually. These additions may come from several different sources, and the curriculum planner must be able to assess the influence of these new job-seekers on the labor market. Each of these sources of new entrants is treated in the following sections.

Graduates of Vocational Programs.   Graduates of existing vocational education programs enter the labor market each year. These individuals may come from comprehensive high schools, area vocational schools, adult programs, postsecondary institutions, technical institutes, four-year colleges, trade schools, job training centers, or other similar vocational education programs. Data about the number of graduates by vocational service area can easily be obtained from each respective source.

Immigration.   People in the United States tend to be mobile, and this fact creates population fluctuations in any community. Immigration implies that people will be moving into communities and thus creating an impact on the labor supply. Since it is difficult to obtain a general estimate of immigrating numbers that the curriculum planner might expect for his or her particular community, each planner must attempt to calculate expected immigration on a community-to-community basis. U.S. census data and state employment commissions are two sources that should be investigated for current information pertaining to specific communities.

Movement from Other Occupations.   People included in this category are individuals who transfer from one job to another. Although these individuals will not alter the total supply figure, they affect the number of individuals available for any one specific occupational title. For example, a carpenter's helper may become sufficiently skilled to become a carpenter; thus, a shift occurs within the labor supply by occupational title. Data about occupational transfers is difficult to obtain, and the curriculum planner may not be able to reflect this change in the labor supply accurately.

Graduates of Nonvocational Programs.   Individuals included under this category are graduates of nonvocational programs who have changed their career plans and accepted positions for which they were not necessarily prepared. This might include graduates from academic curricula in high schools, postsecondary institutions, four-year colleges, or other nonvocational programs. Information about the number of graduates from these schools should be easy to obtain; however, it is more difficult to project the number of graduates who may go into jobs requiring less than a bachelor's degree.

New Entrants.   A new entrant into the labor market is one who is not included in any of the four previous categories and who has not been previously employed. This category consists primarily of dropouts from educational programs and spouses who are now entering the labor market. The number of dropouts from educational programs in any community can be obtained quite readily, whereas it is more difficult to assess the number of spouses entering the labor market.

Current Labor Supply

Two major categories serve to make up the current labor supply. Included are individuals who are currently employed and those who are available but are not employed for some reason.

Employed Individuals.   Employed individuals make up the largest proportion of the current labor supply in any community. However, it must be noted that the current number of people employed never equals the number of jobs that are filled. Some people hold two or more jobs and others may be employed part-time. A curriculum planner desiring data on those employed by types of occupations can easily secure this information from state employment agencies.

Unemployed Individuals.   Individuals in this classification are persons who are able to work but cannot find work for which they are qualified or are not aggressively seeking employment. The number of people unemployed at any one time will fluctuate according to the current economic situation. Data regarding those unemployed can be secured from state employment agencies.

Losses from the Current Labor Supply

As depicted by the funnel in Figure 5–4, combining the additions to the labor supply with the current labor supply will not provide an accurate figure of those available for employment. From this labor supply figure must be subtracted the number of individuals who will not be available for employment.

Information concerning losses to the labor supply will be reflected in data provided by state employment agencies or employers. Losses to the labor market will occur due to retirement, emigration, death, and occupational transfer and will be given as percentage of replacements needed each year. Any one of these categories by itself will not usually represent a sizeable loss to the current labor supply. However, when all losses are added together, the current number of individuals available for employment will be influenced. In addition, there will be individuals who would like to work but who are disabled in some way that prohibits them from entering the labor market. Unqualified individuals are those who do not possess sufficient knowledge of the basic skills to permit them to seek employment. Finally, there will be those individuals who are able and qualified to work, but who choose not to work for some reason.

Real Labor Supply

Real labor supply represents individuals who are available for employment. This includes persons who currently hold jobs and those individuals unemployed but actively seeking employment.

Interfacing Labor Demand and Supply

There remains one critical step the curriculum planner must carry out in determining net labor needs. Net labor needs may be defined as the estimated number of individuals needed to fill a specific occupation but who are not available at that time. This involves an analysis of information obtained during a labor demand study in relation to information obtained during a labor supply study. The form contained in Figure 5–5 will help in determining if established standards can be met in regard to labor needs. This form should aid with the analysis process when the curriculum developer is determining where the curriculum priorities should be placed. A brief treatment of the various information to be placed in this form follows.

Occupational Title

The occupational titles that are placed in this column should reflect titles for which a local school and the curriculum developer wish to assess the labor demand and supply. Specific titles would be those occupations identified by the use of a form such as that contained in Figure 5–1.

Number Employed

This column is used to indicate the number of people currently employed in each particular job title within a community. The procedure used to identify the number employed within a job title may be accomplished by using appropriate labor demand approaches discussed earlier in this chapter or by other means available within a community. The value of this figure becomes important when calculating the annual need for a

FIGURE 5-5. Interfacing labor demand with labor supply to assess net labor needs

Occupational Title	Number Currently Employed	New Positions	Replace-ment[1]	= TLD[2]	Grad. of Voc. Prog.	+ Others[3]	= TLS[4]	Net Labor Needs
___	___	+ ___	+ ___	= ___	___	+ ___	= ___	___
___	___	+ ___	+ ___	= ___	___	+ ___	= ___	___
___	___	+ ___	+ ___	= ___	___	+ ___	= ___	___
___	___	+ ___	+ ___	= ___	___	+ ___	= ___	___
___	___	+ ___	+ ___	= ___	___	+ ___	= ___	___
___	___	+ ___	+ ___	= ___	___	+ ___	= ___	___

[1]Annual Replacement
[2]Total Labor Demand

[3]Estimate of others who may be available for that occupational title
[4]Total Labor Supply

specific occupation based upon annual replacement percentages. This figure is also valuable when past employment numbers are available for a specific occupation such that projection for labor demands can be made by extrapolation.

Labor Demand

The labor demand column enables identification to be made of demand figures for each occupational title under study. The subcolumn indicated by "New Positions" represents positions to be added during the year(s) under consideration. The replacement column provides the opportunity to calculate the number of individuals needed to replace people lost for any reasons outlined as "Losses" in Figure 5–4. The replacement calculation must be made on the projected number to be employed during the year under study and not the current employed number. The end result is the Total Labor Demand (TLD), which indicates the total demand for a specific occupational title beyond the current number of employees. A local community can decide if this should be done for a specific year or years and project into the future to a year congruent to its local philosophy and goals.

Labor Supply

The labor supply column has been divided into two subcolumns, representing vocational graduates coming into the labor market and others representing a source of employees. The vocational graduates represent those individuals coming into the labor market possessing the skills necessary for entry level employment in that occupation. The figure placed in the column headed "Others" represents an estimate of those individuals who might be coming into the labor market. As was pointed out earlier in this chapter, the figure in this latter column would be influenced by immigration, transfer from other occupations, graduates from nonvocational programs, and new entrants, for all of which absolute figures may not be available. The ultimate value of this column is the Total Labor Supply (TLS). This figure represents (for each occupational title) the total number of individuals available for new or replacement positions identified in the Total Labor Demand (TLD) estimated for the year or years under study.

Net Labor Needs

The net labor needs column reflects the estimated total number of individuals needed for a specific occupational title who are not available.

This figure is calculated by subtracting the Total Labor Supply (TLS) from the Total Labor Demand (TLD). The figure obtained as the Net Labor Needs reflects the year or years for which the TLS and TLD were projected. As discussed earlier, Net Labor Needs are, at best, an estimate. The economic situation existing in society, technological advance, human judgment, error, and individuals' changing career choices, all influence the accuracy of the Net Labor Needs. However, if those individuals responsible for collecting data develop a systematic approach to assess Net Labor Needs, the projections developed should be more accurate and provide a much firmer base upon which decisions affecting curriculum programs can be made.

An example of how the form appearing in Figure 5–5 can be used is provided in Figure 5–6. This example is for a local school district with the projection being made for five years into the future.

Example 1. After an employer survey was conducted, it was found that 362 sales representatives were currently being employed. No new positions were projected in the next five years and the typical annual replacement rate was 10 percent. After surveying vocational programs in the community, it was found that 20 seniors graduated each year with competencies in this area, and an estimate was made that 10 individuals per year would seek employment as sales representatives in addition to vocational graduates.

At a 10-percent replacement per year, this would result in 36 individuals being hired each year for five years, for a Total Labor Demand (TLD) of 180. The 20 seniors graduating each year would add to a total of 100 in five years, with 50 additional individuals being available from other sources. Thus, the Net Labor Needs figure for the next five years was placed at 30, or 6 per year on the average.

Example 2. Farm equipment mechanics number thirty-five, with none to be added in the next five years. The annual replacement percentage was found to be 5 percent. No vocational programs were found to exist in the community and it was estimated that no individuals would be qualified to seek employment of this type.

With this example, the replacement percentage indicates that about two replacements would be needed each year, or ten for the five years. In addition, no new positions would be added, giving a TLD of ten. The TLS was zero, with the resulting Net Labor Needs for the next five years as ten.

Example 3. Social secretaries were found to number 475, with 20 new positions to be added each year. The replacement percentage was estimated to be 10 percent per year. In obtaining data from vocational programs in the community, approximately 60 individuals in secretarial programs were found to be graduated each year, and it was estimated

FIGURE 5–6.   Interfacing labor demand with labor supply to assess net labor needs for school district for five years into the future

Occupational Title	Number Currently Employed	Labor Demand			Labor Supply			Net Labor Needs for Five Years
		New	+ Replacement	= TLD[1]	Grad. of Voc. Prog.	+ Others	= TLS[2]	
1. Sales Reps	362	0	+180	=180	100	+50	=150	30
2. Farm Equipment Mechanic	35	0	+10	=10	0	+0	=0	10
3. Social Secretary	475	100	+260	=360	300	+100	=400	-40
4. Dishwasher	150	0	+375	=375	0	+100	=100	275

[1] Total Labor Demand
[2] Total Labor Supply

that an additional 20 individuals per year would be qualified to seek employment as social secretaries.

In this example, the size of the group currently employed and the current replacement percentage require additional calculations. The following table helps to detail this procedure:

	Employed	New Positions	Replacements
Year 1	475	20	48
Year 2	495	20	50
Year 3	515	20	52
Year 4	535	20	54
Year 5	555	20	56
Total		100	260

This provides an estimate for the TLD as 360 for the next five years. Calculating the TLS, the graduates entering the labor market total 300 (60 × 5) and the 100 others who may enter give a TLS of 400. The Net Labor Needs is −40 (360 − 400), or an estimated oversupply of social secretaries.

Example 4.   A high turnover rate of 50 percent was found for dishwashers, with no new positions predicted. About 100 individuals were estimated to be available for this position over the next five years.

In this case, with 75 (50 percent of 150) replacements needed each year, a total of 375 replacements were estimated to be needed over the next five years, for a TLD of 375. The TLS was 100, resulting in the Net Labor Needs for the next five years of 275.

Summary of Projecting Net Labor Needs

The procedure followed to arrive at the Net Labor Needs for a specific occupation is, at best, an estimate. As pointed out throughout this section, certain information is lacking that has an influence on the accuracy of the final projection of Net Labor Needs. First, whether employers or some other source provide information for predicted labor demand, the opportunity for variation from these predictions exists. The economic situation in society, technology, rapid growth, recession, or other unforeseen variables may create a change in expected new positions to be added or in the percentages of replacements experienced. When projecting labor supply, the numbers of graduates from vocational programs can be predicted with some degree of accuracy. The problem arises as to how many persons will actively seek employment in the area for which they were trained. Some may go into military service or change their career plans, and other situations may develop that lower the number of people actually seeking employment in a specific occupation for which they were trained. Combined with these variables is the unpredictable source of new entrants. Thus, when a number is obtained for Net Labor Needs, this represents the best estimate considering what is known at the time the data were collected.

Estimates for Net Labor Needs must be carefully analyzed with regard to established standards. Referring again to Figure 5–6, let us assume that a standard was established as follows: "If twelve farm equipment mechanics would be needed in the next five years, a course should be initiated in Agricultural Machinery Service." Following the Net Labor Needs formula, a curriculum planner would have determined that, in fact, the estimated need for farm equipment mechanics did not meet the established standards.

The Net Labor Needs formula may also provide data that are useful in establishing standards for future curriculum development. For example, a situation may occur that a Net Labor Need is found to be fifty for an occupation in which no vocational program exists. Thus, the curriculum planner may further study this situation to determine if standards should be established in deciding whether vocational courses should be offered that would prepare individuals for employment in that occupation. One note of caution needs to be mentioned if a large Net Labor Need develops for a specific occupation. The example of dishwashers in Figure 5–6 is an excellent illustration. There are certain jobs that experience a high turnover rate, thus resulting in a high job vacancy. The problem may not be a lack of people available to fill such a position, but a shortage due to low wages, poor working conditions, or other undesirable aspects of a job that keep people from seeking employment in it. Another example would be sewing machine operators in a clothing factory. This job tends to become extremely monotonous for some employees, and as a result, a high turnover rate often occurs.

Even with limitations that may exist with forecasting labor supply and demand, vocational education curriculum developers must continue to forecast and predict labor needs for various occupations. Only in this way will vocational education programs remain relevant to the needs of a community. Until the techniques and procedures for predicting labor supply and demand become more sophisticated, and until data used to make these predictions become more reliable, one must continue to use approaches that will provide the best opportunity to determine if established program quality standards can be met.

Projecting Program Costs for Use in Decision Making

The subject of the costs of proposed programs may, at first glance, appear as if it should have been covered in the preceding chapter. However, when considering funding of proposed programs, the curriculum planner must eventually consider resources available in that community to determine if standards relating to financial support are indeed available. Thus, the following section deals with projecting program costs, with the remaining section concerned with identifying resources.

Determining Estimated Program Costs

When considering program costs, there are two basic types that will need to be examined. One type of cost involves the introduction of a vocational curriculum not currently available in the school; the second type involves the cost to incorporate or expand a course offering within a vocational service area that is already a part of the curricular offerings within a school. Discussion of each type of cost follows.

Costs for New Programs.   Projecting costs for a new program may begin by using the outline contained in Figure 5–7.

Instructional and Support Staff.   Estimates for hiring staff vary widely from state to state and even within states. Curriculum planners

---

FIGURE 5–7.   *Projecting costs for new vocational programs*

Item	Support Needed
Staff	
Instructional	$ _____
Support	$ _____
Instructional	
Materials & Supplies	$ _____
Equipment	$ _____
Travel	$ _____
Facilities	$ _____
Other (specify)	$ _____
Totals	$ _____

contemplating the development of new vocational programs should have little trouble in projecting the cost needed to obtain staff associated for the program under consideration.

Instructional Materials and Supplies. Estimated costs for materials and supplies cannot be accurately accomplished unless the curriculum content has been determined. Once the content has been determined (treatment of this topic is found in Chapter 7), it then becomes easier to assess what the costs will be. The forms contained in Figures 5–8 and 5–9 may assist in projecting costs for materials and supplies for any program(s) under consideration; an example has been included on each form. In summarizing costs on the form in Figure 5–9, cost per vocational service can be obtained, cost per vocational course can be determined, and cost per student course and/or per vocational service area can be projected. All of these total cost figures can be transferred to the form in Figure 5–7 where they may be used to assist planners in arriving at the projected instructional materials and supplies cost for a course under consideration.

Equipment. The cost to equip a new facility will vary widely and is largely dependent on the vocational service area and type of equipment

---

FIGURE 5–8. *Projecting costs for materials and supplies*

Class XYZ

Project or Activity	Material	Size	Quantity per Student	Number of Students	Total Quantity Needed
Machine Bolt	Round iron	½"	6½"	40	21.6 feet
	Hex, nuts	½" NC	2	40	80
Wiring Single Pole Switch	Instructional manual	—	1	40	40

FIGURE 5–9. *Summary sheet for projecting costs for materials and supplies*

Course or Vocational Area Machine Technology

Material	Size	Quantity Per Class			Total Quantity Needed	Price Per Unit	Total Cost
		Class XYZ	Class ABC	Class EFG			
Round iron	½ "	21.6'	50.0'	—	71.6'	$0.15 /ft.	$10.74
Hex. nuts	½ " NC	80	300	65	445/20 box	1.44/box	$31.68
Instructional Manual—single pole switch	—	40	—	—	40	7.00 ea.	$280.00
TOTALS							$322.42

needed. Although it is difficult to provide an estimate that will be accurate for all situations, curriculum planners must rely on equipment lists available for each vocational service area from state departments of education or teacher education institutions.

Travel. Expenses for the teachers' travel and field trips for students should be provided. In vocational education, supervised occupational experience projects are a part of the programs; thus, teachers must be provided ample travel expenses in order to supervise and establish educational occupational experience projects for each student. Costs of field trips may also be included under this category.

Facilities. Projecting the cost of new facilities is similar to projecting equipment costs. Construction costs vary widely throughout the United States; thus, for each locality one will need to check closely with local contractors as to costs. Plans and blueprints for vocational service areas are usually available from state departments of education.

Costs for Expanding or Redirecting Current Vocational Programs.
Estimating costs for expanding or redirecting programs or courses to a vocational service area already in existence would be similar to the

process followed for a new program. The form in Figure 5–7 would need to be revised slightly; an example of this revision is provided in Figure 5–10. The major differences is that provision is made for indicating support presently available and an estimate of support needed if the expansion or redirection of a vocational service area were to take place.

Obtaining Assistance in Projecting Costs

The task of identifying and projecting costs is not an easy one, and this type of activity must usually be carried out over a long period of time. The curriculum planner must, therefore, seek the assistance and cooperation of others who can provide pertinent information. Individuals who might be contacted would include vocational teachers aligned with the program or course currently under study, other vocational teachers, specialists in vocational service areas, school finance personnel, or other individuals who have direct knowledge of the service area. Advisory councils can be of particular help, especially when projecting costs of equipment, supplies, and materials. In addition, schools that have recently initiated new programs can be of tremendous help to schools that are just starting a curriculum development study.

Inflation Considerations

The need to consider inflation rates must be considered, since the time from which a program is first conceived to the actual building construc-

FIGURE 5–10. *Projecting costs for expansion of a vocational service area*

Item	Present Support	Support Needed
Staff		
Instructional	$ _____	$ _____
Support	$ _____	$ _____
Instructional		
Materials & Supplies	$ _____	$ _____
Equipment	$ _____	$ _____
Travel	$ _____	$ _____
Facilities	$ _____	$ _____
Other (Specify)	$ _____	$ _____
TOTALS	$ _____	$ _____

tion may be three to five years. Failing to account for rising costs due to inflation may place a school in a situation of having to cut back on some of the facilities, equipment, supplies, or staff when the expense occurs. If this situation materializes, then realizing established quality program standards may be impossible.

Special Considerations in Projecting Costs

As society and technology advance, those individuals responsible for developing vocational curricula must be alert to elements in the environment that have an influence on vocational education programs. *Energy* and its conservation appear to be a major concern to all. The construction of buildings and the conservation of needed utilities are areas that planners must consider as new buildings are constructed or older buildings renovated. *Safety* and the passage of the Occupational Safety and Health Act have an impact on planning vocational curricula. Facilities and equipment designed for the safety of students, teachers, and others will become a greater concern in the future. *Handicapped* individuals are now recognized as one group of students overlooked in the past. Many older buildings did not take into account the handicapped individual. The construction of new facilities and renovation of older facilities will need to accommodate the handicapped. *Flexibility* is the key to vocational programs in the future. Never before in history has the type of jobs changed so rapidly, and in the future, changes will be occurring at an ever-increasing rate. Construction of new facilities must incorporate flexibility so that as programs and courses become obsolete, changes for emerging courses and programs needed for job-entry skills can be initiated with a minimum of expense.

Identifying and Assessing Available Resources

Once standards have been established for resources needed in a quality vocational program, plans must be made to collect data that will indicate if resources are indeed available at the level required. Four basic areas of resources to be examined include funds, facilities and equipment, human resources, and cooperative training stations.

Funds

The monetary resources for vocational programs may originate from local, state, or federal sources, or in some cases, special gifts from indi-

viduals, businesses, or private foundations. The percentage of funds for
each source may vary from state to state or locality to locality, so those
individuals planning vocational programs must determine just how much
is available and from what source. Although the treatment of the topic
here is not lengthy, funds are, nonetheless, one of the most critical factors
in achieving program quality. *Furthermore, as funds are identified for
educational programs, curriculum planners must determine just how
much of those funds will be used for vocational education programs.* With
there being more possibility that the distribution of funds obtained for
any one vocational program might be different than for other vocational
programs, a slight revision to the form in Figure 5–10 permits information about any one vocational course or service area to be analyzed with
relative ease. The revised form is included in Figure 5–11 and provides
the planner with an opportunity to designate the source and amount of
funds received from each funding level.

FIGURE 5–11. *Projecting costs for a new, expanding, or redirection of
a vocational service area and sources of funds*

Vocational Course/Area _____ Year _____

Item	Present Support	Support Needed
Staff		
Instructional	$_____	$_____
Support	$_____	$_____
Instructional Materials	$_____	$_____
& Supplies	$_____	$_____
Equipment	$_____	$_____
Travel	$_____	$_____
Facilities	$_____	$_____
Other (specify)	$_____	$_____
TOTALS	$_____	$_____
Source of Funds		
Local	$_____	$_____
State	$_____	$_____
Federal	$_____	$_____
Private	$_____	$_____
TOTALS	$_____	$_____

Facilities and Equipment

The assessment of school facilities and equipment was discussed in an earlier chapter; however, curriculum planners must not overlook facilities and equipment that may exist in a community. An assessment of community facilities and equipment could take place while an employer survey is being conducted to determine labor demand. The value derived from an awareness of community resources could be pointed out, for example, if an employer owned a piece of equipment valued at $3,000 and the school were able to rent or borrow the equipment. This arrangement might be more economical than investing $3,000 in this equipment and leaving it idle for fifty weeks out of the year.

Human Resources

Effective and quality vocational programs do not rely only on adequate equipment, funds, and materials, but also on competent teachers to conduct the programs. Human resources include support personnel as well as administrators. Thus, a standard must be established regarding the specification of human resources needed for a quality program, and data need to be collected to measure whether this standard can be met.

Cooperative Training Stations

The value of cooperative training stations to student development is frequently supported in the literature. Schools may well desire to establish a standard in this area. Information collected from employers with the use of the form shown in Figure 5–1 permits a school to assess whether or not sufficient training stations are available. Information collected via this form might also be useful for developing a list of those employers who need more information about cooperative programs, and this may lead to further contact and cooperation between the school and community.

Summary

The Vocational Education Acts of 1963 and 1968 and their subsequent amendments, as well as the Perkins Act, were based on preparing youth and adults for placement in entry-level jobs, and with this concept, the need to collect and analyze community-based data for use in decision making in vocational education programs became vitally important. One of the first tasks of curriculum development is to define community boundaries, and these boundaries might fluctuate depending upon the standard being measured. Once standards and geographical boundaries are firmly defined, collection of data can be achieved.

Data are usually needed regarding the types of industries and businesses existing in the community, as well as the number of people employed by occupational title. In addition, attempts to determine new and emerging sources of employment will aid in keeping vocational programs relevant. Labor demand and supply must be assessed to establish Net Labor Needs. The Net Labor Needs reflect the number of individuals not available who are needed to fill newly created jobs or to replace those leaving their occupations. Although many uncontrollable variables will influence the estimates made for future labor demand and supply, vocational educators, especially those responsible for curriculum development, must continue their efforts to arrive at realistic projections.

Vocational education program quality will not be achieved unless adequate resources can be identified and committed to the program. Funding, facilities and equipment, human resources, and cooperative training stations are just a few such resources. Projected costs for initiating new or expanded programs must be assessed to determine if established standards can be met. Consideration must also be given to energy conservation, safety, the handicapped, and program flexibility.

Established program standards related to community-based information have a great influence on the success of quality vocational education programs. Therefore every effort must be made to collect accurate data, so that decisions which affect curriculum development will be based on the best available information.

Related References

Bailey, Thomas. "Jobs of the Future and the Education They Will Require: Evidence from Occupational Forecasts." *Educational Researcher* 20, no. 3 (March 1991): 11–20.

Copa, George H. *Towards a Strategy for Planning Vocational Education*. Minneapolis: Minnesota Research and Development Center for Vocational Education, University of Minnesota, August 1981.

Cunningham, William G. *Systematic Planning for Educational Change*. Palo Alto, Calif.: Mayfield, 1982.

Cyert, Richard M., and Mowery, David C., eds. *Technology and Employment*. Washington, D.C.: National Academy of Sciences, 1987.

Haub, Carl. "Demographics: What Lies Ahead? Shifts, Growth and Change." *VocEd* 59, no. 4 (May 1984): 29–31.

Herman, Jerry J. "External and Internal Scanning: Identifying Variables that Affect Your School." *NASSP Bulletin* 73, no. 520 (November 1989): 48–52.

Involve the Community in Vocational Education, Module LT-F-3, Athens, Ga.: American Association for Vocational Instructional Materials, 1983.

Lamar, Carl S., ed. *Comprehensive Planning for Vocational Education.* Arlington, Va.: American Vocational Association, 1978.

Lewis, Morgan V., and Fraser, Jeanette L. "Taking Stock of National Trends." *VocEd* 59, no. 4 (May 1984): 26–28.

Major Programs, Bureau of Labor Statistics. Report 718, U.S. Department of Labor, Washington, D.C.: U.S. Government Printing Office, 1985.

McCune, Shirley D. *Guide to Strategic Planning for Educators.* Alexandria, Va.: Association for Supervision and Curriculum Development, 1986.

Occupational Projections and Training Data, 1990 Edition. Bureau of Labor Statistics, U.S. Department of Labor, Washington, D.C.: U.S. Government Printing Office, 1990, No. 2351.

Outlook 2000. Bureau of Labor Statistics, U.S. Department of Labor, Washington, D.C.: U.S. Government Printing Office, 1990.

Policy, Planning, and Management in Technical and Vocational Education. Paris, France: United Nations Educational, Scientific and Cultural Organization, 1984.

Warnat, Winifred L. "Preparing a World-Class Work Force." *Vocational Education Journal* 66, no. 5 (May 1991): 22–25.

SECTION III

ESTABLISHING CURRICULUM CONTENT

The initial sections of this book have served to provide a meaningful planning base for the vocational and technical curriculum. School- and community-related data should be thoroughly examined to determine whether or not the curriculum should be offered and, if so, what its general scope should be. Whereas decisions associated with planning are a fundamental part of the curriculum development process, they are not designed to pinpoint content essential to the curriculum. Thus, the planning base must be expanded to include the specific content a curriculum will contain.

This section deals with the processes used to establish meaningful curriculum content. Whether a curriculum is just being formulated or is undergoing revision, it becomes vitally important to ensure that its content reflects the needs of the work world. This section provides curriculum developers with a means of establishing relevant content while placing particular emphasis on approaches that can be used in applied settings.

Although the chapters in this section may be used independently, they have been designed to project a sequence of events in the process of establishing meaningful content. Initially, it is important to determine the range of content that has potential to be included in a curriculum (Chapter 6). After potential content has been identified, the curriculum developer must make decisions regarding which content may be used in a particular educational setting (Chapter 7). Constraints such as time, facilities, personnel, and students can affect the amount of content that can be covered. Thus, the usable content is typically less than that initially identified. An additional element in the establishment of meaningful content deals with developing curriculum goals and objectives (Chapter 8). Certainly it would be possible first to establish goals and objectives and then move on to the identification of content, but the end result might be a lack of content relevance.

The reader should be mindful that this section is not meant to be prescriptive. Whereas some persons may be able to follow the sequence suggested in Chapters 6, 7, and 8, others may find that content has already been derived for their teaching areas.

6

Determining
Curriculum Content

Introduction

Determining curriculum content for vocational and technical education is very rewarding and yet extremely frustrating. The rewarding aspect is the final product: content that may be actually used in the instructional environment to aid vocational students in achieving their fullest potential. The frustrating aspect of determining curriculum content consists of identifying that which is truly relevant to *both instructional and occupational settings.* The paragraphs that follow focus directly on these concerns. Initially, consideration is given to the factors associated with curriculum content determination, including constraints placed upon the curriculum developer. Next, areas of concern associated with selecting a meaningful content derivation strategy are discussed. Finally, a number of strategies are presented, each of which serves as an alternate route to determining meaningful curriculum content.

Factors Associated with Determining Curriculum Content

Perhaps it seems that one could just sit down and decide which content is most important to include in a curriculum, but this impression is far from reality. In a typical educational setting, the curriculum developer is confronted with a variety of factors that may affect the task of determining what should actually be taught. These factors may have great impact on the direction one takes when establishing a content framework. Idealistically, the developer may have unlimited resources and flexibility to shape content in the ways he or she wants to; however, real-world considerations often dictate the scope of the content determination process. Factors such as time and dollars available; internal and external pressures; federal, state, and local requirements; skills needed by employers; academic and vocational education content concerns; and the particular level of content all have potential to affect the means by which content is determined for a particular curriculum.

Time and Dollars Available

Time becomes a critical element in the entire curriculum development process and is obviously a key concern when content is to be determined. The curriculum developer typically is not able to spend an unlimited amount of time deriving content to be taught. Instead, he or she is usually given a prescribed amount of time within which to establish content. This may be a day, a week, a month, or a year, but time is, nonetheless, a finite entity that affects the content determination process. A developer who is given two weeks to establish content for a curriculum will, in all likelihood, use a content determination strategy that can be executed in a relatively short period of time. On the other hand, an individual who is able to spend a year at this same effort has a variety of options available as far as strategies are concerned.

The dollars a developer has at his or her disposal to use in the content determination process can, likewise, affect the scope of a particular effort. Time and money are often considered synonymous in education, since professional salaries constitute such a large portion of the overall budget. Within this context, however, money may be considered in connection with the purchase of items such as travel, printing, postage, secretarial assistance, and the hiring of temporary personnel and/or consultants. When one is examining the ways content might be determined, money is a key factor, since the amount actually available tends to dictate which content derivation strategy is used. Some strategies require no additional funds over what may be available in a typical educational institution's budget. Others require extensive travel or mailings to gather information and, consequently, demand that additional dollars be made available. Thus, the curriculum developer must be very much concerned about time and dollars available in support of content determination activities.

Each of these areas is a constraint placed upon the developer that must be dealt with logically and thoroughly as content is being determined.

Internal and External Pressures

Another factor related to determining curriculum content consists of the subtle (and sometimes not so subtle) pressures exerted by individuals and groups from within as well as outside the educational environment. Certain individuals or pressure groups may feel it is in the best interests of themselves or others to support inclusion of certain content in the curriculum. The reasons behind this sort of support are numerous, since local situations and personalities often enter into the process. Reasons may range from honest concern for students' welfare to quasipolitical tactics. Regardless of the reason behind such pressure, the curriculum developer must recognize that in some cases the cause supported by certain individuals or groups may not be in the best interests of students. For example, emotional concern about content that might be included in a curriculum is no substitute for systematic content derivation. This is not to say that concerns of this type should be ignored. The contemporary curriculum developer must maintain an open mind and search for meaningful curriculum concerns that individuals and groups might possess.

Pressure in support of certain content might be exerted from within an educational environment by several sources. Administrators, vocational and technical teachers, academic teachers, guidance counselors, students, and placement specialists may each feel that certain content must be included in a curriculum and strongly support that conviction. A major responsibility of the curriculum developer is to sort out these concerns and determine which are valid and which are not. If this critical analysis is not accomplished, an invalid concern might receive widespread support and actually be included as content in a curriculum. When a situation such as this occurs, students as well as the school may suffer the consequences.

Pressures from outside the educational environment may emanate from areas such as businesses, industries, self-employed persons, professional organizations, unions, and advisory committees. Since every vocational curriculum must be responsive to the world of work, concerns from these areas cannot be ignored. In certain situations where pressure for specific content is applied from an individual or group outside the educational environment, the validity for a claim must be established. It might be that a particular business firm supports the inclusion of curriculum content dealing with word processing, since they have a need for competent workers in this area; or an occupational advisory committee might believe that metrication should be an integral part of a building construction curriculum. In either case, such concern might be valid and should, therefore, be verified during the content derivation process. Working with the public is an ongoing responsibility of vocational educators and handling the concerns of lay persons is just one part of this responsibility. The curriculum developer must be responsive to public concerns and pressures by examining their implications and determining which claims are valid and justifiable.

Federal, State, and Local Content Requirements

Curriculum content determination is seldom made solely by a curriculum developer or teacher group. In numerous occupational areas there are content requirements specified that serve as a basic framework for curricula. These requirements, which may already be established at the federal, state, or local level, tend to limit the extent to which a curriculum developer can become involved in the content determination process. For example, the Federal Aviation Administration (FAA) specifies the content and hours of instruction required of a person before that individual may be qualified as an aircraft mechanic. This content has been established through national surveys of people working in the occupation. Obviously, major departures from prescribed FAA content might affect not only graduates' competence but also their licensure as aircraft mechanics.

A similar situation exists at the state level with regard to certain occupations. State regulations often specify the content and hours of instruction that must be included in nursing and cosmetology programs, and examinations administered at the state level tend to focus on this content. Consequently, there may be few changes one can make in curriculum content in such areas as these.

State-level content requirements may also be seen in the general education area. The specific general education courses required for completion of an associate degree or high school diploma may be contributing or limiting factors in the design of a relevant curriculum. Excessive general education requirements can limit the extent to which vocational and technical content is provided. Likewise, requirements for extensive vocational and technical content may adversely affect students' general educational development through restriction of course selections.

Local content requirements tend to parallel job opportunities in the particular geographic area. If industries in a locale are heavily involved in the production of textiles, providing relevant core content for all students planning to enter this occupational area would be appropriate. Arrangements might be made with local unions to give credit toward the completion of apprenticeship programs if certain content requirements are met while students are still in school. The content ties between school and work not only benefit the graduate but the employer, the school, and the community. Whereas local content requirements are of a more informal nature, they are equally as important to curriculum building as state and national requirements.

Skills Needed by Employers

In a basic sense, much of the vocational education curriculum content is aligned closely with employers' needs. This focus exists so the educational institution may provide its students with content that is workplace-relevant. Unfortunately, individual employers may not have the most progressive view of what skills their workers need. Factors such as the evolving nature of the workplace and the time lag in knowledge dissemination cause some employers to fall behind others in terms of understanding workplace needs. This is particularly true of future worker needs since employers are more likely to focus on the present rather than the future.

Thus, in the determination of curriculum content, consideration must be given to future as well as current employer needs. This task is made easier through the use of content determination strategies such as the Delphi technique that focus what workers may be doing in the future. However, more general views of the current and future workplace may be drawn from studies that focus on entire industries or businesses or employers-at-large. These studies can provide the curriculum developer with much valuable information about current and future employer needs, needs that may not be discovered through contacts and discussions with individual employers and workers.

One such study, conducted by the American Society for Training and Development (ASTD), focused on workplace basics: skills that employers want their workers to have (Carnevale, Gainer, and Meltzer, 1988). The ASTD report indicates that a new breed of worker is needed—one that may not have to demonstrate as many skills in a narrow area but will have to demonstrate knowledge in a broad range of skills. It is revealed that basic skill requirements will continue to increase in a wide variety of occupations and that the preparation of skill and craft employees with better basic skills may assist America in regaining its competitive advantage. Provided in the ASTD report are descriptions of what employers want. These are organized into a hierarchy of seven skill groups ranging from most advanced to most basic. The groups include

Organizational Effectiveness/Leadership
Interpersonal/Negotiation/Teamwork

   Self-Esteem/Goal Setting-Motivation/Personal and Career
      Development
   Creative Thinking/Problem Solving
   Communication: Listening and Oral Communication
   3 Rs (Reading, Writing, Computation)
   Learning to Learn

Learning to learn is most basic to employees because it enables them to achieve competence in other skills. On the other end of the continuum, workers who are skilled at organizational effectiveness and leadership can contribute more effectively to employer success in the marketplace. As the curriculum content determination process proceeds, it is important to recognize the basic skills that workers must demonstrate in the workplace. The skill groups provided by ASTD can serve as a most meaningful foundation for curriculum content selection and delivery.

   A different set of studies presented by Bailey (1990) further supports the changing nature of the workplace. Bailey and his colleagues conducted extensive examinations of jobs in four employment sectors: apparel, textile, banking, and business services (accounting, management, consultants, systems design, etc.). It should be noted that the nature of work *across* each sector was examined and information could, therefore, be gathered about how jobs are changing and how they will change in the future. The studies strongly support the notion that jobs of the future will require greater and not less skill and that this will occur across both the service and manufacturing areas. Instead of the traditionally held notion that jobs will become deskilled, curriculum developers must recognize that future jobs will require workers to perform a broader range of skills and to demonstrate them at higher levels. Employees must be able to change and develop as an industry or business evolves. Workers of the future should expect their jobs to be more demanding. They must be able to work efficiently as members of teams, "manage more-frequent and more-complex interactions with other individuals, perform a greater number of frequently changing tasks, and otherwise operate in a more uncertain and less well-defined environment" (Bailey, 1990). Workers will, additionally, be required to take more individual initiative and must have a clear understanding of the overall processes, products, services, and markets associated with their employers' firms. The implications for determining vocational education curriculum content are indeed great. Information reported by Bailey as well as Carnavale et al. point to a need for aligning curriculum content with the rich context of the workplace. Thus, although specific tasks, skills, attitudes, values, and appreciations will continue to be important, other capabilities that are needed to survive and grow in the ever-changing workplace will become even more critical. These workplace basics and skills of the future must, therefore, be firmly embedded in the vocational education curriculum.

Academic and Vocational Education Content Concerns

As noted earlier, employers currently need and will continue to need workers who can demonstrate facility in mathematics, science, and communication skills, and this need will continue to grow as the workplace continues to become more and more complex. This situation, coupled with the overarching responsibility of education to prepare persons for both living and earning a living, presents educators with a thorny problem: how to prepare students in terms of both the academic and the vocational education aspects of the curriculum. Concerns related to this area have evolved into the concept of integrating academic and vocational education (to be discussed in Chapter 11). Integration essentially means that academic and vocational education content are brought together and taught together in such a way that the content in each area becomes more relevant. By providing more relevant contexts for both academic and vocational education content it is anticipated that students will learn more and at a more rapid rate than under more-traditional instructional conditions. Since it may be important to identify relevant academic content concepts during the content determination process, the curriculum developer must be aware of specific academic content needs and plan accordingly. For example, if mathematics is to be integrated into a new drafting and design program, the developer may choose to modify drafting and design content determination processes so that mathematics content will emerge instead of remaining firmly embedded in vocational education content. To accomplish this, survey or interview forms can be modified or the curriculum content focus can be broadened to embrace mathematics in a more holistic manner. Basically, the curriculum developer should recognize that when content is being determined it is an opportune time to obtain relevant information about academic as well as vocational education content.

Level at Which Content Will Be Provided

A final factor related to curriculum content determination is the level at which that content will be provided (i.e., secondary versus postsecondary). These different levels have direct impact on content, with the impact being felt in rather subtle ways. At the secondary level, students' educational needs tend to be more basic. Although some students may progress more rapidly to advanced studies in technical areas, the majority focus on developing those academic or general and technical competencies associated with the entry-level work. Instruction is generally geared toward preparation for a specific occupation or closely related family of occupations or, in terms of Tech Prep programs (see Chapter 11), preparation for an associate degree in a technical field. At the postsecondary level, students are typically those who have completed high school and have chosen to pursue education beyond that level. The postsecondary student is usually older and more mature. Thus, content must focus on the needs of this type of student. In many instances, postsecondary vocational and technical education prepares students for an occupational field rather than for a specific occupation. If this is the situation curriculum developers find themselves in, content needs to be identified which has high transferability to a number of occupations within a field.

Selecting a Curriculum Content Determination Strategy

The actual selection of a curriculum content determination strategy appears simple. However, the selection process can be quite complex, with the degree of complexity dependent on a variety of concerns. Of immediate concern to one who is selecting a strategy are the aforementioned factors (time and dollars available; internal and external pressures; federal, state, and local content requirements; and level of content) that may impact on the content determination process. Each of these factors can affect the decision that is ultimately made, and, therefore, all factors should be examined closely and information about them saved for future reference. Once the various factors associated with determining content have been examined, the developer may focus on three additional areas of concern: the educational setting, the occupational setting, and the content determination strategies available. Each of these concerns is discussed in the paragraphs that follow.

The Educational Setting

The setting in which curriculum content will be implemented is most important to study. This enables the curriculum developer to determine which aspects of the setting may affect selection of one strategy over another. Although there are a multitude of questions one might ask about how the educational setting relates to curriculum content, some likely examples might be: What is the current educational philosophy of the school and the attendance area? What support for vocational and technical education emanates from the educational community? To what extent will teachers and administrators assist in the content determination process? How well will educators accept the results of systematic curriculum content determination? These are several questions a curriculum developer should pose.

The Occupational Setting

The occupational setting represents another area of concern for the curriculum developer. As with the educational setting, those aspects of the occupational setting that may result in a better strategy choice must be identified. Several of the questions one might ask about relationships between the occupational setting and curriculum content include: Is the occupation clearly identifiable or is it emerging? Can workers in the occupation be interviewed by telephone or face-to-face? Will permission be granted for workers to complete survey forms and questionnaires? To what extent will businesses or industries assist with data gathering? These are the types of questions that should be asked by the developer as he or she begins to focus on the ways content may be determined.

Content Determination Strategies

A final and most important concern is with strategies that may actually be used to determine curriculum content. Each of the various strategies will be described in detail later in this chapter, but one must first see how these strategies are similar to and different from each other. If we were to draw a straight line and place "more subjective" at one end and "more objective" at the other, we would have a continuum along which each of the strategies could roughly be placed. The *philosophical basis* for determining content is perhaps the most subjective strategy, since a specific philosophy or set of philosophies serves as a foundation for content decisions. This strategy is most typically used to develop curriculum content in academic areas. *Introspection* is used by an individual or group to examine personal experiences and knowledges and to incorporate these into a framework for the vocational curriculum content. This strategy may be classed as quite subjective, since very little (if any) "hard" data are used in the decision-making process. The *DACUM* content determination approach utilizes occupational experts to derive relevant content. Its focus is on development of a single-sheet skill profile that serves both as a curriculum plan and an evaluation instrument. *Task analysis* focuses on the identification and verification of tasks performed by workers in a certain occupation or cluster of occupations. Its procedures enable this strategy to produce quite objective data related to worker tasks. Several other meaningful strategies may be considered by the curriculum developer. These include the *critical incident technique* and the *Delphi technique.* The critical incident technique is useful in identifying curriculum content related to worker values and attitudes. Content in emerging occupations may be identified via the Delphi technique.

The observation may be made that the more objective curriculum content strategies are, the more costly they are to use. For example, task analysis is a very objective process, but this objectivity is obtained at a high cost, since one must send materials or travel to locations where workers are employed. The philosophical approach is very inexpensive and the small investment yields a meager return in terms of objectivity. Realistically, the curriculum developer should *consider using several strategies,* since each has its own particular strengths and weaknesses. When several strategies are used, there is a much greater likelihood that the content developed will be valid.

Philosophical Basis for Content Determination

Philosophy appears to have had the greatest history of affecting curriculum content decisions. Before more sophisticated means of determining content were established, philosophy served as the guiding light for curriculum developers. Even today, the philosophy of vocational education espoused by a particular school, school district, or community college may provide a framework for the various curricula offered. Most of the general education offerings found in our schools today are based solely upon teachers', administrators', and/or school board members' personal philosophies of education. Thus, the fact that philosophy can and often does serve as a foundation for curriculum content is quite evident.

Establishing a Philosophy

A detailed discussion dealing with philosophical foundations of vocational education is beyond the scope of this volume, however, focusing on some examples of philosophy is certainly appropriate. These serve to illustrate the ways that a philosophy might be specified. One must keep in mind that a person's philosophy is basically that which he or she believes. We may say that a philosophy is composed of several belief statements, each of which contributes in some way to the overall makeup of the philosophy. Philosophy tends to vary from individual to individual and group to group just as might be expected of such a value-laden area. Therefore a group may have difficulty reaching consensus regarding some belief statements whereas other statements may be agreed upon unanimously with little or no discussion.

The establishment of belief statements is a rather straightforward activity. Various sources are examined to identify statements that might align with one's personal philosophy. Textbooks, articles, and speeches can all serve as useful sources of information. Philosophies developed by professional associations, community colleges, school districts, and similar units provide a wealth of potential belief statements. Whatever sources may be used, it is important to recognize that these statements represent a potential philosophy. Eventually, a group of concerned and knowledgeable persons must examine each belief statement and agree as to which ones will constitute a philosophical base for the curriculum.

A literature search might serve first to clarify the characteristics of vocational education. For example, a review of numerous sources that included individuals, organizations, agencies, and federal legislation served as a basis for the following statements about vocational education's character:

1. Preparation for gainful employment that requires less than the baccalaureate degree
2. Can include the development of academic skills in concert with development of specific occupational skills
3. A lifelong set of learning experiences ranging from occupational exploration and preparation to on-the-job development
4. May serve to link occupational preparation at the secondary and postsecondary levels
5. Provides a foundation for an employment career in addition to preparation for an entry-level job

The foregoing serves to illustrate how a basic curriculum framework may evolve. If, for example, we believe that vocational education involves "preparation for gainful employment," our belief should certainly have an impact on the curriculum that is established. Based on this belief, any vocational curriculum content that does not relate in some way to the work environment should be seriously questioned.

Belief statements may take many forms. The following represent a range of possibilities in this regard and, in some cases, serve as sources of other belief statements:

1. Each person should be educated in the least restrictive environment in which that person's educational and related needs can be satisfactorally met (Sarkees and Scott, 1985).

2. Secondary vocational education courses should provide instruction and practice in the basic skills of reading, arithmetic, speaking, listening, and problem-solving (National Commission on Secondary Vocational Education, 1984).

3. Lifelong learning is prompted through vocational education (Miller, 1985).

These statements are but a few of the many that may be drawn from the literature and used as a foundation for the vocational curriculum. Dedication to the task of identifying belief statements such as these will ensure that a comprehensive philosophy is developed.

Philosophy as Related to Curriculum Content

Once belief statements have been identified, agreed on, and molded into a philosophy, content may then be identified that aligns with this philosophy. As this process begins, it is almost immediately realized that belief statements are rather broad and tend to cut across several content areas, whereas the technical content appears to be more specific to the individual curriculum. This, perhaps, indicates a basic strength and weakness of the philosophical approach to content determination. The strength has to do with the way a philosophy can permeate an educational institution. A philosophy can, for example, direct the focus of curricula within a school better to meet the needs of groups such as women, minorities, and the handicapped. If those who oversee the operation of a school firmly believe in the statement that "vocational education should be available to all those who can profit by it," their actions should be directed toward the establishment and maintenance of curricula for these groups. This does not mean merely providing a few token offerings but actually aligning curricula with students' needs on a large-scale basis. If it is stated in a philosophy that "a comprehensive placement service should be provided to both currently enrolled and former students," then action should be taken to establish the type of service to align with each curriculum.

These few examples serve to illustrate the broad impact that a sound philosophy can have on curriculum development. However, this impact is not as great in the area of specific technical content, and here is where problems tend to arise in relating philosophy to content. The general nature of a belief statement may not describe specific competencies needed by an individual in the work environment. Thus, the curriculum developer must speculate about what the specific competence should be and hope that this speculation results in the identification of appropriate content.

Introspection

The introspection process basically consists of examining one's own thoughts and feelings about a certain area. However, within the context of curriculum content determination, this strategy may involve either an individual or a group. The person or persons engaged in introspection are typically vocational teachers who each ask themselves the basic question, "What do I feel should constitute the content of this curriculum?" Then a search is made of one's personal employment, teaching experiences, and education to identify what might be most appropriate to include as curriculum content.

The Introspection Process

Introspection typically begins with an examination of ongoing vocational programs and literature related to them. This serves to remind the developer of what content might possibly be included that he or she would not otherwise recall from past experiences. The examination of literature and observation of programs might include traveling to other locations and talking to those who are involved with relevant curricula or examining course catalogs and outlines from other institutions. Concurrent with this, magazines and other related sources are reviewed to identify "ideas" for curriculum content.

Once the examination is complete, the developer considers what content might be best for students, using subjective judgment as the decisive element. Consideration is given to both the education process and the result of that process from the perspective of an experienced vocational teacher. Eventually, a content outline is developed that serves as the basis for the curriculum.

Introspection often becomes a group process where several teachers develop their individual thoughts regarding curriculum content and then meet to decide collectively what form the curriculum should take. This procedure has the advantage of providing a variety of inputs from persons with differing backgrounds and experiences. Teachers who have had different exposure to an occupational area will most likely be in a better position than one individual to determine which content is more relevant to a particular occupation or occupational area. The group process can also serve as a means of keeping personal bias to a minimum. If the group must agree collectively on curriculum content, one person's biases become more difficult to be accepted—unless, of course, all group members share the same bias with this individual.

The foregoing points to a major shortcoming of the introspection process. Whereas moving the curriculum decision-making process from one teacher to a group of teachers may make these decisions more reliable, using introspection does not mean that the content will be any more valid (i.e., relevant and realistic). For example, even though a group of electronics instructors unanimously agrees that curriculum content should consist only of studying vacuum tubes, this still does not make the content precisely relevant to employment in our transistorized society.

Therefore the curriculum developer must recognize that introspection is not always the most valid content determination process. To come up with truly realistic content by this process is often quite difficult, particularly when one considers the nature of individual instructors and the scope of many occupations.

One means of at least partially overcoming this validity problem is through use of occupational advisory committees. The advisory committee is, by its very nature, supposed to be in close touch with reality. Committee members should be able to distinguish between relevant and irrelevant content and provide the curriculum developer with the sort of guidance needed. A basic assumption is that committee members are, in fact, close to the occupation, can determine what content is most relevant and, therefore, should be included in the particular curriculum. However, if this assumption cannot be met, the curriculum developer is not much better off than he or she would be with a teacher group.

The DACUM Approach

A most useful variant of introspection is the DACUM (*Developing A CurriculUM*) approach, which utilizes some basic ideas associated with introspection but shares few of its shortcomings. The reason for this is that DACUM relies on experts employed in the occupational area to determine curriculum content and allows them to be guided through a systematic content determination process. Although the approach has some commonalities with other content determination strategies, DACUM will be examined in a singular fashion because of the success curriculum developers worldwide have had using this approach in content determination.

DACUM was initially created as a joint effort of the Experimental Projects Branch, Canada Department of Manpower and Immigration, and General Learning Corporation. The idea was later adopted and used by Nova Scotia New Start, Inc. and utilized in the determination of vocational curriculum content for disadvantaged adult learners (Adams, 1975). DACUM was felt to be particularly useful for the New Start activity because immediate action needed to be taken on curriculum development and limited dollar resources were available.

DACUM may be defined as "a single sheet skill profile that serves as both a curriculum plan and an evaluation instrument for occupational training programs" (Adams, 1975, p. 24). A unique aspect of the DACUM approach is the way that curriculum content is displayed. A single-sheet skill profile is used to present the skills of an entire occupation, thus reducing the chance of treating one element of an occupation separately from the others. The profile provides an independent specification of each of the behaviors or skills associated with competence in the occupation. These behaviors are stated in a rather simple manner so that the student can understand them and are organized in small blocks on the chart in such a manner that each can be used as an independent goal for the student. The profile can also contain a rating scale that facilitates evaluation of achievement for each of the behaviors. In this manner, the profile may be used as a record of achievement for both student and teacher. As the example in Figure 6–1 indicates, a profile need not only serve as a record of achievement in school, but may also be used as a sort of diploma or documentation of skill development in an occupation.

The development of a DACUM profile involves using a committee of ten to twelve resource persons who are experts in a particular occupation. Employers nominate as resource persons, people who are skilled in the occupation and who are currently serving as a worker or supervisor in the area. Experiences with this approach have revealed that instructors in an occupational field *do not always* contribute effectively to the DACUM process. If vocational teachers are involved in the DACUM process, they might be best utilized as ex officio committee members and be brought in after the basic committee has prepared a preliminary or draft profile.

The DACUM committee functions as a group with all developmental activities taking place when the members are together. Time required to complete a DACUM profile generally ranges from two to four days. A coordinator from outside the committee works with the group to facilitate the development process (Norton, 1985). Examples of previously developed DACUM charts and related materials are provided to committee members so that they may see what the end product will look like.

Following committee orientation, the facilitator guides the group through a series of steps that includes

1. Reviewing a written description of the specific occupation
2. Identifying general areas of competence within the occupation
3. Identifying specific skills or behaviors for each general area of competence
4. Structuring the skills into a meaningful learning sequence
5. Establishing levels of competence for each skill as related to realistic work situations

FIGURE 6–1. *Example of a DACUM profile*

DACUM Profile for

ELECTRONIC PUBLISHING TECHNICIAN

DACUM Panel Members

Calvin A. Cox
Maryland Composition Company
Margaret A. Draper
Corporate Printing Company, Inc.
Nancy Gillio
The Desktop Shop
Sue Olnick
George W. King
Michelle Pierluissi
Spectrum Arts Limited

Kimberly Roelecke
Corporate Printing Company, Inc.
Harry L. Shaw
In Tandem Design, Inc.
Kelly N. Wagner
Waverly Press, Inc.
Craig Ziegler
Graffito Communication and Design

Graphic Communication
Technical Committee

John H. Absalom
Holladay-Tyler Printing Corp.
Marty Anson
Bindagraphics, Inc.
Ronald L. Bray
French Bray, Inc.
Richard Burnham
Graphic Imaging, Inc.
Fred Carter
Waverly Press, Inc.
Calvin Cox
Maryland Composition Company, Inc.
Mary Dahbura
Hub Labels
Randy Dorman
Baltimore Color Plate
Margaret Draper
The Corporate Printing Co., Inc.
Robert D. Guthridge
American Trade Bindery
Helene H. Hahn
Hahn Graphics, Inc.

Jerry J. Hartman
Reese Press
Frank M. Heneghan
McArdle Printing Company
Terrence Heyer
Editor's Press
Theodore J. Kees
Baltimore Typographical Union #12
Arthur H. Kudner
Tidewater Publishing Corp.
Michelle Pierluissi
Spectrum Arts Limited
James A. Ritz
Graphic Technology, Inc.
Lisa Schade
Printing Industries of Maryland
Barbara Westland
Westland Printing
Cathy Zaidlicz
Port City Press

DACUM Facilitator

Nancy Jones
Dundalk Community College
for the
Maryland DACUM Resource Center
Dundalk Community College

Date
February 6-7, 1990
*Maryland State Department of Education/Vocational-Technical
Education and the Graphic Communication Technical Committee in cooperation with
Dundalk Community College.*

Source: Used by permission of Maryland DACUM Resource Center, Dundalk Community College, Baltimore, Md.

FIGURE 6–1. *(Continued)*

THE **Electronic Publishing Technician** supports the creative process by taking a publication through the production stage.

┌──────────────────── **DUTIES & TASKS** ────────────────────┐

A) CREATE TEXT AND PAGE LAYOUT

A1. Select software package*	A2. Set up software to target output device	A3. Set up style sheet*	A4. Set up template*	A5. Set up format definitions*
A6. Format the text	A7. Place graphics	A8. Place page elements	A9. Identify color breaks for pre-press	A10. Identify screens

B) INTERPRET SPECIFICATIONS

B1. Evaluate specifications for completeness*	B2. Evaluate specifications for feasibility*	B3. Evaluate time estimates for feasibility*	B4. Clarify specifications with client/designer	B5. Document changes in specifications
B6. Translate specifications into company terminology*	B7. Mark-up manuscript according to specifications	B8. Create specifications from a visual*		

C) INPUT FILES INTO SYSTEM

C1 Prepare text for input	C2. Prepare graphics for input	C3. Keyboard manuscript	C4. Scan manuscript	C5. Scan graphic image
C6. Input files from magnetic media	C7. Input files from optical media	C8. Receive files via telecommunications	C9. Input graphics from video	

D) MANIPULATE TEXT FILES

D1. Translate the scanned image to text file	D2. Perform file format conversions	D3. Execute translations	D4. Edit text file for format errors	D5. Check for spelling errors using software
D6. Correct spelling errors				

E) MANIPULATE GRAPHIC FILES

E1. Determine method of re- production for graphics*	E2. Translate graphics from one format to another	E3. Manipulate bit-map graphics (paint)	E4. Trace bit-map graphics	E5. Manipulate vector graphics (draw/illustrator)
E6. Crop graphics	E7. Scale graphics	E8. Rotate graphics	E9. Apply reproduction specifications*	E10. Select file format for graphic

*Advanced *(not entry level)*

FIGURE 6–1. *(Continued)*

────────────────── **DUTIES & TASKS** ──────────────────

F) GENERATE OUTPUT

F1. Identify output media	F2. Load/unload media	F3. Select resolution	F4. Generate a proof print	F5. Collate materials for proofing
F6. Output final product	F7. Collate final product and associated materials			

G) CONTROL QUALITY OF PUBLICATION

G1. Proofread text for content	G2. Proof text for adherence to specs*	G3. Review page layout to design specs*	G4. Review page layout to printer specs*	G5. Review graphic elements to design specs*
G6. Review graphic elements to printer specs*	G7. Verify the consistency of the output process	G8. Follow quality control sign-off procedures		

H) OPERATE THE COMPUTER SYSTEM

H1. Maintain an organized filing system	H2. Perform regular back-ups	H3. Archive files	H4. Maintain file library	H5. Install program upgrades
H6. Access network systems	H7. Send files via telecommunictions	H8. Save files to optical media	H9. Save files to magnetic media	

I) MAINTAIN EQUIPMENT

I1. Follow manufacturer's written maintenance procedures	I2. Schedule routine service	I3. Clean equipment	I4. Calibrate equipment	I5. Test the equipment
I6. Troubleshoot equipment malfunctions	I7. Perform minor mechanical adjustments*	I8. Provide for emergency repairs	I9. Keep maintenance logs	I10. Maintain supply inventory
I11. Replenish consummables				

J) FUNCTION IN AN ELECTRONIC PUBLISHING ENVIRONMENT

J1. Manage individual work area	J2. Plan work flow within individual jobs*	J3. Document time use	J4. Provide technical assistance for planning job*	J5. Coordinate resource use with co-workers
J6. Report deviations from job plan	J7. Document material use	J8. Document use of contracted services	J9. Resolve minor operations problems*	J10. Keep abreast of field
J11. Update technical skills	J12. Comply with company policies and procedures			

FIGURE 6–1.   *(Continued)*

Traits and Attitudes

Will be:

Creative
Flexible
Optimistic
Punctual
Reliable
Detail oriented
Self-motivated
Organized
Dependable

Will possess:

Sense of urgency
Foresight
Ability to work well under
    pressure
Common sense
Good eyesight
Good hand-eye coordination
Desire to learn
Ability to learn quickly
Ability to accept
    constructive criticism
Initiative
Ability to work well with
    others

Knowledge/Skills

Skills

Mechanical skills
Word processing functions
Visualize end product
Computer literacy
Typing skills
Time management skills
Communication skills (client/
    co-workers)
Memory skills
Organizational skills
Problem-solving skills
Measurement skills
Questioning skills
Produce a mechanical

Knowledge

Spelling and Grammar
Proofreaders' and editors' marks
Typesetting and graphic terminology
Math/arithmetic,
    geometry, algebra (copy fittings)
Reading skills-high school (manuals . . .)
Understanding production processes
Typography (fonts, measurement,
    points, etc.)
Photographic process
Software (publishing, layout,
    draw, paint illustrator,
    word processing)
Elements of design
Color theory
Color separation
Screens

Tools and Equipment

PICA rule/inches rule
Proportion wheel
Computers - several platforms
    MAC
    IBM
    Front-end system
    SUN
Type book
Type gauge
Densitometer
PMS book
Process color guide
Scanner
Loupe
Processors
Laser printers
Typesetter
Image setter
Thermal printer
Copy machine
Templates
Waxer
Clip/art
Sizer
Type face overlay
Exacto knife
Light table
Drafting tools
Non-reproducible blue pencil
Calculator
Color calibrator
FAX
Modem
Screen gauge
Mouse
Graphics tablet
Trac ball
Software
Keyboard
Line printer
Periodicals
Manuals
References

The Maryland State Department of Education does not discriminate on the basis of race, age, color, sex, national origin, religion or disability in matters affecting access to or participation in programs or organizations. For inquiries related to departmental policy, contact the Equal Opportunity Office.

For additional copies of this chart or further information on Maryland's Technical Committee Project, contact the Curriculum Management Specialist, Division of Vocational-Technical Education, Maryland State Department of Education, 200 West Baltimore Street, Baltimore, Maryland 21201. (301) 333-2062.

MARYLAND
VOCATIONAL
CURRICULUM
MANAGEMENT
SYSTEM

Once the DACUM profile has been developed, the product may serve as a basis for developing instructional content and materials that focus on student attainment of specified skills. It should be noted that teachers tend to become involved *after* the profile has been produced. This procedure has the advantage of identifying only those skills that are most relevant to the work setting. This does not mean teachers are disenfranchised; they are recognized for their overall technical expertise and ability to organize, sequence, and detail curriculum content.

The DACUM approach to curriculum development has some distinct advantages. First, the committee procedure results in a relatively low development cost. The major expense would be payments to committee members, and in many cases, a business or industry will gladly release an "expert" from his or her duties to assist in this process. Second, the time frame for conducting the DACUM activity is quite short. Thus, in a relatively brief time, instructors may use the profile to prepare for their classes. No time is spent waiting for forms to return or worrying about nonrespondents. Third, and perhaps most important, is the way that DACUM enables curriculum content to be derived without academic intervention. DACUM's advantage over the traditional introspection process is quite clear. The process allows more relevant content to be identified and incorporated into a curriculum. At first glance, the DACUM approach appears no different from the traditional trade and job analysis process. One should note, however, that these approaches rely on the instructor to determine what the content should be with little direct consideration given to input from persons employed in the actual work setting.

Task Analysis

Few content determination strategies have seen such widespread use as task analysis. This particular approach has been employed by vocational educators in varying forms for a number of years. However, during the mid-1960s, several developments occurred that resulted in major refinements to the task analysis process. These refinements have enabled curriculum developers to make more objective decisions regarding content that should be included in various curricula. Of particular note was research conducted at the Personnel Research Laboratory, Lackland Air Force Base, Texas, which resulted in the development of a procedural guide for conducting occupational surveys (Morsh and Archer, 1967). This guide has enabled educators to study systematically the behavioral aspects of job requirements. Further refinement and use of the task analysis process by groups such as the Vocational-Technical Education Consortium of States (V-TECS) has shown this approach to be quite applicable to public vocational and technical education.

Task Analysis Fundamentals

Basically, task analysis may be defined as the process wherein tasks performed by workers employed in a particular job are identified and verified. The worker's *job* consists of duties and tasks he or she actually performs. *Duties* are large segments of work done by an individual that typically serve as broad categories within which tasks may be placed. Examples of duties would be organizing and planning, typing, maintaining equipment and tools, and loading and hauling. *Tasks,* on the other hand, are work activity units that form a significant aspect of a duty. Each task has a definite beginning and ending point and usually consists of two or more distinct steps. Examples of tasks performed by workers would be planning menus, filing materials, computing depreciation, and winterizing vehicles. Basic to the task analysis process is the gathering of information directly from workers. Obtaining information from this source ensures that workers are actually providing input for curriculum content decisions. Just as the name "task analysis" implies, potential tasks are identified and then verified by job incumbents, with the resultant analysis serving to determine which tasks are actually associated with a particular job.

Conducting the Task Analysis

There are several possible ways that a task analysis may be conducted, but the key to success lies in being both thorough and systematic. For this reason, much of the discussion that follows is drawn from procedures utilized by the Vocational-Technical Education Consortium of States (V-TECS) in the conduct of their task analyses. V-TECS is a cooperative effort among a number of state agencies to develop catalogs of performance objectives, criterion-referenced measures, and guides in selected occupational areas. The consortium is administered by the Southern Association of Colleges and Schools, Commission on Occupational Education Institutions, Atlanta, Georgia. Catalogs based on task analyses are completed or underway for hundreds of job titles ranging from child care to turf management. The experience of this consortium over the past several years has enabled V-TECS to develop a set of task analysis procedures that is extremely functional. There are, of course, other sources of information for persons who are planning to conduct task analyses. However, most references are, at least in part, based upon Morsh and Archer's (1967) work. Those interested in marketing education occupations may explore parallel competency identification efforts conducted by the Marketing Education Resource Center, Inc., Columbus, Ohio.

What, then, are the basic steps involved in task analysis? Typically they include reviewing relevant literature, developing the occupational inventory, selecting a worker sample, administering the inventory, and analyzing the collected information.

Reviewing Relevant Literature

The first step in conducting a task analysis consists of examining literature in the occupational area. This review is useful in determining the extent to which other analyses may have already been conducted. If meaningful analyses have been completed, there is usually no reason to go any further with the analysis process. A second use of the literature review is to develop lists of potential tasks and equipment associated with the occupational area. Tasks may be listed for one or several jobs, with the exact scope of the analysis being determined by the curriculum developer. Thus, an occupational area typically consists of two or more jobs in a related area or cluster. Equipment lists serve to identify the extent to which equipment is used and, once verified, serve as meaningful aids in laboratory planning and similar areas.

Developing the Occupational Inventory

After task equipment and work aid lists have been gleaned from the literature, duplicate items are deleted and, wherever appropriate, relevant items are added. Lists are then incorporated into an inventory that will eventually be completed by incumbent workers. The equipment list is generally placed on a separate sheet of the inventory, together with spaces for workers to check items used in the current assignments. A sample page from a printing occupations list is provided in Figure 6–2.

In order to keep track of the various jobs examined in a task analysis, standard numbers and job titles provided by the *Dictionary of Occupational Titles* (D.O.T.) may be used. The D.O.T. classification scheme is utilized by the U.S. Department of Labor and might prove especially helpful when an instructor is eager to know what tasks are appropriate to various jobs in an occupational area.

Tasks are grouped under appropriate duty headings, with the exact number of headings being dependent on the particular occupational area. Duties provided in a V-TECS occupational inventory for plumbing include: organizing and planning, directing and implementing, inspecting/ evaluating, training, joining pipe, installing hangers and supports, building distribution lines, building drains, installing traps and cleanouts, installing vents, installing fixtures, installing hot water/steam systems, and maintaining plumbing systems (used by permission of Vocational-Technical Consortium of States [V-TECS]).

For this particular inventory, a total of 293 tasks was included. In this manner, a comprehensive picture of the job is provided so that mean-

FIGURE 6–2. *Page from a printing occupations tool, equipment, and work-aid list*

TOOLS, EQUIPMENT AND WORK-AIDS LIST

Directions: Please place a check to the right of each tool, piece of equipment, or work aid that you use in your current job. Add any tools/ equipment/work aids that you use which are not listed.	used in present job?					MVCRC use only
	Daily	Weekly	Monthly	Yearly	Never	
1. Automatic Letterspace						
2. Burnishing Roller						
3. Color Pencils						
4. Color Wheel						
5. Collator-Stitcher-Trimmer						
6. Computer-Aided Design Software						
7. Contact Vacuum Frame and Point Light Source						
8. Date Stamp						
9. Data Conversion System						
10. Densitometer						
11. Developing Trays						
12. Digital Scanner						
13. Digitized Typesetting System						
14. Drawing Board						
15. Drawing Curves						
16. Double Head Stitcher						
17. Electronic Publishing Software						
18. Enlarger						
19. Film Dryer (Automatic)						
20. Film Processor						
21. Graduated Cylinder						
22. Handjack						
23. Jogger						
24. Laminator						
25. Light Source						

Source: Used by permission of Vocational-Technical Education Consortium of States (V-TECS). State of origin: Massachusetts.

ingful reactions are obtained from workers. After task and equipment lists have been developed in preliminary form, they are reviewed by a sample of incumbent workers and supervisors to obtain reactions directly "from the field." Feedback from these individuals may result in anything from technical and grammatical refinements to the addition of relevant items. This is obviously an important part of the task analysis process, since the inventory can be verified.

An equally important aspect of inventory development deals with the areas marked by incumbent workers. These consist of scales to check whether or not tasks are done in the present job, and they permit the indication of time spent doing the tasks. Unfortunately, time spent on a task does not indicate that it is more or less important than other tasks. Some very important tasks take a very short time to complete. Data collected from workers are used to determine whether or not a particular task is of sufficient importance to warrant its inclusion in the curriculum. Figure 6–3 contains one task-list page from an inventory for biomedical equipment technicians.

The items in Figure 6–4 are representative of background information that is usually gathered. Workers' names and addresses may be needed in the event that some responses require clarification, whereas "How long have you worked in this occupational area?" may be used to categorize workers' responses in accordance with their work experience. A curriculum developer using this approach is advised to keep informational items to a minimum and only include items that are absolutely essential.

Selecting a Worker Sample

Although, in some instances, information may be gathered from an entire population of workers, this procedure is usually not followed. Workers in a particular occupational area may number several thousand or even hundred thousand; thus, data must be gathered from an appropriate sample of that population. Sampling not only cuts costs in terms of printing and mailing, it also reduces the magnitude of data to be analyzed. Numerous references are available that describe procedures for determining the appropriate sample size. Regardless of the sampling procedure used, any sample selected must be truly representative of the population. An appropriate sampling technique will ensure that results from the worker sample can be generalized to the population.

Administering the Inventory

Once the inventory has been developed and the sample selected, data can be gathered from incumbent workers. Perhaps the most expeditious

FIGURE 6–3. *Page from an occupational inventory task list for biomedical equipment technicians*

OCCUPATIONAL INVENTORY Duty/Task List	Page 21 of 37 Pages

DIRECTIONS
A. 1. DO Mark (X) by the tasks you perform now in the column labeled "Mark If Done in Present Job" and Add any tasks you do now which are not listed.
B. 1. DO NOT Mark tasks you have done in past jobs.
    2. DO NOT Mark tasks performed by others whom you supervise.

DUTY H: MAINTAINING EYE, EAR, NOSE AND THROAT (EENT) EQUIPMENT	MARK IF DONE IN PRESENT JOB	OFFICE USE ONLY
TASKS		
1. Adjust digital biometric rulers.		
2. Adjust eye chart projectors.		
3. Calibrate audiometers.		
4. Calibrate audiometric impedance bridges.		
5. Calibrate caloric irrigators.		
6. Calibrate lensometers.		
7. Calibrate optical laser systems.		
8. Calibrate perimeter vision testers.		
9. Calibrate tonometers.		
10. Calibrate treatment cabinets.		
11. Calibrate tympanometers.		
12. Perform preventive maintenance on audiometer booths.		
13. Perform preventive maintenance on audiometric impedance bridges.		
14. Perform preventive maintenance on audiometers.		
15. Perform preventive maintenance on bronchoscopes.		
16. Perform preventive maintenance on colorimeters.		

Source: Used by permission of Vocational-Technical Education Consortium of States (V-TECS). State of origin: Illinois.

FIGURE 6–4. *Background information sheet for a secretary occupational inventory*

OCCUPATIONAL INVENTORY: WORKER BACKGROUND INFORMATION
DOMAIN: SECRETARY

FOR OFFICE USE   INVENTORY NUMBER /////

Name _____

Street Address_____

City_____ State _____Zip Code_____

Directions: Please answer the following questions as accurately as possible.

1. Please place a check mark in the box to the left of the title that best describes your present job.

___ Secretary, Secretarial Stenographer (201.362-030)
___ Stenographer, Clerk-Stenographer (202.362-014)
___ Clerk Typist (203.362-010)
___ Typist (203.582-066)
___ Other (Specify)_____

2. How long have you held the job title marked above?

Years ____ Months_____

3. How long have you worked in this occupational area?

Years ____ Months_____

4. Which of the following best describes the nature of the organization in which you work:

___ Government agency
___ Educational Institution
___ Private business (manufacturing/technology)
___ Private business (service)
___ Other (please specify) _____

5. Approximately how many workers are employed by the organization you work for?

___ 1-100
___ more than 100

Source: Used by permission of Vocational-Technical Education Consortium of States (V-TECS). State of origin: New York.

approach is to mail the inventory out and rely on workers to complete and return it. Unfortunately, this is not always successful, since inventories usually contain twenty to thirty pages and hundreds of tasks. When care is not taken to follow up on those who fail to return forms, the result may be a low return rate. If fewer than 60 percent of the selected sample complete and return inventories, the generalizability of results to a population of workers may be seriously questioned. Therefore a high return rate should be secured whenever the inventory is mailed to workers. An alternative approach is to sample employers and make contact with persons at the managerial level to solicit the cooperation of their employees. By dealing directly with employers, the curriculum developer is able to obtain support "from the top" and thus encourage a good return rate. Workers whose employers support the inventory process may feel a strong personal obligation to complete and return the inventory promptly. A third alternative would be to interview workers at the job location. This is often an expensive proposition, but it may be the only effective way to gather data from workers in certain occupational areas.

Analyzing the Collected Information

After the data have been collected from workers, responses are typically processed via computer. This is certainly the most expeditious route to take, since each inventory contains so many different tasks and items of equipment. If, for example, 200 workers each completed an inventory with 300 tasks and 75 equipment items, 75,000 bits of data would be produced!

In the determination of what actually constitutes a meaningful task the recommendation is made to establish some appropriate cutoff point. For example, this might be "80 percent of the workers perform the task." Whatever standard is eventually established, it must be remembered that the vocational curriculum typically prepares students for entry-level employment. Tasks should not be arbitrarily eliminated just because they are not performed by seasoned veterans, since these same tasks may be performed by a high percentage of novice workers. By taking information from the workers' background information sheets such as time spent on a job, a determination may be made of which tasks are performed by more experienced and less experienced workers.

The Critical Incident Technique

Even though the critical incident technique has been available for many years, its use in deriving curriculum content has been quite limited. This technique is comprised of "procedures for collecting direct observations of human behavior in such a way as to facilitate their potential usefulness in solving practical problems" (Flanagan, 1954).

An incident is any observable human activity that enables "inferences and predictions to be made about the person performing the act"

(Flanagan, 1954). Incidents are classified as critical when the observer sees their purpose and consequences as being clear. A major contribution that the critical incident technique can make to curriculum content identification is its potential to deal more directly with isolating important values and attitudes. Whereas task analysis and similar approaches are useful in the identification of content, they tend to focus more exclusively on technical content and less directly on affective concerns. With the critical incident technique, one can select those behaviors that are attitude- or value-laden and thus provide a firmer foundation for affective content in the curriculum.

The technique may be illustrated by using an example of a concern that many curriculum developers have. Assume that a certain curriculum has a poor record of graduates holding jobs. Placement has been high and no difficulties have been identified with the workers' technical competence, yet persons who have been placed on jobs tend to be dismissed at a much higher rate than those who studied other curricula. When approaching this problem, one would first want to identify those nontechnical essentials that make the difference between job success and failure. To accomplish this, supervisors are asked to record in the form of anecdotes or stories those job behaviors that contributed to worker dismissal. The data gathered are then used to build a composite picture of job behavior.

In order to obtain the necessary information, a critical incident form is devised that allows supervisors who have day-to-day contact with workers to record specific instances of workers' inappropriate affective behavior. The form provided in Figure 6–5 may be used for this purpose. Each supervisor completes a form for each critical incident that he or she can remember. In addition to a description of the incident, information may be requested about the amount of time the worker has been employed. This assists in isolating incidents associated with entry-level type workers. Examples of some incidents gathered from supervisors are presented in summary form:

1. A worker was consistently "sick" on Mondays, using up sick time as soon as it was awarded.
2. Worker activity consisted of only that which was specifically assigned. The worker showed no initiative to find work to do.
3. Over a three-week period, the worker was late to work ten times. For each instance of being late, the worker had a questionable excuse.

The above incidents are merely illustrative and must be combined with many others to arrive at any meaningful inferences. Typically, from 100 to 200 incidents are gathered, with the actual usable number being somewhat less. The reported incidents are then conceptually grouped into

---

FIGURE 6–5. *Critical incident record form*

Directions: Think of the workers you dismissed over the past six months. Focus your
attention on any one nontechnical thing that one of your workers may have
done that contributed to his or her dismissal. In other words, think of a *critical
incident* related to nontechnical failures of your workers. Please do not place
any person's name on this form.

WHAT LED UP TO THE INCIDENT?

EXACTLY WHAT DID YOUR WORKER DO THAT WAS CLASSIFIED AS A NONTECH-
NICAL FAILURE?

HOW DID THIS INCIDENT CONTRIBUTE TO HIS OR HER DISMISSAL?

WHEN DID THE INCIDENT HAPPEN?

---

categories with general headings. Categories associated with the area of
nontechnical failures might consist of the following:

1. Punctuality
2. Interpersonal relations
3. Interpretation of company policy
4. Personal initiative

Other categories could, of course, be added, with the exact number being
determined by the incidents that have been gathered.

The utility of this information is quite evident. Categories and their
associated incidents serve as a foundation for curriculum content that
focuses on developing appropriate attitudes and values. Curriculum developers must recognize that instruction based upon this type of content
is not provided on a lesson, project, or similar basis. Affective education
must be infused into the curriculum in such a way that students develop
appropriate values and attitudes across their entire school experience
instead of just during formal classroom or laboratory sessions.

The Delphi Technique

A more recently developed research tool, the Delphi technique, has much applicability when curriculum content is being determined. As its oracular name implies, the Delphi technique focuses more directly on the future of a particular area. Originally developed by the RAND Corporation for predicting alternate defense futures, it has seen widespread use in many areas of education. The Delphi technique has been found to be a most useful tool in setting priorities, establishing goals, and forecasting the future. Obviously, this technique would be of much value when persons desire to reach consensus regarding the content of a particular curriculum. All too often there is more content available than time in which to teach the material. The curriculum developer must provide a means of ensuring that the most relevant content is included and the least relevant content is excluded. A second use of the Delphi technique is related to emerging occupations. When curriculum development is conducted for a new occupation that has few workers or teachers, the opportunity to come up with valid curriculum information by regular means is quite remote. As an alternative to the approaches mentioned earlier in this chapter, the Delphi technique enables experts to speculate individually and then reach consensus collectively regarding the content necessary to prepare workers, even in areas where no workers exist at the present time.

Basically, the Delphi technique consists of a series of interrogations of samples of individuals (experts) by means of mailed questionnaires. The focus is on some curricular content area in which each individual is knowledgeable. Since respondents never meet face to face, the group is not biased by one individual's outlook. Anonymity enables each respondent to be more thoughtful and creative. Several rounds of questionnaires are typically used. The initial questionnaire requests a list of content that each participant feels should be included in the curriculum. This is followed by a second round, with each participant receiving a list of all opinions. The listing is reviewed, and then each item is rated in terms of its importance to the curriculum. During the third round, participants are asked to review consensus ratings of items and, based on the results, possibly revise their opinions. The fourth round provides participants with a chance to review updated consensus ratings and make final revisions (if any) to their individual ratings.

Although the Delphi technique can provide much meaningful information, the entire process consumes a considerable amount of time and relies on participants who have a great deal of stamina. However, even with its obvious disadvantages, the Delphi technique may be the only route to take for certain curricular areas. It is best thought of as a first step in the content determination process, one that may perhaps be used because no other data source exists.

Synthesis of Strategies

It is evident that much diversity exists among curriculum content determination strategies. The range of possible data that may be gathered presents an interesting challenge to any curriculum developer. An answer to the following question may serve to provide direction: Given certain resources, which strategy or strategies might be the most useful in determining content for a specific curriculum or program? Although obtaining an answer is not simple, the task may be made more manageable via a comparative analysis of strategies as presented in Figure 6–6. This figure displays the relative merits of strategies in terms of several key areas: ease of data collection, objectivity, validity, and applicability for deriving vocational education curriculum content. Even though the various "ratings" are of a relative nature, they provide a feel for some of the subtle and not so subtle differences among various strategies. It should be recognized that in the application of these strategies to vocational and technical education, consideration is given to three content areas: awareness of work, exploration of work, and preparation for work. These strategies correspond to some degree with many education frameworks and programs now in existence. Awareness and exploration content, for example, might fit into technology education, consumer home economics, and prevocational offerings.

Several areas of concern should be noted. First, it appears that ease of data collection comes at the expense of validity. Strategies that require more complex and thus more costly data collection processes tend to be the more valid means of deriving content. A second area of concern has to do with overlap among the various strategies. For example, a given educational philosophy might affect the introspection process or the reactions to a Delphi survey. The recognition that strategies are not mutually exclusive should aid curriculum developers in selecting them and in carrying out content derivation processes. It is all too easy to oversimplify the curriculum-content development process.

Strategies seem to apply more readily to one area than others. For example, using a philosophical basis works best for identifying awareness content but is less useful with exploration and preparation content. This fact may be related to the specific nature of some strategies and the broader aspects of others. Although task analysis may be used to focus on the specific aspects of an occupation, it does not incorporate the futuristic aspects of the Delphi approach which are so useful for identifying tomorrow's as well as today's content. It should be reemphasized that the use of multiple strategies has the greatest potential for deriving high-quality content. Each strategy has its own strengths; however, these strengths follow a rather narrow band of content. The application of several well-chosen strategies to a particular area should produce content that is more relevant to the needs of today's students, who are tomorrow's workers and citizens.

FIGURE 6–6. Analysis of curriculum content determination strategies

Strategy	Ease of Data Collection	Objectivity	Validity	Applicability to Vocational and Technical Education		
				Awareness of Work	Exploration of Work	Preparation for Work
Philosophical Basis	+	–	?	+	?	–
Introspection	+	–	?	?	?	?
DACUM	?	+	+	–	–	+
Task Analysis	–	+	+	–	?	+
Critical Incident Technique	–	?	+	–	+	+
Delphi Approach	–	?	?	+	+	?

158

Summary

This chapter has focused directly on the business of determining curriculum content. Efforts made to determine content must take into account the various factors that can affect the entire process. The actual time and dollars available to determine what content should be included in a curriculum constitute potential constraints for the developer. Likewise, internal and external pressures and concerns must be examined to determine which types of content are valid and justifiable. Requirements already established at federal, state, and local levels must be identified and taken into account as the curriculum is being established. Skills needed by employers must be considered, and relationships between academic and vocational education must be acknowledged. The level at which content is provided needs to be examined in relation to the students served so that their needs may be fully met.

Other areas of concern to the curriculum developer include the educational setting, the occupational setting, and the various content determination strategies available. The unique aspects of an educational or occupational setting might result in the choice of one strategy over another. Strategies range from the more subjective philosophical basis and introspection to the more objective task analysis. The critical incident technique has greatest utility in the values and attitudes area, whereas the Delphi technique is most useful for determining content in emerging occupational areas. Since the curriculum developer may not be able to gather complete information when one strategy is used, several strategies should be utilized to identify meaningful content. This will make the final curriculum better able to meet all student needs.

Related References

Adams, R. E. *DACUM Approach to Curriculum, Learning and Evaluation in Occupational Training.* Yarmouth, Nova Scotia: Department of Regional Economic Expansion, 1975.

Bailey, Thomas. "Jobs of the Future and the Skills They Will Require." *American Educator* vol. 14, no. 1 (Spring 1990), pp. 10–15, 40–44.

Carnevale, Anthony P., Gainer, Leila J., and Meltzer, Ann S. *Workplace Basics: The Skills Employers Want.* Alexandria, Va.: American Society for Training and Development, 1988.

Faber, Dennis M. *DACUM: A Practical Response to Corporate Training Needs.* Baltimore, Md.: Maryland DACUM Resource Center, Dundalk Community College.

Flanagan, John C. "The Critical Incident Technique." *Psychological Bulletin* 51, no. 4 (July 1954): 327–358.

Miller, Melvin D. *Principles and a Philosophy for Vocational Education.* Columbus, Ohio: National Center for Research in Vocational Education, 1985.

Morsh, Joseph E., and Archer, Wayne B. *Procedural Guide for Conducting Occupational Surveys in the United States Air Force.* Texas: Lackland Air Force Base, Personnel Research Laboratory, September 1967.

National Commission on Secondary Vocational Education. *The Unfinished Agenda, The Role of Vocational Education in the High School.* Columbus, Ohio: National Center for Research in Vocational Education, 1984.

Norton, Robert E. *DACUM Handbook.* Columbus, Ohio: National Center for Research in Vocational Education, 1985.

Sarkees, Michelle D., and Scott, John L. *Vocational Special Needs, 2nd ed.* Homewood, Ill.: American Technical Publishers, 1985.

7

Making Curriculum Content Decisions

Introduction

Decision making is perhaps one of the highest-level skills that a person can develop. It is a skill that permeates our society and is recognized as a part of virtually all professional, vocational, and technical occupations. Naturally, decision making is an integral part of the curriculum development process. Decisions must be made regarding numerous areas, including whether or not to offer a curriculum, how curriculum content may be identified, and what the substance of a curriculum should be. Chapter 3 provided an overview of the decision-making process and showed how decision making applies to curriculum planning. This chapter applies the process in an equally important area: curriculum content. Initial consideration is given to the purpose and scope of the content decision-making process. This is followed by a description of how constraints are identified that may affect content decisions. Next comes a discussion of the ways that potential content may be related to identified constraints. Finally, the curriculum framework is described, and the ways it may be utilized are detailed. In sum, this chapter serves to emphasize further the role of decision making in the curriculum development process and to point out how it may be applied to curriculum content decisions.

The Content Decision-Making Process

Curriculum content decisions arise as often as there is a need to determine what a curriculum's actual parameters will be. However, decisions of this type must not be taken lightly. When content is simply thrown together and arranged in a sketchy syllabus, the result is new problems rather than an effective curriculum. Basically, sound content decisions serve to bridge the gap between the identification of potential content (as detailed in Chapter 6) and the development of objectives (as explained in Chapter 8). Obviously, it is impossible to teach all the content that is identified as part of a task analysis or similar content determination strategy. The curriculum developer must, therefore, make some key determinations regarding which content is more beneficial to students and which content is less beneficial.

The content decision-making process may be expressed according to the following formula:

$$\text{Potential Curriculum Content} - \text{Constraints}$$
$$= \text{Usable Curriculum Content}$$

Potential curriculum content consists of that which has been determined potentially relevant to students through one or more of the strategies described in Chapter 6. *Constraints,* on the other hand, are those factors that might place serious limitations on the teaching of certain content. *Usable content* is that which best contributes to the students' welfare and, given existing constraints, can be taught. Although this formula may tend to oversimplify the process, it reflects how the curriculum developer can delineate content to the point where it is most meaningful and manageable for use in designing instruction.

Identifying Constraints Related to Curriculum Content

In order that constraints may be clarified, it is necessary to focus on the limitations present in the teaching-learning process. These logically take the form of statements related to either given or anticipated curricular outcomes. For example, it may be that there are only twelve months available to prepare certain student groups for employment. The twelve-month period then becomes one constraint that serves as a focal point when decisions are made regarding curriculum content. If, however, two years' preparation time were available, time would still be a constraint but one of lesser importance, since greater flexibility would be available in the selection of content. Whereas constraints may be associated with virtually every aspect of the curriculum, it is perhaps more productive to give consideration to four areas. These are the student, the teachers and support staff, the curricular arrangement, and the employment setting. The four areas tend to overlap; however, they will be discussed individually in the pages that follow.

The Student

Vocational and technical students represent a major force in the shaping of curriculum content. Student characteristics can have great impact on curriculum content and should, therefore, receive close scrutiny as the content selection process takes place. Initial consideration must be given to students' entering characteristics. What are the students' general and applied skills? Are they interested and motivated? What are their maturity levels? These and other related questions are of particular relevance, since such factors greatly affect the amount and type of content that can actually be covered. While recognizing that it is not always beneficial to use group data when a curriculum focuses on meeting the needs of individual students, the curriculum developer may need to obtain some group information during the decision-making process. Assume that content is being determined for a printing technology program. Data from prospective students indicate that 50 percent read at or above the eighth-grade level; the remainder read below this level. If it has been established that printing technology content mastery requires an eighth-grade reading level or better, a number of implications for content can be drawn regarding the students who are poorer readers. These might include the need for remedial reading instruction, tutorial help, a printing technology instructor who is also skilled in teaching reading, or an arrangement whereby reading instruction would be integrated with the printing technology instruction. All of these have implications for the amount of printing technology content selected, since time would need to be spent providing some students with basic reading instruction.

The Teachers and Support Staff

Several relevant questions may be posed about teachers and support staff as potential constraints in the content decision-making process. These include: What content are the vocational teachers qualified to teach? Are a sufficient number of teachers available to provide needed course work in general content areas (e.g., mathematics, science, English)? Are teachers across the institution capable of integrating general and vocational education content? Are qualified personnel available to provide adequate support services such as guidance, placement, and counseling? Since other questions will certainly come to mind, it is crucial to consider each in light of how teachers and support staff may ultimately affect the curriculum content. If, for example, a vocational teacher has sole responsibility for student placement as a part of his or her regular teaching load, content coverage may suffer while placement activities are being carried out. On the other hand, when placement is a responsibility shared by the teacher and the placement staff, more time is available to the teacher for dealing with important curriculum content areas.

The Curricular Arrangement

This category of constraints represents perhaps the broadest range of concern in curriculum content decisions. It goes beyond the basic scope of vocational and technical education content and into the total set of requirements and standards associated with a curriculum. Questions posed by the curriculum developer in relation to this area would include (but not necessarily be limited to): What time is or can be made available to teach the students? What content coverage, if any, is required for certification or licensure of graduates? What kind of general education content coverage is required? What dollars are available for equipment, resources, and supplies in support of certain content? Time becomes a basic limiting factor in relation to the amount of content that can be included in a curriculum and serves to act as a framework for the content that can be chosen. Required content coverage likewise limits the developer in his or her selection of content. It may be found in some instances that very little latitude is given to local personnel in content selection. This is particularly true in the health occupations area, where state requirements tend to dictate what should be included in a curriculum.

Although dollars have been a general concern during the curriculum-planning process, it is sometimes easier to pinpoint what costs are associated with specific content after the potential content is identified. If, for example, certain information-processing content must be supported by a computer and related hardware, this situation may well affect whether or not the content is included in a particular curriculum. It is important to examine each item of potential content and determine whether or not dollars are available to deal with the area in a professional manner. Content that is "too expensive" to teach may well suffer at this juncture; however, a decision needs to be made regarding which content is most important in relation to available dollars. Decisions in this area are often tentative and subject to reexamination after a year or so when hard cost data are available.

The Employment Setting

A final set of constraints may be drawn from the work environment that graduates are entering. In this regard, several important questions may be raised. These include: What minimum employability level is expected of graduates? What occupational areas will the graduates be prepared for? Which experiences (if any) may be best obtained in the work settings? These three questions are essentially related to the transition from school to work. If content essential to meet entry-level employment requirements is not included, graduates will be at a tremendous disadvantage. Content with too narrow a focus can also adversely affect the opportunities available to graduates. Consideration must be given to content breadth but not at the expense of depth. This requires a great deal of insight and creativity on the part of the curriculum developer, since both breadth and depth are important; however, sometimes other constraints (e.g., available time) will not allow both to be dealt with adequately.

Examining Content as It Relates to Constraints

Once various constraints have been identified (see Figure 7–1), the curriculum developer is then in a position to examine each constraint as it affects the potential curriculum content. It should be noted that this is a highly subjective process and one that attempts to arrive at the best fit of content and constraints more from a logic base than a data base. This means the developer must place considerable reliance on available information sources, logic, and intuition. An additional problem associated with content is the fact that constraints may cut across the various content elements. One constraint area such as state-mandated content coverage may have tremendous impact on a variety of content. Given the difficulty of relating constraints to content, it is often best to utilize a group of knowledgeable persons in the examination process (an advisory committee, a group of experienced teachers, or some combination thereof). It is useful to have a number of people review both content and constraints and give their personal ideas about congruence of the two. Input from persons such as these greatly aids the curriculum developer in making the most meaningful decisions.

Content Versus Constraints

Examining content in relation to constraints can be a very difficult proposition, especially when a great deal of potential content must be

---

FIGURE 7–1.   *Checklist for preparing to make curriculum content decisions*

Directions: Before major curriculum content decisions are made, check to be sure that information is available about the areas described below.

1. Student Entering Characteristics
   - ☐ General and applied skills
   - ☐ Interest and motivation
   - ☐ Maturity levels
   - ☐ Special needs
   - ☐ Other

2. Teachers and Support Staff
   - ☐ Content teachers can teach
   - ☐ Provision for teaching supporting coursework
   - ☐ Provision for integrating general and vocational education content
   - ☐ Availability of support staff (e.g. guidance, placement)
   - ☐ Other

3. The Curricular Arrangement
   - ☐ Time available to teach students
   - ☐ Required vocational content coverage
   - ☐ Required general content coverage
   - ☐ Funding available for equipment, resources, and supplies
   - ☐ Other

4. The Employment Setting
   - ☐ Minimum expected employability level of graduates
   - ☐ Employment areas graduates will be prepared to enter
   - ☐ Learning experiences best obtained in employment settings
   - ☐ Other

---

eliminated from the curriculum. However, given the alternative of selecting content for a meaningful curriculum or not establishing any curriculum at all, the process is most useful. It sometimes becomes a problem to point out exactly where one should begin looking for the congruence between content and constraints. Certain individuals may prefer to start with the employment setting, since it constitutes a basic focal point for content. Others may see the student as a key starting point, since students represent the fundamental input to any curriculum. Regardless of the constraints chosen to be examined first or last, it is essential to remember that each must be reviewed and considered in relation to all others.

In order to illustrate the examination process, assume that a curriculum developer wants to consider content in relation to constraints for a curriculum associated with supply technology (a fictitious area). Initially, the decision is made to look at content as it relates to the curricular arrangement. This is followed by examining the employment setting, the student, and lastly, the teacher and support staff. Scrutiny of potential constraints associated with the curricular arrangement reveals the following:

  No certification or licensure of graduates is required.

  Content must align with state requirements for a two-year Associate of Applied Science degree.

  Total productive instructional time in supply technology may not exceed 500 hours.

  Dollars are available to provide student transportation to school-owned work sites and to enable the teacher to coordinate students' cooperative work experiences with employers in the immediate area.

These items serve to indicate the kind of limitations a curricular arrangement can impose on content. Certainly the instructional time limitation has much impact on the amount of content that can be covered. The associate-degree requirement has numerous implications for general-education content coverage. This means the curriculum must include post-high-school-level content in areas such as English, mathematics, and science, all of which would be specified in state requirements. The availability of dollars for transportation and travel allows greater flexibility in content coverage outside a school's facilities. For example, opportunities to establish cooperative work experience arrangements and offer laboratory experiences away from the school give the instructional staff a great deal of latitude in the ways content may be delivered.

Moving into the employment area, the following are found to exist:

  Graduates may be employed as entry-level workers in the occupational area.

  Different physical requirements exist with regard to employment in different businesses and industries.

  Persons working in the occupational area have the opportunity to advance to supervisory positions if they become qualified.

These three statements provide useful input for content decisions because they help to point out the direction the curriculum should take. Since it is noted that graduates may be employed as entry-level workers, content coverage should prepare persons to attain at least this minimum level. Assuming that entry-level skills were detailed when potential content was identified, the curriculum developer may use these skills as a basis for content selection. At this point, however, some conflicts may arise between content coverage needed and time available to teach the content. Problems related to content coverage are not easily resolved and, in most instances, end up in a compromise between what is needed and what can actually be done. The indication that physical requirements exist in different occupational settings has major implications. Whereas it would be possible to prepare persons for a variety of occupations with businesses and industries, this must be considered in light of student characteristics. Variations in employment requirements might serve to limit the enrollment of certain groups (e.g., handicapped) if these requirements are not taken into account as content is selected. Thus, the employment settings prepared for can seriously affect the types of students to be enrolled in a curriculum.

With regard to students involved in the curriculum, the following information was identified:

Entering students' ages range from eighteen to forty-one years.

All entering students are sincerely interested in the curriculum.

Of the entering students, 30 percent have deficiencies in the mathematics area.

Of the entering students, 20 percent have deficiencies in the reading area.

The variation in students' ages gives some indication of heterogeneity among learners. How content relates to this factor depends on the time available and the resources that may be used to individualize instruction. If both time and resources are available, more content may be taught to this diverse group. Student interest and motivation do not become as much of a problem at the postsecondary level as they do at the secondary level. In this case, student interest is apparently good and the instructors can, therefore, focus on productive educational pursuits. When students are not motivated and lack interest, particularly because of lack of maturity, instructors who are not creative may spend much time on nonproductive activities such as maintaining discipline and order. This can have a marked effect on the content that is covered, sometimes resulting in a large reduction in productive teaching time. In terms of students' general subjects deficiencies, a decision must be made about the extent to which general subjects instruction will be provided. If this is an integral part of the curriculum (e.g., integration of general and vocational education content), time must be taken away from other content areas. The result could be a curriculum that does not fully prepare students for employment. An alternative would be to have general subjects instruction and demonstrated mastery of that instruction serve as a prerequisite to enrollment in the curriculum. This arrangement serves to maintain the curriculum's integrity and, at the same time, not restrict enrollment. However, the result could be that some program enrollees become discouraged and quit because they are forced to "endure" the study of general subjects before they can take supply technology courses. The data reported about students' general subjects skills make it obvious that some remediation is required. A basic question remains: How can this be taken care of without seriously reducing the amount of curriculum content?

Information regarding a final area, teachers and support staff, is as follows:

Teachers are available who qualify to instruct in the range of possible content areas.

Support personnel are not available to assist with placement of graduates.

Ratio of students to guidance counselors is 500 to 1.

It is clear that instructor qualifications should align with content to be taught. Otherwise, it might be necessary to eliminate certain content that would be beneficial to students. Although this example poses no particular problem, the curriculum developer should be aware of potential difficulties with teacher qualifications. Careful consideration should be given to instructor qualifications *before* individuals are hired rather than after they have taught for a year or so. Since it appears that teachers are to be responsible for the placement of graduates, time must be allocated to this activity. The time commitment to placement entails a corresponding reduction in content coverage. Certainly it is recognized that instructors can be responsible for a number of supplementary activities, but placement is too important to be a "catch-as-catch-can" responsibility. Whoever is designated to work in the placement area must have adequate time provided to do an acceptable job. This, of course, means that time may well be taken from teaching. Since implications could be made that guidance counselors have little time for each student, the teacher may, either formally or informally, assume some of this responsibility. Whereas a teacher may often counsel his or her students, excessive amounts of time spent counseling may detract from curriculum content coverage. It is, therefore, important to determine how much support is actually provided by the teaching staff, since this area has direct impact on curriculum content.

Implications of Content and Constraints

The foregoing has served to point out ways in which various factors can affect the content included in a curriculum. Whereas it would be impossible to spell out all the constraints related to content, the curriculum example has provided a point of reference for those making curriculum content decisions. In terms of implications for the curriculum developer, there are several items that may be of value. First, it is important to recognize that examining content in relation to constraints is an inexact process. Curriculum development has not advanced to the point where we can base content decisions solely on conclusive evidence. Thus, the curriculum developer must use sound professional judgment based on input from other qualified professionals.

A second implication concerns the aspects of different locales. Each educational setting, whether a community college, high school, or adult learning center, has unique characteristics. Corresponding to these characteristics are staff, students, facilities, administration, supervision, and a host of other factors that tend to make each setting somewhat different from others. Although the constraints and examples discussed on those pages provide a framework for the determination of meaningful curriculum content, individual educational settings may be unique in the ways that content relates to constraints. The curriculum developer needs to be aware of this situation and should examine each curriculum as a set of offerings and experiences having unique qualities, content, and constraints.

A final implication has to do with the creativity of a curriculum developer. The adequacy of content coverage is often a function of one's creative efforts in arranging, modifying, and sequencing curriculum content. Much can be gained by applying creative talents to the task of establishing content. The creative curriculum developer does not always approach problems with traditional solutions. He or she should keep in mind that instruction need not take place within the confines of an educational institution. When applied to content decisions, creativity has the potential to build curricula that better meet student, teacher, and community needs.

The Curriculum Framework

Educators often express concern about the ways curriculum content and associated areas may be documented. This concern has evolved from a perceived gap between curriculum as defined in its broader sense and instruction as defined in its narrower sense. Whereas the curriculum encompasses all those experiences provided under the direction or auspices of the school, it is apparent that documentation of content often does not extend beyond the course level. Of particular note is the course syllabus, which serves as a formalized course outline. This type of document does little more than provide students and visitors with some idea about content scope and sequence. Although the syllabus is important to instruction, this sort of documentation covers but a small part of the total curriculum.

Another form of instructional communication is the course of study, the importance of which cannot be underestimated. It is certainly useful for a teacher to have program or course units and plans delineated so that instruction may be conducted most efficiently. However, the vocational course of study typically fails to include any information about nonvocational content as well as numerous other items such as teacher and support staff capabilities. Thus, although the course of study serves a most useful function from an individual vocational or technical teacher's vantage point, it does not clarify the total scope of the curriculum.

Vocational and technical curriculum guides represent an additional form of documentation and communication. The curriculum guide is typically developed by a committee or group at a state or regional level and is used by vocational and technical teachers in their particular instructional areas. Representative course titles may include Horticulture, Welding, Quantity Food Preparation, and Secretarial Science. Curriculum guides often serve as guidelines for instruction in vocational areas and provide the instructor with meaningful information about suggested content coverage including time allocations. These guides are particularly useful for beginning teachers who, unlike their seasoned counterparts, do not have the experience on which to base content decisions. Since their applicability is quite general, curriculum guides may not be utilized until they are adjusted to specific local conditions and constraints. Although development at a higher level ensures wider applicability of such a guide, local constraints may sometimes negate the use of certain elements contained in it.

The foregoing concerns point to the need for a comprehensive curriculum document, one that takes a host of factors into account at the local level and serves as a foundation for the total curriculum. This document is termed the *curriculum framework*. The preparation of a curriculum framework document makes the course of study, curriculum guide, and syllabus of no less importance. It merely serves to complement and enhance each by providing an overall frame of reference for curriculum substance and structure.

Nature of the Curriculum Framework

Some may look at the development of a curriculum framework document as just more busywork; however, this is certainly not the case. Complaints have been leveled at vocational educators for many years regarding the lack of articulation in regard to academic areas, and most conventional curriculum documents have tended to perpetuate this separation. The curriculum framework document serves to involve a variety of teachers, since it considers the range of learning experiences encountered within the curriculum. Whether it be vocational, technical, mathematics, or science content, information can be clearly documented for use by all persons associated with the curriculum. The document can provide a much-needed means of communication for all who are involved in the curriculum development process. This includes not only vocational and academic faculty but support personnel and administrators as well. Basic to the establishment of such a document is a recognition that professionals view and understand the role each person has in the total curriculum.

The curriculum framework serves to display meaningful curriculum experiences and activities as well as identified constraints. It is extremely important to clarify exactly what will be provided in the curriculum and the reasons why. Spelling out the content and constraints associated with a curriculum enables everyone to see just what limitations are imposed on the content. An additional benefit has to do with accountability. When content and constraints are detailed, it is easy to understand why certain areas are emphasized in a curriculum. Without this information, one may only speculate about the various reasons for certain content selections. This particular condition is frequently evident in curriculum guides and courses of study where content is present but the logic behind its selection is not included.

Additionally, the curriculum framework serves as a basis for developing specific objectives. Some persons may feel that the most logical approach to curriculum development consists of identifying objectives and then selecting content that aligns with them. Although this strategy can work, it reflects content being built on conjecture rather than on a comprehensive information base. If objectives are to be most meaningful, they must flow from the identified content for a curriculum. This helps to ensure content coverage that is of greatest value to vocational and technical students (and ultimately, graduates).

Developing the Framework

The establishment of a curriculum framework document is a simple and straightforward task. In reality, much of the work has already been accomplished if proper planning has been done. In order to illustrate the use of available information in preparing a framework, an example of a table of contents is provided in Figure 7–2. As may be noted by the various headings, much of the needed information would have been identified as determinations were made about the content to be included in the curriculum. Initially, the institution's philosophy and goals are stated. These serve to tie the curriculum to a broader perspective, that of the total institution. Next, the various items that have impact on curricu-

FIGURE 7–2. *Table of contents from a curriculum framework document*

I.	Philosophy and Goals of the Institution	1
II.	Students Served	2
III.	Instructional and Support Staff	4
IV.	Curricular Arrangement	6
V.	Employment Setting	10
VI.	Content Coverage	12
	A. Vocational and Technical	12
	B. General Education	17
	C. Cocurricular Activities	20

lum content are documented. These include the students served, instructional and support staff, the curricular arrangement, and the employment setting. It is important that each be detailed enough so any professional will understand the curricular focus. Content is then detailed to include vocational, technical, and general (e.g., mathematics, science, English) coverage. Information regarding cocurricular activities (e.g., student vocational organizations and athletics) is also provided, since large portions of time may be allocated to these areas. Tentative time allocations for content coverage may also be included in the framework; or, in the case of a competency-based, individualized curriculum, average estimated completion time can then be used. Developing the curriculum framework document is essentially a process of bringing information together that has already been developed and ensuring that it is fully documented. While this process is going on, it is most beneficial to involve all those who will eventually use the curriculum. Included would be vocational and academic teachers, support personnel, administrators, and students. Widespread involvement assists in the identification of potential problems and enables a variety of persons to give their personal reactions to the document. This is most important since the curriculum framework document serves as a basis for instructional planning and delivery activities that are likely to include the integration of general and vocational education content.

Summary

Making sound curriculum content decisions has been pointed out as an essential element of the curriculum development process. The content decision-making process involves an examination of potential content and constraints to determine what content can actually be used in the curriculum. Constraints associated with the curriculum appear in relation to four distinct areas: the student, the teachers and support staff, the curricular arrangement, and the employment setting. It must be recognized that these factors tend to limit the content that can logically be taught. Thus, the curriculum developer must select the best content for a given educational setting. The curriculum framework document provides an overall structure for planning instruction. It is comprehensive in scope, including vocational, academic, and related content. Since this document serves as a basis for the development of specific curricular objectives, it is important that content be identified which will be of greatest value to students.

Related References

Doll, Ronald C. *Curriculum Improvement: Decision Making and Process, Seventh Edition*. Needham Heights, Mass.: Allyn and Bacon, 1989.

Sarkees, Michelle D., and Scott, John L. *Vocational Special Needs*. Homewood, Ill.: American Technical Publishers, 1985.

8

Setting Curriculum Goals and Objectives

Introduction

The establishment of sound goals and objectives represents one of the most crucial steps in curriculum development. Without quality objectives, a curriculum may wander from topic to topic and result in students being unprepared for employment. One can often find references in the literature to goals, general objectives, specific objectives, terminal objectives, enabling objectives, performance objectives, as well as others. Realistically, a clear understanding of each goal and objective is needed if the curriculum developer is to comprehend and deal with their basic similarities and differences.

This chapter deals with the different types of curricular outcomes as well as the way goals and objectives may be prepared for use in vocational and technical education. Specific examples have been included to help clarify differences between goals and objectives and to indicate how they may be better prepared.

Curriculum Outcomes

The development of meaningful outcomes for the curriculum can be one of the most frustrating and time-consuming tasks facing an educator.

This is especially true if the individual preparing them is unfamiliar with the various types of goals and objectives. Before dealing directly with objectives, it must be realized that in vocational education outcomes are of prime importance. Outcomes can be in terms of program graduates or the extent to which students demonstrate competence after specific curriculum content has been taught. Furthermore, curriculum developers must recognize that some outcomes are more measurable than others and, in fact, some may be unmeasurable.

Measurable Outcomes

Measurable outcomes in vocational and technical education can take many forms; for example, a student identifying twenty carpentry tools, baking a cake according to the directions in the recipe, correctly applying a mathematical formula in a problem situation, or completing a job application form. In reality, measurable outcomes represent those results that can be assessed with quantifiable data or in an objective manner.

Unmeasurable Outcomes

The other extreme represents outcomes that tend to be unmeasurable. Examples of these outcomes might be that a student develops an appreciation of the value of work in society, develops the ability to use leisure time wisely, or forms an attitude conducive to working in a group setting. As can be seen, measuring student performance associated with these outcomes would be most difficult. This is not to say unmeasurable outcomes are undesirable in vocational education. The three examples just cited, as well as other similar types of outcomes, represent important aspects of vocational education.

Any vocational curriculum will have both measurable and unmeasurable outcomes; thus, objectives that are developed should speak to both types. A basic rule to be followed by the developer is that a sufficient number of measurable outcomes be identified in order to assure student competence as determined by objective student performance measures in critical vocational or technical areas. This enables vocational programs to be evaluated more accurately in terms of graduates' competence and assists in making vocational education more accountable when the curriculum is being evaluated.

Types of Goals and Objectives

The establishment of sound, realistic goals and objectives requires the developer to be familiar with their similarities and differences. A discussion of goals and objectives follows, with examples provided to help clarify the unique aspects of each.

Goals

Goals are broad (unmeasurable) aims or purposes of a total educational curriculum or, in some cases, the broad outcomes expected within a specific program. The purpose of each goal is to give direction and provide a basis for the development of more detailed general and specific objectives. Since numerous goals have been developed at the national, state, and local levels, it is often quite easy to find statements that align closely with a particular school or curriculum.

A review of goal statements for a typical local school illustrates how goals are usually stated. These goals tend to be broad and unmeasurable and attempt to reflect the philosophy of the community. Examples of goal statements for a local high school might include the following:

Students will:

Become competent in the fundamental academic skills.

Become qualified for further education and/or development.

Participate as responsible citizens.

Develop positive and realistic self-images.

Exhibit a responsibility for the enhancement of beauty in their daily lives.

Practice sound habits of personal health.

Broad goals are often established for specific curricular areas. As an example, the following selected goals might be appropriate for consumer and homemaking education:

The Consumer and Homemaking Education Department at Washington High School will:

Provide preparation for the vocation of homemaking for youth and adults of both sexes.

Contribute to homemaking abilities and the employability of youth and adults in the dual role of homemaker and wage earner.

Encourage interest in home-economics-related occupations and home-economics careers.

Develop intelligent consumer habits in the marketplace.

By closely scrutinizing these examples, one can visualize the difficulties that might arise if measurable outcomes were to be sought from these goals. Goals can and do serve a useful purpose in giving further direction for the development of specific objectives; however, they never serve as substitutes. Broad goals can also provide a basis for discussion in determining the direction that an educational program should be taking.

General Objectives

General objectives are similar to goals in that they tend to be broad statements and are usually unmeasurable. The major difference seems to occur in the use of general objectives. General objectives are more apt to be used for a vocational or technical education course or to appear as general objectives in a specific course syllabus. In reality, goals and general objectives are sometimes interchanged to the point where a clear distinction between the two is impossible. Examples of general objectives might include:

> The general objectives for Accounting I at Coolidge Community College are to develop:
>
> Specific skills associated with entry-level employment as an accountant.
>
> Relevant related knowledge associated with the accounting occupation.
>
> Appropriate human relations attitudes associated with the accounting occupation.

Although these three general objectives may appear at first glance to focus on specific preparation for a certain occupation, it soon becomes evident that they defy measurement. Skills, knowledges, and attitudes have not been specified; thus, a teacher would have difficulty determining when a student has fulfilled the objectives. Using these objectives to answer a question such as "What skills will these students be able to perform when you are through teaching them?" can become extremely difficult and perhaps even embarrassing!

Specific Objectives

Specific objectives—or performance objectives, as many prefer to call them—are precise, measurable statements of particular behaviors to be exhibited by a learner under specified conditions. The performance objective is different from a general objective in clarity and specificity in that the activity to be performed is described as well as the level of acceptable performance, and the condition under which the performance must take place.

For each general objective developed, at least one performance objective must be established to indicate precisely what is expected of the student. In fact, several specific or performance objectives usually need to be developed for each general objective in order to assure that students develop the competence associated with the general objective. Examples of specific objectives include:

Given a 6' folding rule, a 2' length of ⅜" diameter copper tubing, holding device, hacksaw, and reamer, measure and cut 6" from a length of copper tubing. A tolerance of ± ⅛" will be allowed for the cut piece. All burrs must be removed from cut ends.

Given sample specimens of grass, identify the blade, sheath, collar, and ligule with 100-percent accuracy.

The establishment of performance objectives permits the student to know precisely what performance is expected and to what degree it must be demonstrated. Performance objectives give clearer direction for the teacher in the selection of technical information and curriculum materials. Furthermore, each performance objective serves as a contributor to the achievement of general objectives and ultimately to the fulfillment of curriculum goals.

Foundations of Educational Goal Formation

Goal statements may be found at all levels of education. Virtually all of these statements tend to be quite broad and stated in unmeasurable terms. Before the development of a goal statement begins, one should become familiar with goals that have been already established at various educational levels and that may have a direct influence on the development process. The development of goals is certainly related to philosophy; however, further discussion will not be devoted to the impact of philosophy on educational goals and programs, since this topic was discussed in Chapter 6.

National Goals for Education

The preparation of national goals for education dates back to the early efforts to provide quality education for our youth. One of the first and most influential efforts dealing with goal development that still has much impact today produced the *Seven Cardinal Principles* (The Reform of Secondary Education, 1973). These principles were

To secure a command of the fundamental processes

To develop good habits of citizenship

To maintain good health and habits of safety

To develop ideals for worthy home membership

To develop a sense of ethical character

To furnish a background for vocational efficiency

To develop socially desirable leisure-time activities

Although these goals were developed to meet the needs of society in 1918, the substance of each can still be found today in many goal statements.

Several other major national efforts were conducted after 1918 to revise the original seven cardinal principles. In 1938, four broad goals were outlined in the *Purposes of Education in American Democracy*. The White House Conference on Education in 1955 developed fourteen basic goals of education, and in 1961, the National Education Association stressed the common thread of education as the "ability to think."

Since the late 1970s there have been numerous national studies conducted by private and public organizations that have produced suggested reform movements for education. A common thread running through many of these reports indicates that the purposes of education are to develop in students the basic skills of communication (especially reading, writing, and arithmetic needed to succeed in a democracy), to create in students the ability to think and to think creatively, to develop those human relations skills that are essential for interacting with others in our society, and to ensure that students can function in an information-based society.

Recent national goals were presented as an outgrowth of the historic governor's summit at Charlottesville, Virginia. President Bush set six goals for U.S. schools to prepare students for the twenty-first century. These goals were:

Goal 1: Readiness for School

By the year 2000, all children in America will start school ready to learn.

Goal 2: High School Completion

By the year 2000, the high school graduation rate will increase to at least 90 percent.

Goal 3: Student Achievement and Citizenship

By the year 2000, American students will leave grades four, eight, and twelve having demonstrated competency in challenging subject matter including English, mathematics, science, history, and geography; and every school in America will ensure that all students learn to use their minds well, so they may be prepared for responsible citizenship, further learning, and productive employment in our modern economy.

Goal 4: Science and Mathematics

By the year 2000, U.S. students will be first in the world in science and mathematics achievement.

Goal 5: Adult Literacy and Lifelong Learning

By the year 2000, every adult American will be literate and will possess the knowledge and skills necessary to compete in a global economy and exercise the rights and responsibilities of citizenship.

Goal 6: Safe, Disciplined, and Drug-Free Schools

By the year 2000, every school in America will be free of drugs and violence and will offer a disciplined environment conducive to learning (*America 2000: The President's Education Strategy,* 1991).

Another recent national report that has implications for curriculum development at the local level was *What Work Requires of Schools: A SCANS Report for America 2000.* Basically, this document highlights common elements that all workers will need in the future workplace. Five competencies identified in this report, with specific skills delineated for each, are presented in Figure 8–1.

National Goals for Vocational Education

Nationwide efforts to formulate broad goals for all of vocational education were not fully evident until the early 1960s. However, individual vocational service areas did develop goal statements prior to 1960, many of which provided direction for local programs. The main impetus to develop goals for vocational education was the Panel of Consultants on Vocational Education appointed by President John F. Kennedy in 1961. Emerging from the efforts of the panel were five general recommendations; these have served as a basis for the development of goals at the national, state, and local levels. The recommendations were that in a changing world of work, vocational education must:

Offer training opportunities to the twenty million noncollege graduates who would enter the labor market in the 1960s.

FIGURE 8–1. *FIVE COMPETENCIES*

Resources: Identifies, organizes, plans, and allocates resources
  A. *Time*—Selects goal-relevant activities, ranks them, allocates time, and prepares and follows schedules
  B. *Money*—Uses or prepares budgets, makes forecasts, keeps records, and makes adjustments to meet objectives
  C. *Material and Facilities*—Acquires, stores, allocates, and uses materials or space efficiently
  D. *Human Resources*—Assesses skills and distributes work accordingly, evaluates performance and provides feedback
Interpersonal: Works with others
  A. *Participates as Member of a Team*—contributes to group effort
  B. *Teaches Others New Skills*
  C. *Serves Clients/Customers*—works to satisfy customers' expectations
  D. *Exercises Leadership*—communicates ideas to justify position, persuades and convinces others, responsibly challenges existing procedures and policies
  E. *Negotiates*—works toward agreements involving exchange of resources, resolves divergent interests
  F. *Works with Diversity*—works well with men and women from diverse backgrounds
Information: Acquires and uses information
  A. *Acquires and Evaluates Information*
  B. *Organizes and Maintains Information*
  C. *Interprets and Communicates Information*
  D. *Uses Computers to Process Information*
Systems: Understands complex inter-relationships
  A. *Understands Systems*—knows how social, organizational, and technological systems work and operates effectively with them
  B. *Monitors and Corrects Performance*—distinguishes trends, predicts impacts on system operations, diagnoses deviations in systems' performance and corrects malfunctions
  C. *Improves or Designs Systems*—suggests modifications to existing systems and develops new or alternative systems to improve performance
Technology: Works with a variety of technologies
  A. *Selects Technology*—chooses procedures, tools or equipment including computers and related technologies
  B. *Applies Technology to Task*—Understands overall intent and proper procedures for setup and operation of equipment
  C. *Maintains and Troubleshoots Equipment*—Prevents, identifies, or solves problems with equipment, including computers and other technologies

Source: What Work Requires of Schools: A SCANS Report for America 2000. Washington, D.C.: The Secretary's Commission on Achieving Necessary Skills. U.S. Department of Labor. U.S. Government Printing Office, June 1991, p. 12.

Provide training or retraining for the millions of workers whose skills and technical knowledge must be updated as well as those whose jobs will disappear due to increasing efficiency, automation, or economic change.

Meet the critical need for highly skilled craftsmen and technicians through education during and after the high school years.

Expand the vocational and technical programs consistent with employment possibilities and national economic needs.

Make educational opportunities equally available to all regardless of race, sex, scholastic aptitude, or place of residence (*Education for a Changing World of Work,* 1963).

These recommendations were instrumental in the wording of the Vocational Education Act of 1963, which focused on all vocational education service areas in a changing world of work. Thus, the primary goal of vocational education as reflected in these recommendations is to prepare learners for entry into and advancement of their chosen careers.

A more recent effort to state the national goals for vocational education was documented in the *The Unfinished Agenda*. Members of the National Commission on Secondary Vocational Education (1984) who prepared this report stated that vocational education should be concerned with development of the individual student in five areas:

Personal skills and attitudes;

Communication and computational skills and technological literacy;

Employability skills;

Broad and specific occupational skills and knowledge; and

Foundations for career planning and lifelong learning (*The Unfinished Agenda,* 1984).

Since the Vocational Education Act of 1963 was initiated and the subsequent Carl Perkins Act of 1984 was enacted, each of the vocational service areas has updated its national goals for the purpose of bringing these goals in line with the new emphasis on the world of work, and eventually to stimulate states and localities in the development of new goals and objectives.

One such example is in Technology Education. A National Standards Project in this area identified a series of goal statements to guide future program direction. These statements were developed to help guide state and local program development by advocating that program goals are established from stated philosophy to provide direction for program development, implementation, and evaluation.*

---

*Goodheart-Willcox Co., Inc./International Technology Education Association. Reprinted with permission.

1. The program goals encompass the major purposes of technology education.
   a. Emphasis is placed upon assisting students in developing insight and understanding of our technological society.
   b. Emphasis is placed upon improving student ability to make informed and meaningful career choices.
   c. Emphasis is placed upon preparing students for entry into specialized, technical, training and/or advanced professional programs in technology.
   d. Emphasis is placed upon preparing students for lifelong learning in a technological society.
   e. Emphasis is placed upon developing student skills, creative abilities, positive self-concepts, and individual potentials in technology.
   f. Emphasis is placed upon applying tools, materials, machines and processes, and technical concepts safely and efficiently.
   g. Emphasis is placed upon developing student problem-solving and decision-making abilities involving human and material resources, processes, and technological systems.
   h. Emphasis is placed upon reinforcing the basic skills and interrelating the content of technology with other school subjects.
   i. Emphasis is placed upon developing leadership ability, encouraging and promoting responsibility, and developing positive social interaction through AIASA.
2. Program goals are consistent with local, state, and national standards and emerging developments in technology education.
3. Program goals are developed with input from teachers, administrators, students, representatives from business and industry, and other consultants.
4. Program goals are written and are on file.
5. Program goals are utilized by teachers and administrators for planning, implementing, and evaluating courses.
6. Program goals are reviewed annually and revised when necessary (*Standards for Technology Education Program,* 1985).

Goals for Vocational Education at the State Level

Consistent with the new thrust put forth by vocational education at the national level in relation to the world of work, many states have redefined their goal statements. Although goals from many different states could have been used as examples, the goal statements for Virginia have been included here to enable the reader to form an idea of a statement of goals for vocational education at the state level. Virginia, in stating its broad goals, first developed what it called a "mission statement." The following goals were taken from the *Virginia State Plan for Vocational Education, 1989–1990* (1988):

Mission Statement

The mission of the State Board of Vocational Education is to ensure that the vocational education needs of all youths and adults in Virginia are met consistent with the needs of the workplace.

Goals

Consistent with the needs of the workplace, and with individual aptitudes, interests, and educational needs, youth and adults in Virginia will:

1. Develop an awareness of employment or self-employment opportunities and requirements for making career choices and for determining their educational programs.
2. Acquire the competencies needed for employment or self-employment in occupations of their choice and for which there are employment opportunities.
3. Acquire the competencies needed for consumer use of goods and services, for home and family living, and for personal needs.
4. Develop competencies needed for successful transition from school to work with emphasis on leadership skills, the American private enterprise system, responsible citizenship, and personal employability skills.
5. Benefit from programs improved and updated through a comprehensive vocational education delivery system.
6. Benefit from programs which are developed through collaborative efforts with business, industry, and government, and which effectively use public and private resources.

Goals for Vocational Education at the Local Level

Goals for vocational education at the local level may be stated separately or they may be included in the broad goal statements for all of education. Broad goals such as those which follow are not uncommon for public education at the local level.

The primary goals of public education in Knox County are twofold: to help pupils realize their greatest personal potential for happiness and success, and to educate them in order that they may become worthwhile citizens of the home, school, and community.

The faculty of Butler Community College believe that the basic mission of education is to provide all persons, regardless of economic status or locality, the opportunity to develop to the highest capacity of their own ability, and thus strengthen our system of self-government and freedom as a people.

Other schools may choose to list several goals in statement form and thus end up with five, ten, or even more separate goals.

For the most part, goals for vocational education at the local level should be closely aligned with goals at the state level. However, an exact duplication of state goals is not recommended, since each school and community should develop goals consistent with its unique local needs. For example, goals for vocational and technical education at Butler Community College that were referred to earlier might include the following points:

Vocational and technical education at Butler Community College strives to:

Provide vocational and technical education of excellence that relates to the specific needs and interests of the students and the community;

Develop the marketable skills of students who do not plan to continue their formal education after they have left the community college;

Encourage each student to be a worthy citizen;

Develop among students a spirit of tolerance and understanding through supervised work experience so that all students may become active participants in a democratic society;

Cultivate an atmosphere in which students can develop self-discipline, intellectual curiosity, and moral worth.

This entire discussion of goals from the national level to the local level has been designed to provide a foundation from which goals may be developed. A broad review and understanding of goals already developed at various levels and for a particular curriculum should assist in the development of more relevant and realistic goals.

Preparing Goals

Although it has been indicated that their preparation can be frustrating, the actual development of goals is relatively easy. The frustrating aspect of goal preparation occurs when a group of individuals attempts to reach agreement on a set of goals that reflects the true purposes of the organization. The development of broad goals for a vocational education curriculum must take three factors into consideration. These include ensuring that (1) individuals who will be affected by the goals are involved in their development, (2) the goals being developed are consistent with goals established at other educational levels, and (3) careful consideration is given to each goal developed. This is important because each goal must be supported by relevant objectives. Each of these factors will be discussed in the sections that follow.

Individual Involvement

The need for involvement of many individuals in the development of goal statements has been stressed in vocational education for many years. Vocational education curricula must be designed for students, and it is philosophically sound that students assume active roles in their education. This implies that regardless of the level for which goals are being developed—students, parents, educators, citizens, and others—the people concerned should be involved as the goals are being established. Involvement can occur via advisory councils, review by concerned individuals, or other appropriate means. Persons are more apt to accept and use established goals if they have actively participated in the preparation of them.

Consistency of Curriculum Goals with Other Goals

Goals that are established at the state, local, or vocational service-area level should be consistent with those goals established at the national level. Specifically, any set of goals in vocational education should speak to the preparation of individuals for entry-level employment and their preparation for full participation in a democratic society. Furthermore, goals at the vocational service-area level in a local school should align with those goals developed for the total vocational education program at the local level, with the local goals for education, with the goals at the state level, and so forth. Goal formation throughout the educational system has been illustrated in Figure 8–2, which shows graphically the ways that goals relate to each other.

In Figure 8–2, the influence of goal formation tends to move from upper left to lower right. For example, national goals for education influence state-level goals for education, which in turn influence local goals for education. National goals for education likewise influence national goals for vocational education and ultimately local goals for vocational education service areas. Whereas the influence of goal formation moves from the national to the local level, a reverse influence may also occur. Persons who establish goals at the local level for vocational service areas may use these goals to influence the way state goals for

FIGURE 8-2. *Structure of goal formation*

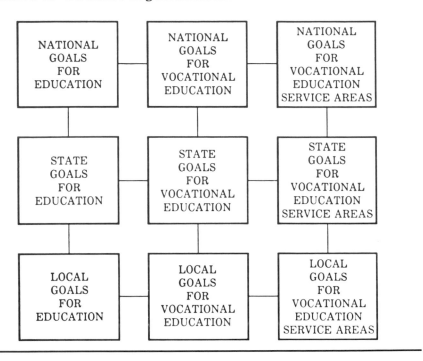

vocational education may be affected. There is a variety of factors that tend to influence goal formation, regardless of the level for which goals are being developed. Thus, the developer must be aware of goals that have already been established at other levels and determine how they can give direction to goal formation at the local level.

Goals and Objectives

Although the development of objectives typically follows the establishment of goals, it is most useful to give some thought to possible related objectives for each goal statement as it is being devised. Since each objective developed should correlate with a goal statement and each goal statement should relate to one or more performance objectives, the developer may find it beneficial to consider which objectives might be classified with certain goals. If this step is carried out, it should make the accomplishment of broadly stated goals a much easier task, since related objectives will help define what these goals actually are.

Preparing Objectives

It is widely acknowledged that objectives serve as facilitators of a sound curriculum and that, without them, instruction may be irrelevant or ineffective. However, once the question is raised about how generally or specifically an objective should be stated, controversy seems close behind. Teachers, administrators, and even students often cannot agree on what constitutes a "good" objective.

As was mentioned earlier, some curriculum outcomes may be unmeasurable and others are readily measurable. Even though the difficulty of preparing meaningful objectives is fully recognized, it is firmly believed that every effort should be made to develop relevant, measurable objectives for key areas in the curriculum. If key measurable objectives are not developed, it will be impossible to determine when students have attained whatever they are supposed to attain or even to measure their progress. In the preparation of measurable objectives, several factors must be considered. These include the identification, selection, classification, and specification of objectives (Kibler et al., 1981).

Identification

When consideration is first given to preparing objectives, the developer must identify which kinds of objectives he or she hopes to prepare. Earlier, a distinction was made between general and performance objectives. Since general objectives are typically broad and unmeasurable, it would seem logical to focus attention on preparing performance objectives because they most closely align with the learner's needs. Consequently, this discussion will deal directly with developing performance objectives, since they play such an important role in communicating curriculum outcomes to others. In terms of further clarifying performance objectives, it should be noted that there are two types: the terminal objective and the enabling objective. These two types are both used in the curriculum, each having a distinct purpose.

Terminal Objective. The terminal objective represents performance in the worker role or a close approximation of that role. It focuses on the way a student should perform when in the intended work situation. The terminal objective should, therefore, be valued in and of itself and be stated at a level that will be meaningful to the student later in life. For example, a terminal objective might specify that the student close a sale. In order for this to be classified as a terminal objective, a performance must take into account that an actual sale has been closed with a customer in a sales setting. A terminal objective that focuses on straightening a damaged fender should specify that a customer's car is repaired and that repair time is within the limits specified in the manufacturer's flat rate manual. When it is not feasible to assess performance in an actual employment setting, every effort should be made to simulate this condition as closely as possible. Appropriate terminal objectives that focus on key aspects of the occupation can often be developed and used in the school laboratory or, in certain cases, within the classroom. This allows the teacher to utilize realistic objectives even when work stations or settings outside the school are not readily available.

Enabling Objective. The enabling objective focuses on what the student must learn if he or she is to attain the terminal objective. The enabling objective serves to guide the student from where he or she is at the beginning of instruction to where he or she should be at the end of the instruction. It may focus on basic factual knowledge, awareness, fundamental skills, or attitudes. Basic to any enabling objective is the contribution it makes to achieving one or more terminal objectives. If this supportive relationship does not exist, one may question the value of having the enabling objectives in the first place. As an example of how enabling objectives might relate, let us consider a terminal objective that focuses on completing a successful job interview. Enabling objectives that might conceivably contribute to this terminal objective include exhibiting proper dress and grooming, understanding questions that should and should not be asked, and demonstrating skill in answering questions posed by prospective employers.

Selection

Once the appropriate types of objectives have been identified, it is necessary to select those that will actually be used in the curriculum. During the selection process, a number of relevant factors must be considered. These include the content, the students, and the available resources.

Content. At this point in the curriculum development process, it must be assumed that relevant content has already been identified. Chapter 6 has pointed out the ways that curriculum content may be identified, whereas Chapter 7 has focused on making content decisions. The next logical step in this process is selecting and developing those objectives that align with the chosen content. By using meaningful content as a basis for establishing objectives, the curriculum developer may be assured that each terminal objective will focus on an important aspect of the occupation. Using relevant content as a base for developing enabling objectives is of equal importance. Enabling objectives should be selected that are logically related to performance in the worker role. Although there is nothing wrong with developing objectives that focus on areas such as knowledge, understanding, and appreciation, it is important for the developer to ensure that these objectives contribute to the achievement of terminal objectives, and ultimately, to meaningful performance in the world of work.

Students. While a close examination of students' concerns may have already been accomplished as curriculum content decisions are being made, it is important that consideration be given to the ways objectives can be aligned with students' needs. For example, enabling objectives in a power-sewing-machine-operator program might well be different for handicapped students than for nonhandicapped students. In this case, the difference in objectives is a function of identified disabilities that do not allow the student to progress through a program in the same manner. The end may remain the same, but the means to this end varies in relation to student needs. The selection of appropriate objectives is not limited to handicapped students. Similar concerns may exist with disadvantaged, gifted, and adult learners. Regardless of the student group to be served, the curriculum developer has an obligation to identify those objectives that will enable each student to achieve his or her optimum potential.

Resources. Resources have likewise been discussed in the context of curriculum content decisions. Whereas basic resources may be available to operate the curriculum, specific resources needed to aid students in achieving certain objectives may not be on hand. It might be that although a great deal of standard equipment is available for students enrolled in an appliance repair program, this equipment is not appropriate to assist them with an enabling objective focusing on troubleshooting strategy development. In this case, a need exists for different equipment or some sort of equipment simulator. If resources cannot be made available, consideration must then be given to selecting different objectives for the curriculum.

Classification

As objectives are being prepared, it is most beneficial to classify them according to the basic behavior they describe. Classifying objectives is necessary in order "1) to avoid concentrating on one or two categories to the exclusion of others, 2) to make sure that instruction is provided for prerequisite objectives before attempting to teach more complex ones, and 3) to assure that appropriate instruments are employed to evaluate desired outcomes" (Kibler et al., 1981). Numerous classification schemes have evolved over the last two decades, each of which has attempted to assist educators in organizing objectives logically and systematically.

Several of the more useful classification schemes are described briefly in the paragraphs that follow.

Classification of objectives in the cognitive domain is most thoroughly detailed in a document by Bloom (1956). A taxonomy is presented for objectives "which deal with the recall or recognition of knowledge and the development of intellectual abilities and skills" (Bloom, 1956). Six major classes included in the taxonomy consist of knowledge, comprehension, application, analysis, synthesis, and evaluation. These classes represent the hierarchical order of different cognitive objectives. Curriculum developers may find this classification scheme quite useful when cognitive objectives are being prepared, since levels of the taxonomy can correspond with the way objectives are sequenced and taught.

A companion publication focuses on classifying affective objectives (Krathwohl et al., 1964). The authors establish a taxonomy for objectives "which emphasize a feeling tone, an emotion or a degree of acceptance or rejection" (Krathwohl et al., 1964). The affective domain consists of five major classes: receiving (attending), responding, valuing, organizing, and characterizing. This taxonomy also distinguishes among levels, with "receiving" representing the lowest level and "characterizing" the highest. By using this taxonomy, affective objectives may be distinguished from each other and more effectively incorporated into the curriculum.

Classification of objectives in the psychomotor domain is dealt with most comprehensively by Harrow (1977). Psychomotor objectives "emphasize some muscular or motor control, some manipulation of material or objects, or some act which requires a neuromuscular coordination" (Krathwohl et al., 1964). Given that specialized psychomotor skill development is an integral part of most vocational and technical education curricula, it is certainly important to examine objectives in this area. The following five classes of psychomotor objectives have been established: perception, set, guided response, mechanism, and complex overt response. Although it may be difficult to distinguish between some of these classes, the taxonomy provides a much needed framework for curriculum developers.

Interestingly enough, authors of the aforementioned classification schemes all note that questions may be raised about the rigid distinctions among the cognitive, affective, and psychomotor domains. Perhaps it is useful to examine the broad objectives that encompass all three domains. This possibility has been explored and documented by Harmon (1969). Harmon's classification scheme, which has proved useful in establishing job training programs, includes three classes of objectives: verbal performance, physical performance, and attitudinal performance. As noted in Figure 8–3, subclasses under each class assist in distinguishing among the various types of performance objectives that may be used in vocational curricula. As Harmon indicates, some performance objectives deal with two or more numbers. The strength of Harmon's classification scheme

lies in its flexibility. Since most terminal objectives in vocational education curricula deal with more than one class of behavior, it is often
difficult (if not impossible) to consider a single class or domain. By using
the classification shown in Figure 8–3, objectives may be arranged more
logically and systematically, giving full consideration to the complexities
of vocational and technical education. If it were desired to classify an
objective dealing with finding a malfunction in a tractor engine, several
numbers could be used to describe collectively what is entailed; e.g., 2.5
(perform an appropriate skilled action in a problem-solving situation)
and 3.3 (respond with limited or controlled responses in given social
situations). Physical performance would be directly related to locating
the malfunction, whereas attitudinal performance would be associated
with safe practices followed during the troubleshooting process. Only a
brief introduction has been given to this as well as other classification

FIGURE 8–3. *A classification of performance objective behaviors*

1.0 Verbal Performance Objectives
    1.1 Recall a name; list a set of names; state a simple rule or fact.
    1.2 Explain an ordered set of actions (how to do a task).
    1.3 Respond to a series of statements or questions.
    1.4 Solve a specific symbolic problem.
    1.5 Solve a general type of symbolic problem.

2.0 Physical Performance Objectives
    2.1 Make physical identifications (point to things).
    2.2 Perform simple physical acts
    2.3 Perform complex actions (with instructions or by rote).
    2.4 Perform physically skilled actions.
    2.5 Perform an appropriate skilled action in a problem-solving situation (de-
        termine what is to be done and then do it).
    2.6 Determine acceptable quality in physical products.

3.0 Attitudinal Performance Objectives
    3.1 State or list probable consequences of a given action.
    3.2 Evidence memory of correct social responses over an extended period of
        time.
    3.3 Respond with limited or controlled responses in given social situations.

Some objectives do not fall into any of these categories. Some objectives involve two or more types of behaviors. For example, often personal/social objectives involve both attitudinal and physical behaviors. In these cases, it is easy to
classify a performance objective using two numbers.

Source: From Paul Harmon. "A Classification of Performance Objective Behaviors in Job
Training Programs." *Educational Technology* (January 1969): 5–12.

schemes, but there can be no doubt that each has the potential to assist in systematically classifying curriculum objectives.

Specification

In order for performance objectives to be useful, they must be clearly delineated. Just as it becomes quite difficult to hit a target when one does not know what the target is, the vocational educator must first have clear objectives if he or she expects to develop relevant instructional strategies. Numerous references are available that describe how performance objectives may be specified, but they typically include the three elements espoused by Mager (1975): the activity, the conditions, and the standard.

Activity.   This element of the performance objective is used to indicate what the student should actually do. It is important to state exactly what activity is to be performed so that the student and the teacher will both be able to communicate clearly with each other. Since each performance objective is designed to be measurable, provision must be made to ensure that it is readily observable. It is not enough to state simply that the student should "understand the binary system." A clear indication should be made of what a student must do to show that he or she understands it. This might include the following: "Convert 85° Fahrenheit to centigrade," or "Convert 50 miles to kilometers." In the specification of activities it is important to keep away from ambiguous terms such as *know, understand, enjoy, appreciate, have faith in,* and *believe.* Instead, terms such as *list, construct, solve, write, recite, define, state, recall, select,* and *measure* should be utilized. Using more precise terms aids greatly in the communication process and in the meaningful measurement of objectives.

Conditions.   The second element of any performance objective is the conditions under which the performance is to be observed. Several kinds of conditions may be considered as the objective is being developed. These include the range of problems a student must learn to solve, tools and equipment that may be used, auxiliary materials such as books and manuals, environmental conditions, and special physical demands. If a student were asked to "formulate and prepare a growing medium for a common plant," conditions might include provisions for soil, sand, peat moss, and artificial soil amendments such as perlite, calcified clay, and vermiculite. If it is important that a student be able to multiply numbers without any aids, this should be indicated; however, if a calculator may be used, this needs to be specified. Conditions are most useful in further clarifying student performance, especially when they serve to point out any differences in performance created by these conditions.

Standard. A final element included in each performance objective is the standard of acceptable performance. This element serves to establish the student performance level or levels used in a curriculum. Standards can focus on several areas of performance such as speed, accuracy, frequency, or some form of production. For most complex skills in vocational education, multiple standards are specified. An objective dealing with "formatting three business letters on a personal computer," "according to prescribed business letter formats," and "within a half-hour time limit," specifies several areas of expected student performance. Whereas any one of these standards would be important in itself, collectively they focus on realistic performance that a student would be expected to perform on the job.

In the establishment of standards, it is important to keep in mind that variations may exist across a particular curriculum. Standards at the first-year level may require less of the student than would those used in the final phases of instruction. Minimum standards in first-year keyboarding might be "Fifty words per minute with no more than three errors"; standards set for program graduates might be "Seventy words per minute with no errors." Although these standards are merely illustrative of the possibilities that might exist, it must be realized that entry-level work performance is not usually required of students just beginning a program. It is essential to develop meaningful standards that align with student development within the curriculum and to ensure that standards associated with terminal performance correspond with what is expected in the worker role.

Sequencing Objectives within the Curriculum

Although much has been discussed in the literature about the ways objectives may be sequenced within the curriculum, little empirical evidence exists to support one approach over any other. The lack of concrete information in this area makes one wonder if students learn in spite of sequencing rather than because of it. Even though problems exist in pinpointing a basis for correct sequencing of objectives, it is nonetheless important that this activity take place. Perhaps the best way to think of sequencing is as "common sense logical ordering" (Gagné and Briggs, 1988). When the time comes to arrange objectives in the best possible manner, it is the professional educator's responsibility to establish this sequence. This reliance on professional judgment tends to make sequencing more of an art than a science.

When designing any piece of instruction, two important questions facing instructional designers are: (a) How should the instructional events be sequenced over time? (e.g., In what order should the ideas be taught? When should the definitions be given? Where should the practice be placed?) and (b) How should the interrelationships among these ideas be taught to the students? (e.g., How is idea A related to idea B? Where does idea C stand in relation to ideas A and B?). Therefore, strategies for sequencing and synthesizing aim to help instructional designers break the subject matter into small pieces, order the pieces, teach them one at a time, and then pull them together based on their interrelationships (Van Patten, Chao, and Reigeluth, 1986).

As the sequencing activity gets underway, it is important to consider factors that can affect the sequencing as well as ways objectives might be sequenced. Sequencing is not an exact process; however, the curriculum developer must be aware of how objectives can be arranged if he or she expects to make reasonable decisions about sequencing.

Sequencing Factors

Several factors can have impact on the way that objectives are sequenced. These are essentially practical considerations that relate to the entire curriculum; however, each must receive due consideration when the sequencing process takes place.

Logistics.   Sequencing plans must be examined in light of logistical considerations within a particular school. Since sequencing is often contingent upon what may be available and when, the logistics of providing instruction become extremely important. Consideration needs to be given to facility needs, instructional staff availability, seasonal variations, equipment availability, and necessary travel arrangements. These as well as other areas have to be examined closely, since they can affect an otherwise perfect sequencing of objectives.

Preparation for Work.   Regardless of the particular approach taken to sequencing, it is important to provide each student with some saleable skills early in the curriculum. Certainly this may be a narrow range of skills and only a small part of the curriculum, but it is essential to do so, since some students may choose to drop out prior to completion of the course. By providing for development of some marketable skills toward the beginning of a curriculum, students who leave should be in a better position to compete on the job market.

Face Validity.   No matter how logically objectives may seem to be sequenced, the arrangement is only successful to the extent that it is accepted by teachers. In this situation, face validity encompasses the extent to which teachers accept sequencing as being logical and meaningful. Whereas face validity may have nothing to do with the actual quality of sequencing, it is certainly of no less importance. The way objectives are sequenced must be accepted by instructional staff if they will eventually be expected to use this sequence in their respective classes.

Approaches to Sequencing

Numerous approaches to sequencing objectives have been suggested in the literature. Some are drawn from a theoretical base whereas others are quite pragmatic, but most have not been validated to any great extent. Thus, the curriculum developer is often faced with a trial (and, it is hoped, a no-error) situation. The approaches that will be discussed are representative of those found to be useful by certain teachers in certain instructional settings. The ultimate test of any approach to sequencing lies in its acceptability and utility within a particular curriculum.

Sequencing Based on Relationships. One possible approach to sequencing objectives integrates the combination of two different types, the concept-related and the learning-related. The premise for this approach is the relationship between different objectives. It must be remembered that the purpose of sequencing objectives is to help assure that learning occurs, with each objective placed in optimum relationship to other objectives.

In order to sequence objectives, the relationship between all objectives must first be determined. The relationship could be one of the following affiliations (*Interservice Procedures,* 1975):

1. A dependent relationship, in that mastery of one requires prior master of another.
2. A supportive relationship, in that some transfer of learning takes place from one learning objective to another.
3. An independent relationship, in that two objectives are totally unrelated to and independent of each other.

Figure 8–4 contrasts these relationships, gives examples of each, and illustrates how the relationship affects sequencing. When two or more objectives have been determined to have a dependent relationship, it is a fairly simple process to determine which objective is dependent on another and the logical sequence in which they must occur. Objectives that are supportive to each other can occur in any order, as long as they occur close together in order to maximize the transfer of learning. In addition to this basic rule, there are several other good reasons for placing supportive objectives near one another in the sequence. A teacher may have some instructional areas that require identical or similar learning con-

FIGURE 8–4. *Types of relationships between objectives*

	DEPENDENT	SUPPORTIVE	INDEPENDENT
RELATION-SHIP	Skills and knowledges in one objective are closely related to those in other objectives.	Skills and knowledges in one objective have some relationship to those in other objectives.	Skills and knowledges in one objective are unrelated to those in other objectives.
MASTERY	To master one of the objectives, it is first necessary to master another.	The learning involved in mastery of one objective transfers to another, making learning involved in the mastery of the other easier.	Mastering one of the objectives does not simplify mastering another.
EXAMPLES	In business education, the typing of a letter cannot be accomplished without first mastering the keyboard. The efficient use of a computer is totally dependent upon the prior learning of the keyboard.	In horticulture, pruning a shrub has a supportive relationship to pruning an apple tree. In both examples, learning to do one would help considerably in learning to do the other.	In auto mechanics, "adjusting a carburetor" is independent of "torquing engine head bolts." In both examples, knowing how to do one would not help much with the other.
SEQUENCE ORDER	The objective must be arranged in the sequence indicated by the above hierarchy.	The objectives should be placed close together in the sequence to permit optimum transfer of learning from one objective to another.	In general, the objectives can be arranged in any sequence without loss of learning.

Source: Adapted from *Interservice Procedures for Instructional Systems Development,* Phase II: Design. Fort Eustis, Va.: U.S. Army Transportation School, 1975, p. 83.

ditions or conditions that are difficult or expensive to provide at any given time. For example, a situation may exist where several objectives require the use of a land laboratory located 500 yards away from the school building. Another example would be a situation where several objectives require an expensive piece of equipment or facility and the teacher has access to these resources for a limited amount of time.

Sequencing Based on Taxonomic Classification. Kibler et al. (1981)* have proposed a procedure for "sequencing" objectives through a taxonomic classification based upon a task analysis approach. Six classifications identified for grouping objectives were proposed:

1. Knowledge
   a. Of terminology.
   b. Of conventions.
   c. Of criteria.
   d. Of methodology.
   e. Of theories and structures.
2. Comprehension
   a. Translation.
   b. Interpretation
3. Application
4. Analysis
   a. Of elements.
   b. Of relationships.
   c. Of organized principles.
5. Synthesis
   a. Production of a unique communication.
   b. Production of a plan or proposed set of operations.
6. Evaluation
   a. Judged in terms of internal evidence.

The application of this classification system to sequencing assumes that a teacher would begin instruction at the lower levels of cognitive thinking (knowledge) and guide students to a higher order of thinking (synthesis).

Sequencing Based on Practical Educational Experience. As noted earlier in this section, little is found in the literature to guide the curriculum developer in sequencing objectives. Educators' practical experiences

---

*From Kibler et al. *Objectives for Instruction and Evaluation,* Second Edition, Boston, Mass.: Allyn and Bacon, Inc., 1981, pp. 111–13.

become handy at this point. What follows are some sequencing "rules" that teachers have found helpful as they place objectives in sequence based on the content to be taught.

simple	to	complex
earliest	to	most recent
closest	to	farthest
east	to	west
small	to	large
part	to	whole
concrete	to	abstract
specifics	to	generalizations
observing	to	hands-on
skill acquisition	to	skill application
familiar	to	remote
less difficult	to	more difficult
more interesting	to	less interesting
theory	to	application
known	to	unknown

Although the effectiveness of various sequencing techniques is still under question, several conclusions have been reached about sequencing in general:

1. *Sequencing effects are long-range.* The advantages or dis-advantages of using any particular sequencing scheme are not likely to show up immediately. Therefore, end-of-course evalua-tive measures should be used for evaluating the effectiveness of sequencing techniques. Within-course evaluative measures of small portions of the material are not likely to reveal the true effects of sequencing.

2. *Sequence is important to low-aptitude students.* Students who have a high aptitude for the subject matter will learn the materi-al in spite of sequencing. The lower the aptitude of the learner for the content, the more important it becomes that *some* type of sequence and structure be provided.

3. *Sequence is important when students are given unfamiliar ma-terials.* Students who are familiar with materials will learn re-gardless of the order of presentation. But as material becomes increasingly unfamiliar to the student, the importance of the sequence increases.

4. *Sequence is important when used to help teach nonredundant materials.* Some curricular materials are especially redundant, stating important points over and over again. Sequencing is not

especially important with these materials, because the student can pick up the second time anything missed at first. But if the materials are nonredundant (state their points only once), it is important that they be sequenced according to some rationale.

Although these various approaches to implementation may seem rather abstract, it is because they have not been attached to specific vocational or technical content. That task is essentially one that the curriculum developer and his or her colleagues must perform. Unique content often dictates unique content arrangements; the various types of sequencing discussed here can provide a sound base for sequencing efforts.

Summary

This chapter has focused on goals and objectives as two essential elements in the vocational education curriculum. A strong distinction has been made between measurable and unmeasurable curricular outcomes. It was also recognized that one cannot assess all outcomes associated with a curriculum. Goals that have broad, unmeasurable outcomes can serve as a foundation for further curriculum building. Objectives represent the measurable outcomes in a curriculum. Their development requires detailed and systematic effort if objectives are to communicate exactly what is expected of the learner. Basic elements included in each performance objective include the activity to be performed, the conditions under which it should be performed, and the standards of acceptable performance. Finally, several types of sequencing arrangements have been presented, each of which has the potential to aid curriculum developers in sequencing objectives best to meet students' needs.

Related References

America 2000: The President's Education Strategy. Washington, D.C.: U.S. Government Printing Office, 1991.

Bloom, Benjamin S., ed. *Taxonomy of Educational Objectives, Handbook I: Cognitive Domain.* New York: David McKay Company, 1956.

Cross, Aleene A., ed. *Vocational Instruction.* Arlington, Va.: American Vocational Association, 1980.

Education for a Changing World of Work. Panel of Consultants on Vocational Education. Washington, D.C.: Office of Education, U.S. Department of Health, Education, and Welfare, 1963.

Evans, Rupert N., and Herr, Edwin L. *Foundations of Vocational Education, 2nd ed.* Columbus, Ohio: Charles E. Merrill Publishing Company, 1971.

Gagné, Robert M., and Briggs, Leslie J. *Principles of Instructional Design.* New York: Holt, Rinehart and Winston, 1988.

Harmon, Paul. "A Classification of Performance Objective Behaviors in Job Training Programs." *Educational Technology* 9, no. 1 (January 1969): 5–12.

Harrow, Anita J. *Taxonomy of the Psychomotor Domain.* New York: Longman, 1977.

Heines, Jesse M. "Writing Objectives With Style." *Training/HRD* 17, no. 7 (July 1980).

Herman, Jerry. "Site-Based Management: Creating a Vision and Mission Statement." *NASSP Bulletin* 73, no. 519 (October 1989): 79–83.

Holmes, Glen, and Sherman, Thomas H. "Applying Computer Spreadsheet Technology to Front-End Instructional Design Tasks." *Performance & Instruction* 28, no. 3 (March 1989): 7–10.

Interservice Procedures for Instructional Systems Development, Phase II: Design. Fort Eustis, Va.: U.S. Army Transportation School, 1975.

Kibler, Robert J.; Cegala, Donald J.; Miles, David T.; and Barker, Larry L. *Objectives for Instruction and Evaluation, 2nd ed.* Boston: Allyn and Bacon, 1981.

Krathwohl, David R.; Bloom, Benjamin S.; and Masia, Bertram B. *Taxonomy of Educational Objectives, Handbook II: Affective Domain.* New York: David McKay Company, 1964.

Mager, Robert F. *Preparing Instructional Objectives.* Palo Alto, Calif.: Fearon Publishers, 1975.

National Commission on Secondary Vocational Education. *The Unfinished Agenda, The Role of Vocational Education in the High School.* Columbus, Ohio: National Center for Research in Vocational Education, 1984.

The Reform of Secondary Education. A Report to the Public and the Profession. New York: McGraw-Hill Book Company; The National Commission on the Reform of Secondary Education, 1973.

Standards for Technology Education Programs. South Holland, Ill.: The Goodheart-Willcox Company, 1985.

Van Patten, James; Chao, Chun-I; and Reigeluth, Charles M. "A Review of Strategies for Sequencing and Synthesizing Instruction." *Review of Educational Research* 56, no. 4 (Winter 1986): 437–471.

Virginia State Plan for Vocational Education, 1989–1990. Richmond, Va.: State Board of Education, 1988.

What Work Requires of Schools: A SCANS Report for America 2000. Washington, D.C.: U.S. Department of Labor, U.S. Government Printing Office, June 1991.

SECTION IV

IMPLEMENTING THE CURRICULUM

The final section of this book follows directly from planning and content determination. The preceding sections have dealt with planning the curriculum and establishing curriculum content; however, they have not focused directly on the ways a curriculum may be implemented in a school setting. This section provides meaningful information for curriculum developers responsible for the implementation of relevant vocational curricula.

Once curriculum content has been established, quality materials must be obtained to aid in planning and conducting meaningful student learning experiences. These materials may already be available from various sources. Thus, the task of the vocational educator is to identify and select materials that can aid students in reaching predetermined objectives (Chapter 9). If materials are not available and must be developed, Chapter 10 provides information that is useful in guiding the materials development process, whereas Chapter 11 is designed to provide the curriculum developer with a broad understanding of strategies that may be used to implement the curriculum.

Evaluation must be a continuous process in order to ensure that the curriculum is relevant for today's needs and for future needs of society. Chapter 12 emphasizes the comprehensive nature of evaluation and provides direction for evaluating both programs and materials. Although treated as a separate chapter, it must also be recognized that evaluation is an integral part of curriculum development, all the way from planning through content determination and implementation.

9

Identifying and Selecting Curriculum Materials

Introduction

Many different resources are employed to achieve an effective teaching-learning environment. One important resource consists of curriculum materials, which are often synonymous with instructional materials. These materials play a key role in helping to motivate, teach, and evaluate students. Some individuals even go so far as to say that curriculum materials are the crucial factors in determining whether an individual learner succeeds, not the teacher.

Whereas arguments could be made against such a statement, educators must not underestimate the role that quality curriculum materials can have in an effective teaching-learning environment. Chapter 9 deals specifically with identifying and selecting the best curriculum materials available.

Curriculum Materials

Curriculum materials may be of many different types and forms. When discussing them, one of the first areas to clarify is a definition. The following paragraphs will serve as a basis for future comments on these materials.

A Definition of Curriculum Materials

Curriculum materials are resources that, if used properly, can assist a teacher in bringing about an intended desirable behavior change in individual students. These materials must not be confused with teaching techniques or methods. One way to consider the difference between the two is that curriculum materials are tangible resources used by the teacher and/or students, whereas teaching techniques are mainly approaches to teaching where success depends heavily on the professional skill of the teacher. For example, in role playing, student success in the teaching-learning environment depends on the skillful direction of a teacher, whereas the effective use of workbooks depends not only on the skillful use of the workbook by a teacher, but also on the quality of the workbook itself.

Types of Curriculum Materials

In general, curriculum materials may be classified into three categories: printed matter, audiovisual materials, and manipulative aids. Materials classified in these categories may be used separately or in combination with each other when applied in a teaching-learning situation.

Printed Matter.   Curriculum materials classified as printed matter are those that rely mainly upon reading for comprehension and are currently printed on paper. Types of printed material include

1. Manuals
2. Workbooks
3. Pamphlets
4. Study guides
5. Reference books
6. Standard textbooks
7. Magazines
8. Newspapers
9. Modules

Audiovisual Materials.   Audiovisual materials may involve seeing and hearing at the same time, although not in all cases. Furthermore, audiovisual materials require some type of equipment for their use. For example, slides require a slide projector. These materials include (but are not limited to)

1. Pictures
2. Graphics
3. Transparencies
4. Filmstrips
5. Posters
6. Audiotapes

7. Records
8. Films
9. Film loops
10. Slide series
11. Videotapes
12. Microcomputers

Manipulative Aids. Instructional materials classified as manipulative aids are those that must be physically handled. Examples include

1. Puzzles
2. Games
3. Models
4. Specimens
5. Puppets/figures

6. Learning kits
7. Experiments
8. Trainers
9. Simulators

Need for Securing Curriculum Materials

A master teacher must make wise use of all potential resources when planning for and conducting instruction. This implies that innovative teachers rely upon a variety of curriculum materials to supplement and complement their professional expertise in teaching situations. This is not to be construed that instructional materials are the sole basis on which an effective teaching-learning situation rests. The point is that curriculum materials can make teaching more effective for a teacher and more efficient for a learner.

A second reason for securing curriculum materials is the lack of time a teacher usually has to develop his or her own materials. Time may be the critical factor as to whether a teacher develops certain materials or purchases the completed product from a publisher or other source. Many teachers do not have ample time to devote to curriculum material development. Thus, if any such development is undertaken, it is usually restricted to the transparency, slide, model, or handout.

Costs constitute a third factor in determining whether materials should be purchased or developed. If a teacher fully accounts for his or her time that is required to develop quality materials in addition to needed monetary inputs, the savings experienced, if any, in materials development may not be sufficient to warrant the effort.

Quality control is another concern in the development of curriculum materials. Some teachers may have the time to develop certain materials; however, sufficient time and resources may not be available to field test, revise, and retest them in order to assure a quality product. Materials available through commercial sources may not always be of superior quality; however, the materials may have been tested and used to determine their effectiveness prior to marketing. Thus, the purchase of curriculum materials that have already been developed may result in a higher-quality product than those that could be developed using resources available to the vocational teacher.

In some cases, a teacher may not find desired instructional materials from commercial sources and thus must rely on developmental efforts to provide them. Whereas this chapter is concerned with the identification and selection of materials already available, Chapter 10 deals specifically with the process involved in developing such materials.

Selecting Curriculum Materials

The person selecting quality materials for a curriculum must take several factors into consideration. All of these factors are important, and the failure to examine materials in relation to each of these factors may result in the purchase of items that cannot be used to achieve the desired learning outcomes.

The assessment of curriculum materials must be carried out in a logical, planned order. Factors that the developer should consider when selecting materials include (1) general information (a description of the materials); (2) acceptable standards of quality relating to areas of bias, readability, content, presentation, learning, support, and cost-benefit; and (3) strengths and weaknesses. Each of these factors is discussed on the following pages, and an example of a complete Materials Assessment Form is included in Appendix A. In addition, sample exercises are provided to illustrate how materials can be assessed and selected.

General Information

The first step in the selection process is to obtain an overall understanding of the material. Section I, General Information, of the Materials Assessment Form may be used as a guide in this process. Completing Section I enables an individual to develop an overall understanding of the materials. Space is provided to indicate the title, author, publisher, and supplier of the publication. In addition, the year and place published, cost, and format of packaging can be indicated. Space is also provided to indicate vocational subject area, potential students for which the material is intended, and how the material is to be applied in an educational setting.

Assessment Areas

Section II of the Materials Assessment Form focuses on specific areas by which materials under consideration should be evaluated. While any number of assessment scales could be used, the ultimate decision a reviewer must make is whether the materials are acceptable or unacceptable according to some type of predetermined standards. Discussion on each of the specific standards follows, while the complete Section II of the Materials Assessment Form is in Appendix A.

Bias.   Today public concern with bias has strong implications for vocational educators when materials are selected. In the past developers of materials gave little consideration to whether photographs or words were biased. Thus, highly biased materials were unintentionally produced which ultimately had an effect on students' attitudes and opinions. Bias may occur as any of the following:

Job denigration	Age discrimination
Sex-role stereotyping	Racial bias
Ethnic bias	Religious bias

In addition to bias, materials such as magazines containing advertising must be analyzed to determine if any content is objectionable. For example, an ad may use language that is offensive to a minority group, or a photograph may depict one race as superior to another.

Peterson and Vetter (1980) have developed an "Awareness Guide" for use by educators that will help to alert readers to areas where sex bias may occur. This guide is shown in Figure 9-1.

Pratt (1980) has developed an extensive procedure to determine bias in publications through content analysis. This procedure is referred to as ECO analysis (evaluation coefficient analysis). Briefly, this procedure involves (1) identifying the subject (idea, individual, or concept) to be studied; (2) listing all value terms (either positive or negative) about the subject; and (3) calculating an ECO analysis by totaling the number of positive terms multiplied by 100 and divided by the combined total number of positive and negative terms. A coefficient of 0.0–50.0 represents material containing unfavorable content toward a subject, whereas a coefficient of 50.0–100 indicates material with favorable content.

Readability.   The importance of determining the reading level can easily be appreciated, especially if a teacher attempts to use materials designed for tenth- to twelfth-grade level students with students who read at the eighth-grade level. If this occurs, students will have difficulty reading the material and the information may not be understood.

If a readability score is desired, several procedures are available. The more traditional approach used in the past was the simplified Flesch formula, and the procedures to follow when using this technique can be found in various resources. Two other approaches that might be used are

FIGURE 9–1. Sex bias awareness guide

Reminders

Balance in the materials is important. Do not make a judgment based on one page.

There are ways to give **constructive** criticism:

Focus on the words and pictures—not on the author, illustrator or publisher.

Suggest a better way to write the words or draw the pictures.

Be positive rather than negative in your suggestions:

Wrong: "The pictures throughout Chapter 12 are very biased against males."

Right: "I am enclosing some rough sketches suggesting how the pictures in Chapter 12 might include both males and females."

Focus on the big issues and don't be nitpicky.

Words are powerful. Some attempts to make our language more sex fair have been criticized. However, without carrying it to the point of ridiculousness, here are some uses of words that you should look for. Do the words . . .

Tie gender to occupation? The carpenter . . . he? The house-keeper . . . she? Woman doctor? Male nurse?

Always say, "he and she" rather than "she and he"; "boys and girls" rather than "girls and boys"?

Reflect neutrality wherever possible? Chairperson? Salesperson? Repairperson?

Check List

In the **illustrations and words** . . .

	Biased against Females	Biased against Males	Balanced Males & Females
1. Are both males and females shown in traditionally sex-biased occupations? Both female and male secretaries?	☐	☐	☐
2. Is there any evidence of tokenism? One female in a group of ten male construction workers? One male in a group of female dental assistants?	☐	☐	☐
3. Is either sex consistently shown in serving, assisting and other secondary roles? Women as supervisor of nurses with males as orderlies?	☐	☐	☐
4. Are males and females portrayed in leadership roles? Women executives? Male day-care supervisors?	☐	☐	☐
5. Are work roles tied to social roles? Are men shown making coffee? Are women the only part-time workers?	☐	☐	☐
6. Are traits such as independence, decisiveness, drive, ambition, creativity and loyalty indicated for both females and males?	☐	☐	☐
7. Are there unnecessary references to physical attributes? The "burly" truck driver? The "good looking" receptionist?	☐	☐	☐
8. Are suggestions for grooming and personal appearance directed to both males and females?	☐	☐	☐

Source: From Marla Peterson and Louise Vetter. "What to Do About Those Biased Materials." *VocEd* 55, no. 4 (1980): 34–36. Copyright © 1980 the American Vocational Association. Used with the permission of *VocEd* and authors.

the cloze procedure and forecast formula (Ross, 1979).* Each will be discussed in the following paragraphs.

Cloze Procedure. The steps to follow with this approach are

1. Select sample paragraphs from materials students are to read.
2. Type the sentences from these paragraphs as follows:
   a. Type first sentence of paragraph as it appears.
   b. For the second and succeeding sentences, type the sentence, but omit every fifth word until there are fifty blanks (all blanks should be the same length).
   c. The last sentence of the passage should be typed completely as it appears.
3. Have students read the entire passage as you have typed it.
4. Have students reread the entire passage and complete the blanks with what they perceive to be the missing words.
5. Score their responses: to be correct responses, the words supplied by the students must be exact (minor misspellings are considered correct).
6. Interpret the scores according to the following scale:
   23 or more correct responses—students are operating at the independent reading level; they can read and understand the materials without teacher assistance.
   19–22 correct responses—students are functioning at the instructional level; teacher assistance is needed with using more difficult words and understanding the content.
   Fewer than 19 correct answers—students are frustrated; material is too difficult to understand, even with teacher assistance.

The cloze procedure requires the teacher to use the materials with student assistance. If a teacher desires to measure the readability levels of curriculum materials before using the materials, he or she could use the common simplified Flesch formula mentioned earlier or a shorter procedure known as the forecast formula.

Forecast Formula. The forecast formula is a simple and inexpensive approach to use in determining the readability level of materials. The steps to follow are

1. Select a 150-word passage from the material to be measured.
2. Count the number of one-syllable words.

---

*From Novella M. Ross. "Assessing Readability of Instructional Materials." *VocEd* 54, no. 2 (February 1979): 10–11.

3. Use the following formula to determine reading grade-level (RGL):

$$20 - \frac{\text{Number of one-syllable words}}{10} = \text{RGL}$$

An example will help to clarify the use of this formula. Assume a 150-word passage has 80 one-syllable words. Using the formula, the calculations would be as follows:

$$20 - \frac{80}{10} = 20 - 8 = 12 \text{ RGL}$$

Thus, the reading grade-level for this particular passage was judged to be twelfth grade. To make a valid assessment of the materials, eight to ten passages must be reviewed using the formula. The passages may be averaged to determine the average reading grade-level for the material.

Content. A very crucial assessment area that must be included when reviewing materials concerns the content. Specific attention should be focused on the content accuracy, whether the content is up-to-date, and appropriateness of the material for the intended students.

Presentation. Presentation refers to whether the material is presented in an easy-to-use format, contains sufficient illustrations and examples, and has visual appeal to the student.

Learning. To be most effective, curriculum materials must be based on sound principles of learning. For example, does the content build on previously learned material (principle of association)? Are situations provided for the student to make application of the content (principle of practice)? Are the materials appealing to the student's senses (principle of effect)? Do the materials prepare the student for what is to follow (principle of readiness)? Materials developed with these learning principles in mind will enable the teacher to take the materials and incorporate them into the teaching-learning environment in a most effective manner.

Support. Very few curriculum materials are used alone in an educational setting. Often, special equipment or other resources must be obtained in order to use the materials. The question a reviewer must consider is whether the amount of additional support is reasonable in relation to the objectives to be achieved and content to be covered.

Cost-benefit. One of the major factors to consider in purchasing curriculum materials relates to the cost. A later section in this chapter deals with those factors a curriculum developer must consider when determining priorities for materials purchase. The question a reviewer must answer is How reasonable is the cost in relation to other materials available or other instructional methods that may be appropriate and possible?

Strengths and Limitations

As curriculum developers review materials in detail, certain strengths and limitations will become more obvious. Section III of the Materials Assessment Form provides the reviewer with an opportunity to highlight unique strong points of the material and note specific limitations. While any notes made in this section of the form may not in and of themselves determine whether the materials are acceptable, just being aware of them will enable the reviewer to be better informed when the decision must be made to determine if materials are acceptable or unacceptable.

Assessment Summary

Section IV of the Materials Assessment Form provides an opportunity for the reviewer to summarize ratings assigned to standards in Section II of the form. After the ratings of acceptable, questionable, unacceptable, or does not apply are recorded, the reviewer can then form a judgment regarding the overall assessment for the material under consideration.

Selecting Computer Software: A Special Case

The influx of microcomputers into educational programs will no doubt increase in the future, in terms of computer-assisted programs and instructional packages. Many of the points highlighted in the earlier section of this chapter dealing with the selection of instructional materials also apply to microcomputer software. However, the uniqueness of this resource poses some different problems when selection of software packages is at hand. The form contained in Appendix B gives several guiding statements that can be followed in helping to select the right software for a particular situation. The form helps point out what hardware and software are needed to use the material correctly and whether the material has been arranged in a logical order.

Textbook Selection

Whereas the preceding section focused on a procedure for the comprehensive review of any curriculum materials, an examination of the literature will reveal specific selection forms for use with certain types of curriculum materials. Warming and Baber (1980) developed what they call a "harmonious, holistic approach" to the selection of textbooks. The form consists of a twenty-item inventory referred to as "Touchstones for Textbook Selection Inventory." The complete form is in Figure 9–2; a teacher could use this inventory in assessing the desirability of textbooks under consideration.

Curriculum Materials for Learners with Special Needs

The factors to consider for the identification and selection of curriculum materials for learners with special needs are no different from those discussed in the prior sections of this chapter. However, care must be taken by vocational educators to ensure that the materials considered and eventually selected for learners with special needs complement their unique learning characteristics. It is imperative that the special-needs student be the focal point when the selection of any curriculum materials is being made. Two general areas that vocational educators must consider when selecting materials concern individual students' vocational potential and the unique characteristics that make each student special.

Vocational Potential

The vocational teacher must assess each individual's vocational potential and, once this assessment is made, arrive at implications for the selection of appropriate curriculum materials. The assessment of these general student characteristics is important regardless of the type of special need a student has. Assessment of a student's vocational potential might focus on the following areas:

1. General and specific skills and abilities
2. Aptitudes, interests, and needs
3. Personality and temperaments
4. Values and attitudes
5. Motivation
6. Physical capacities
7. Work tolerance

FIGURE 9–2. *Touchstones for textbook selection inventory*

	Excellent 5	Adequate 3	Inadequate 1
1. Appropriate readability level			
2. Author(s) reputable in field			
3. Indicates successful field-testing of text and assessment instruments			
4. Published by reputable firm			
5. Table of contents exhibits logical development of subject			
6. Meets course objectives			
7. Language appropriate for intended students			
8. Presents major concepts thoroughly and accurately			
9. Defines difficult/important ideas and vocabulary in context or in a glossary			
10. Contains visual illustrations of key concepts			
11. Levels of abstraction appropriate for readers			
12. Provides chapter objectives			
13. Provides chapter summaries			
14. Format interesting and material well presented			
15. Avoids stereotypes and sexist language			
16. Provides for concrete application of abstract concepts			
17. Recommends resources and research projects			
18. Suggests alternative resources for students experiencing difficulty			
19. Provides teacher's guide or manual			
20. Provides for assessment of instructional objectives			
Subtotals			
Total score			

Text _____

Author_____   Reviewer _____

Publisher _____

Publication date_____   Some inventory users will wish to assign extra weight to certain "touch-

Date of review _____   stones."

Source: From Eloise O. Warming and Elizabeth C. Baber. "Touchstones for Textbook Selection Inventory." *Phi Delta Kappan* 61, no. 10 (June 1980): 695. © 1980 Phi Delta Kappan, Inc.

The characteristics that a student possesses in each of those areas should be considered.

Unique Characteristics

The individual qualities that make a student special have a direct impact on the type of curriculum materials that are appropriate for that student. One needs only to review the various categories of special-needs learners to begin eliminating certain types of curriculum materials. Special-needs learners may be

Mentally retarded	Orthopedically handicapped
Hard of hearing	Learning disabled
Deaf	Affected with other health impairments
Speech impaired	Gifted or talented
Visually impaired	Limited English proficiency
Emotionally disturbed	

It is not possible in this volume to deal with every possible kind of uniqueness possessed by special-needs learners and the direct implications for identification and selection of appropriate curriculum materials. An obvious example would be that for a visually impaired learner, materials must be selected that highlight the hearing mode of learning and/or the use of Braille. Many resources are available to the vocational teacher that deal in depth with the various characteristics of special-needs students and with the suggested teaching-learning strategies that work best for particular students.

Sources of Curriculum Materials

The number of sources from which curriculum materials can be obtained is limited only by ingenuity and innovative thinking. Many sources can be identified in any one community. However, curriculum developers and teachers must look beyond their own communities to assess what is available. To help reduce the amount of time spent identifying such sources, there are specific people and firms that should be contacted first. These include

Commercial publishers	Military service
Journals	Companies
Magazines	Curriculum networks
Curriculum centers	State educational agencies
ERIC System	U.S. Government Printing Office

Additional Sources of Materials

Some materials must be purchased, but many of them may be secured free of charge. Local newspapers, catalogues, road maps, charts, animals, and automobiles that have been damaged in accidents are just a few examples of resource materials. The list is endless and is limited only by a teacher's imagination in relation to the topic being discussed in class.

Planning to Secure Curriculum Materials

The tendency to overlook the purchase of much-needed curriculum materials in vocational education is a serious mistake. For example, if vocational teachers are allotted $3,000 to spend for their department, they will usually spend most, if not all, of the money for equipment, supplies, and tools needed for laboratory instruction. Although these resources may be critical to the effectiveness of the program, the need for continual expenditures in the laboratory area may lead to a critical shortage of materials for both the classroom and the laboratory. Thus, special attention should be given to the development of short- and long-range plans for securing curriculum materials.

Short-Range Planning

Short-range planning for curriculum materials consists of determining which materials are essential for the coming years. The criterion for determining essential materials would be which items include information that a teacher desires to teach during the year. Another factor might be which materials could be used in a variety of situations or learning environments. For example, basic texts or visual aids that contain pertinent information might represent a higher priority the first year than workbooks that could not be used again. Another consideration would be the amount of money available. As an illustration, assume that sufficient money were available to buy printed resource materials. It might be better to buy these materials the first year and schedule the purchase of transparencies for the second year, since some transparencies could be made by the teacher during the year.

Long-Range Planning

The value of giving consideration to long-range planning in purchasing curriculum materials becomes evident when one starts to look at the prices of such materials. Very few budgets will permit any teacher to order all the materials desired for a given year. Thus, it is vital that a long-range plan be developed for securing them. Materials that might be included in long-range plans would be those that treat more advanced subject matter. Another way to approach this decision would be to consider those materials that build on prior student knowledge or learning sessions. As mentioned in the preceding section, limited budgets must be considered. Materials that entail a high cost or require special equipment might be included in the long-range plan if current situations would prevent their being used effectively.

Developing a Plan for Securing Materials

The establishment of priorities for securing commercially produced curriculum materials usually evolves from a subjective thought process. Although this may be sufficient in certain cases, development of a logical, systematic procedure may be a more objective basis upon which decisions can be made regarding their purchase. For this reason, a materials priority form has been developed to assist teachers, curriculum planners, or administrators either as individuals or as groups in arriving at priorities for the purchase of materials. This form is provided in Figure 9–3 with illustrative data.

Curriculum materials identified as a lesser priority for short-range needs and not purchased would need to be considered later as the long-range plans are implemented. Again referring to Figure 9–3, if the fourth-priority materials in the short-range plan (Auto Electrical Systems) were not purchased, those materials might later become a first priority as the time draws near for the purchase of materials identified in the long-range plan.

Summary

The impact of curriculum materials on the effectiveness of a teaching-learning environment cannot be underestimated. For this reason, educators must develop some type of logical procedure for identifying and selecting curriculum materials.

First, one must consider exactly what curriculum materials are. Basically, they are resources that assist a teacher in bringing about a desirable change of behavior in students. Curriculum materials may consist of printed matter, audiovisual materials, and/or manipulative aids. Certainly teachers can and should develop some of the materials needed, but eventually a situation will exist where materials need to be purchased.

FIGURE 9–3. *Materials priority form*

Course: ___Auto Mechanics___

Number of Students: ___10___

Year: ___19 × 1___

Material	19 × 2 Short-range Needs			19 × 3 Long-range Need by Year		
	Cost Each	Total Cost	Priority	Cost Each	Total Cost	Priority
1. ABC of Auto Mechanics	$ 5.00	$ 50.00	3	$	$	
2. ABC of Auto Mechanics Transparencies					100.00	2
3. Beginning Auto Mechanics	12.50	125.00	1			
4. Intermediate Auto Mechanics				12.50	125.00	1
5. Advanced Auto Mechanics				15.00	150.00	4
6. Auto Electrical Systems	7.50	75.00	4			
7. Acme Transmissions				10.00	150.00	3
8. Computer Software for Troubleshooting Auto Engines	20.00	200.00	2			
Total Cost		$550.00			$525.00	

Educators must consider several important factors before a decision is made to purchase or not to purchase a specific item. Factors to consider in selection of materials include an overall general description of the material, bias, readability, content, presentation, learning, support, and cost-benefit. The selection of materials for learners with special needs must focus on the unique characteristics of these learners.

Sources of curriculum materials are limited only by one's ingenuity and creativity. General areas of sources are commercial publishers, journals and magazines, curriculum centers, ERIC system, state educational agencies, the U.S. Government Printing Office, the military, and private companies.

Securing curriculum materials should follow a logical and systematic plan. Short-range planning is used to identify those materials that are basic for the units of instruction to be taught in the near future. Long-range planning serves to identify materials that represent advanced units of instruction occurring at a later date. But by following a systematic process, teachers, either individually or as a group, will be more likely to secure materials that are appropriate for the instructional units planned and to eliminate others.

Related References

A Guide to Selecting and Using Textbooks. South Holland, Ill.: Goodheart-Willcox Company, 1990.

Alexander, Wilma J. "The Problem of Software." *VocEd* 57, no. 3 (April 1982): 39, 54.

Budke, Wesley E., and Selkow, Charles. "Resources for Updating a Curriculum." *Vocational Education Journal* 61, no. 5 (August 1986): 31–33.

Camp, William G.; Moore, Gary E.; Foster, Richard M.; and Moore, Barbara, A. *Microcomputer Applications for Students of Agriculture*. Danville, Ill.: The Interstate Printers and Publishers, Inc., 1988.

Chase, Shirley A. "One-stop Curriculum Shopping." *VocEd* 60, no. 2 (March 1985): 43–44.

Chase, Shirley A. "Using Military Curriculum Materials." *VocEd* 56, no. 5 (June 1981): 10, 12.

Dahl, Peter R.; Appleby, Judith A.; and Lipe, Dewey. *Mainstreaming Guidebook for Vocational Educators—Teaching the Handicapped*. Salt Lake City: Olympus Publishing Company, 1978.

Farr, J. N.; Jenkins, J. J.; and Paterson, D. G. "Simplification of Flesch Reading Ease Formula." *Journal of Applied Psychology* 35 (October 1951): 335.

Fry, Edward. "A Readability Formula for Short Passages." *Journal of Reading*, vol. 33 no. 8 (May 1990): 594–597.

Gall, Meredith Damien. *Handbook for Evaluating and Selecting Curriculum Materials*. Boston: Allyn and Bacon, 1981.

Handbook of Instructional Resources and References for Teaching the Gifted. Boston: Allyn and Bacon, 1980.

Johnston, Brenda A. "Readability in Written Instruction." *Performance & Instruction Journal* 24, no. 3 (March 1985): 18–19.

Make Learning Easier: A Guide for Improving Educational/Training Materials. Rome, Italy: Food and Agricultural Organization of the United Nations, 1990.

Mangano, R. Michael; Hofen, Susan; and Foster, Phillip R. "In Search of Resources for Handicapped Students." *VocEd* 55, no. 6 (June 1980): 38–39.

Mehlinger, Howard D. "American Textbook Reform: What Can We Learn from the Soviet Experience." *Phi Delta Kappan* 70, no. 1 (September 1989): 29–35.

Miller, Samuel K. *Selecting and Implementing Educational Software*. Boston: Allyn and Bacon, 1987.

Peterson, Marla, and Vetter, Louise. "What to Do About Those Biased Materials." *VocEd* 55, no. 4 (1980): 34–36.

Pratt, David. *Curriculum Design and Development*. New York, N.Y.: Harcourt Brace Jovanovich, 1980.

Reynolds, Dorothy F. "Locating Instructional Materials for Energy Education." *VocEd* 57, no. 3 (April 1982): 17–20.

Robenstein, Judith. *Microcomputers in Vocational Education*. Englewood Cliffs, N.J.: Prentice-Hall, 1986.

Ross, Norella M. "Assessing Readability of Instructional Materials." *VocEd* 54, no. 2 (February 1979): 10–11.

Schmidt, B. June. "Procedures for Evaluating Microcomputer Software Used in Vocational Education." *The Journal of Vocational Education Research* 9, no. 1 (Winter 1984): 10–23.

"Sources of Information for Equipment and Teaching Aids—1982 Buyers Guide." *VocEd* 57, no. 1 (January/February 1982): 53–69.

Tauber, Robert T. "ERIC Update." *VocEd* 59, no. 5 (August 1984): 48.

Vaughn, Jane. "Finding the Right Software." *Vocational Education Journal* 61, no. 6 (September 1986): 37–38.

Warming, Eloise O., and Baber, Elizabeth Coe. "Touchstones for Textbook Selection." *Phi Delta Kappan* (June 1980): 694–695.

10

Developing Curriculum Materials

Introduction

Even with the variety of vocational and technical curriculum materials available today, the curriculum developer is often faced with the need to produce new materials. This need becomes evident when materials are required for a certain instructional situation and are not available. Furthermore, a need may be established when the available materials are not appropriate for an intended audience or when their use is limited by other factors that might prohibit a teacher from using them with established instructional objectives.

This chapter deals directly with factors associated with the development and dissemination of curriculum materials. During the development process, consideration must be given to factors such as the time and dollars available, the audience, and the development alternatives. In addition, the actual development process must take on a logical and orderly format to assure that usable materials are produced.

Determining the Need for Curriculum Materials

Ultimately the need for curriculum materials must be determined in relation to content. Once the content has been established, plans must be made to secure meaningful materials that align with established instructional objectives. Two different situations could exist at this time.

After an exhaustive search has been conducted, the conclusion may be reached that curriculum materials are not currently available from either public or private sources. Thus, the logical alternative would be to develop the needed materials. On the other hand, a search may produce several items that are related to the instructional content but for some reason the materials may appear to be deficient in certain areas. Therefore, educators would be faced with the task of developing or adapting the curriculum materials.

Factors to Consider in Curriculum Materials Development

The development of quality curriculum materials depends on several factors, with any one of them having great impact on product quality. Thus, individuals who assume leadership for any development effort must carefully consider all areas that might affect the quality of the final product. Furthermore, management of the development process must be such that materials can be produced at a smooth and steady pace, thereby helping to ensure that quality materials are developed. Factors that must be considered when developing curriculum materials include the time available, the dollars available, and the audience for which the materials are intended. Each of these factors will be discussed in the following paragraphs.

Time Available and Needed

One of the most critical factors to consider when the development of curriculum materials is undertaken is the time available to devote to a development project in relation to the time needed. The development of quality materials can be very time-consuming when the total effort is considered. When time is a concern, one must think not only about the time needed to develop the product, but also the time needed for testing, revising, printing, and disseminating the finished item. This time may be as short as a few weeks or more than a year in duration, depending on the quantity of materials to be produced.

Whereas the time needed to develop quality materials is crucial, consideration must also be given to the time available from those individuals who are to be involved in the development. Persons who have little available time can only be expected to contribute minimally to a developmental effort, and thus the number of materials produced would be fewer or the length of time required to develop the materials would need to be extended.

Expertise Available

Regardless of the experience and knowledge possessed by those individuals involved in curriculum materials development, there will often be instances where outside assistance should be sought. Special assistance might be needed with regard to technical information, editing, media, and duplication.

Technical Information. Accuracy of the technical information is a basic concern of those who develop curriculum materials. For the most part, materials are developed by those who are knowledgeable in a particular technical area, however, there are some instances when outside technical assistance may be desirable. For example, if materials are being developed that include some federal or state laws or interpretation of statutes, then the review of the materials by a lawyer might be appropriate. Another example where technical assistance might be desirable is when materials will be disseminated over a large audience, for example a state or region. Securing input from others in this situation might avoid materials being developed that were not applicable to all of the geographic areas intended.

Editorial Assistance. Curriculum materials producers often do not have the necessary writing expertise in grammatical matters to handle all problems that arise during the development process. Thus, persons who are competent in the editorial area need to be contacted for assistance prior to the time materials are utilized by student groups. After materials have been prepared in draft form, they should be reviewed for correct grammar, punctuation, and spelling.

Media. Curriculum materials are seldom used alone in a teaching situation. Typically, they are utilized in conjunction with overhead transparencies, microcomputers, slides, audiotapes, or a variety of other media. For this reason, the curriculum materials developer is advised to contact a media specialist as the development process begins and to obtain help in the selection and use of media. Helpful suggestions can be obtained in areas such as how to arrange material attractively and how much media will cost.

Duplication. After materials have been developed, they need to be duplicated in quantity and distributed if any use is expected. Thus, individuals developing materials need to secure estimated costs of duplication, turnaround time (time from submission to delivery), and the style and format that would be best suited for the material being developed and the intended audience.

Although printing curriculum materials on paper still appears to be a most popular approach, the need to explore alternative methods of duplication may become more critical, especially as wood becomes scarce and the cost of paper rises. The use of microfilm, microfiche, diskettes, and other methods of reproducing information will need to be considered in the future.

Dollars Available

One of the most important factors to consider when developing curriculum materials is the monetary resources available. Obviously, the amount of accessible money can have great impact on the quality of materials developed. The relationship between the dollars available and curriculum materials development can be pointed out in several ways. First, compensation may need to be made to outside experts who are asked to provide assistance. For example, seeking input from a lawyer regarding legal concerns may result in a substantial expense. A second set of expenses is associated with the actual development of materials. This might include, but not be limited to, pencils, paper, resource materials, typing, and general supplies. Third, costs will occur when the materials are duplicated. This cost, which involves the printing of materials and associated media, is often quite expensive, and therefore must receive close attention. A fourth cost is related to the dissemination of materials, which might include workshop expenses, travel costs for the developer and teacher, or postage charges. And fifth, the time required of those individuals actually developing the material represents a monetary investment. Thus, when one considers all the expenses associated with curriculum materials development, some thought must be given to the current budget as it relates to the development effort and whether an additional source of funds needs to be identified.

If materials are being developed over a lengthy time period, some provision must be made for inflation. For example, if materials that are now being developed will not be duplicated until a year from now, current printing prices may not be appropriate figures to use when preparing operational budgets for the next year. Failing to allow for inflation may later result in reducing the quantity of items printed.

Decisions to Make Regarding Materials Development

As educators begin the task of curriculum materials development, there are several crucial decisions to be made. These decisions could be thought of as the what, why, who, when, and where of materials development.

What Materials Should Be Developed and Why? The answer to this question is quite obvious. If the material needed to complete an instructional unit successfully is not available, then the typical response is to develop it. However, a more complex situation arises when individuals with different philosophical beliefs attempt to decide exactly what information to include in the material and what to delete.

Who Should Develop the Materials? This type of decision is critical, since individuals developing the materials must be knowledgeable in the technical area for which the items are to be used. These individuals must be up-to-date as to the latest developments in their area of concern. Furthermore, they must have the ability to put their thoughts down on paper in a clear, logical, and concise manner. Other considerations include the time available to devote to a project of this magnitude as well as the involvement of the person or persons actually willing to undertake the task.

When Should the Materials Be Developed? The decision associated with this question depends to some degree on the individuals involved. If the material developers are responsible for teaching, time that can be devoted to materials development will probably be somewhat restricted. Of course, more time could be devoted to materials development during the summer or if an individual were released from some or all of his or her teaching load. Regardless of when the materials are developed, blocks of time—at least two to three hours per work session—are needed in order for developers to be productive and efficient.

Where Should the Materials Be Developed? Although this may seem to be a minor consideration, functional space is important for those who develop materials. The space must be adequate such that materials can be laid out and readily used while the development process is underway and that the developer is not cramped for writing space. Furthermore, a location is needed where the developer is free from unnecessary distractions or interruptions.

Target Population

The target population represents the audience for which the materials are being developed. There are basically two factors to consider with regard to target population as the development process begins. First, consideration must be given to the grade level(s) of the group(s) who will be using the materials. This will not only influence the reading level at which the material is written, but also the depth to which technical information will be covered. A second consideration deals with the use of materials on a local, state, regional, or national basis. Curriculum materials developers want to be sure that the materials being developed will be applicable to the entire audience and not be limited due to differences in geographical locations.

Dissemination

Dissemination involves the process of distributing materials produced to those who have a need. A planned dissemination scheme is important to help ensure that materials are adopted and used. To overlook this step may result in quality materials being shelved, which would be a great waste of money and human effort. The dissemination of curriculum materials is treated in greater depth later in this chapter.

Support Needed

In addition to the need for adequate physical facilities in support of preparation efforts, several other types of support are needed. Reference materials are needed as materials are being developed. In fact, multiple copies of certain references may be needed if a team approach to development is used. If overhead transparencies are to be developed to supplement written materials, overhead projectors, screens, thermofax machines, and other types of equipment will be needed.

In addition to the above support items, moral support needs to be provided by those who are giving leadership to the project. The development of quality curriculum materials in vocational and technical education is an essential part of curriculum development, and this process should be encouraged and supported by vocational administrators and supervisors when the need arises.

Development Alternatives

One factor that must be considered is the way materials will actually be developed. Basically there are two approaches to development: individual or team. There are distinct advantages and disadvantages to each approach, which will be discussed in the following paragraphs.

Individual Development.   Although input may be obtained from others, such as superiors, colleagues, and subject matter experts, responsibility for the actual writing, testing, revision, and completion of materials falls upon one individual. The advantages of such an approach are management-related. With only one person involved, problems experienced when working with a group of professionals are not present.

Several distinct limitations are associated with the individual approach. The most obvious limitation concerns the limited amount of materials that can be developed by one individual compared with a group of developers. Another limitation is the reluctance of others to adopt materials developed by one individual. For a variety of reasons, teachers tend to prefer materials developed through the combined efforts of several knowledgeable individuals. In addition, the amount of time needed to develop materials is longer with the individual approach; thus, more time needs to be allotted for the development process. Concern can also be raised as to the product quality. With one individual responsible for carrying out all the development steps, several steps may be slighted or eliminated completely if the project falls behind anticipated completion dates.

Team Development.   The team approach offers some unique opportunities for curriculum materials development. This approach basically relies on a group of individuals who all have one objective in mind—the development of quality materials. Several different team arrangements may be used. One consists of the total team being divided into small groups that each have responsibility for the development of a different set of materials. When the materials produced by each group are combined, they constitute a complete set of curriculum materials. Another arrangement utilizes one group to develop the materials and another to assume responsibility for reviewing and testing. This arrangement enables the reviewing and testing to be conducted by persons who are not intimately involved with the development effort and thus ensures a less biased estimate of the materials quality. Ideally, a team effort approach provides for an equitable division of responsibility with activities being assigned on the basis of each individual team member's expertise.

Many limitations associated with the individual approach to materials development can be minimized through a team approach. For example, a greater volume of materials may be developed in a shorter period of time. Furthermore, concerns that individuals might have about the materials' quality would be fewer, since input was secured from several people during the development process.

Each of the factors to consider in curriculum materials development is certainly important, to say that one factor is more important than another cannot be justified. Any one of these factors can seriously affect materials quality or the projected outcome of the development effort. Thus, all factors must be considered and a determination made as to how each might limit the quality of materials.

The Curriculum Materials Development Process

Curriculum materials development must follow a systematic and logical process from beginning to end. Whether an individual or team approach is used, it is important to keep in mind that development consists of several stages, each of which contributes to the overall materials quality. When each stage in the development process is followed, materials produced will be of higher quality and well worth the effort involved.

Stages in the Development of Curriculum Materials

The various stages included in the curriculum materials development process are important contributors to materials quality. These stages are presented in the order one should follow when carrying out development activities.

1. Prepare a preliminary development plan.
2. Determine curriculum content to be investigated.
3. Determine terminal and enabling objectives.
4. Identify special curriculum materials needed.
5. Review the literature to determine what materials are available.
6. Identify materials lacking in the content area.
7. Establish priorities for needed materials.
8. Finalize the development plan.
9. Conduct an intensive literature review.
10. Obtain relevant references and resources.
11. Prepare a first draft of the materials.
12. Edit the first draft.
13. Prepare a second draft.
14. Pilot-test the second draft.
15. Prepare a third draft.
16. Field-test the third draft.
17. Prepare the final draft.
18. Duplicate the materials.

Prepare a Preliminary Development Plan.   The preliminary plan serves to establish general guidelines to follow during the materials development process. The individuals who are involved in developing this plan include those responsible for providing leadership to the overall project as well as teachers or other persons who will be actively involved in the preparation of materials. Representatives from those who will be teaching the curriculum content and using the materials should also be included when the preliminary planning is taking place. Specific concerns that may be brought up during this preliminary planning include the curriculum content to be focused on, the person(s) who will assume responsibility for stages 2 through 7, and the projected timetable for the first seven stages. Although the preliminary plan is not usually a formal document, it serves to provide direction for activities to follow and establishes a tangible frame of reference for those who will develop and use the materials.

Determine Curriculum Content to Be Investigated. The actual process that should be followed in making curriculum content decisions was detailed in Chapter 7. At this stage in the materials development process, a decision needs to be made as to which part(s) of the curriculum supporting curriculum materials should be developed. Let us assume that a two-year marketing education program has just been established at a local school. The marketing education coordinators realize that materials are available for one part of the curriculum, but they are not sure if materials are available for another segment. Thus, the most logical decision at this time would be to focus on that part of the curriculum where supporting materials may not be available.

Determine Terminal and Enabling Objectives. The identification of curriculum content will not, by itself, clearly indicate what students are to accomplish as a result of content taught. Therefore, before a determination can be made of the materials needed to teach a specific segment of the curriculum, terminal and enabling performance objectives must be established. Detailed information about developing these objectives is provided in Chapter 8. These objectives provide specific direction as to what technical information must be included in the materials. Once technical content has been clarified through objectives, development of relevant curriculum materials may then proceed.

Identify Special Curriculum Materials Needed. This stage provides the opportunity to identify special curriculum materials known to be needed while teaching the technical content. An example may serve to point out the necessity of this stage. Assume that a curriculum has been established for deaf students. In this particular curriculum, any materials involving audio communication would be of limited usefulness in the classroom or laboratory. Time would be better spent identifying materials that rely on visual communication to transfer knowledge. In summary, this stage provides the opportunity to reflect on the characteristics of the audience for which the curriculum is designed and to identify materials that can best be utilized by them.

Review Literature to Determine What Materials Are Available. The ultimate goal of this stage is to determine what materials are already available pertaining to the curriculum content under consideration. Special efforts should be focused upon contacting those sources of curriculum materials identified in Chapter 9. Failure to review the literature extensively may ultimately result in materials being developed that are already available. Individuals who are assigned the task of reviewing the literature must not be too narrow in their thinking, and they should exhaust all possible sources in their search for appropriate materials. In fact, some materials may be found that could be appropriate if subjected to an extensive revision.

Identify Materials Lacking in the Content Area. The identification of materials lacking in the content area should become evident during the preceding stage and be listed for further discussion. Furthermore, curriculum materials developers may want to hold a brainstorming session to identify some creative approaches or materials needed to present information in a different or more interesting manner.

Establish Priorities for Needed Materials. The situation may arise where several different materials have been identified as being needed, but available resources will not permit the development of every item. When this occurs, priorities need to be established as to which materials are more important than others. Although it is difficult to provide precise guidelines to use in establishing priorities, there are several factors to be considered. These include competencies of the teachers who will be using the materials, the type and level of other available materials related to the content, and the projected length of time needed to develop each identified item.

Finalize the Development Plan. At this stage in the development, those persons who first met during the preliminary stage should reconvene to discuss what has occurred during each of the first seven stages. In fact, one of the actions taken during this stage is to decide whether the materials development plan should continue through the completion of a final product or whether it is most logical to cease at this point. Special factors to be considered tie in with ones discussed earlier in this chapter: namely, time available and needed, expertise available, and dollars available.

If the decision is made to develop materials identified as high-priority items, assignments must be given to those who will carry out the work. At this time it is also appropriate to involve other individuals who may need to become concerned with other aspects of the development. For example, if five different areas of curriculum materials are identified for development, additional people may need to be brought in to develop materials in each area. Other decisions to be made include target completion dates for various stages, estimated costs, and other details regarding the operational framework of the entire materials development process. Another consideration at this point would be whether a team approach or individual approach might be used. For example, if a group of teachers could be assembled during the summer, the team approach might permit a greater quantity of material to be developed in a relatively short period of time. A team approach also provides more flexibility for testing in the latter stages of the development process.

Discussion at this time must also focus on the desired format the materials are to take. Although philosophical differences will tend to alter the format between different individuals and situations, several major headings can serve to give direction for the format. These headings include

Cover Page
Table of Contents
Directions for Use
Technical Content
Bibliography

Conduct an Intensive Literature Review. This stage becomes most important when any great length of time passes between the initial review of literature and the actual development of curriculum materials. New materials are becoming available each day, especially those designed as part of software packages, and those responsible for the actual preparation of materials certainly need to review the latest ones available. Another activity that might prove beneficial at this time would be to contact individuals or organizations who are currently developing materials. The situation could develop where materials that closely align with established high-priority items are being developed by individuals or curriculum centers in other locations.

Obtain Relevant References and Resources. All references and resources that may be of assistance in the preparation of materials should be secured and made available to persons who will be responsible for developing them. These items should be available before an initial draft of the materials is prepared.

Prepare a First Draft of the Materials. Preparation of the initial draft may be the most time-consuming activity in the development of curriculum materials. Based on the performance objectives and identified content, individuals charged with the responsibility of actually preparing the materials can now begin the task of merging technical content with sound educational principles.

Edit the First Draft. Once the first draft of materials has been completed, a thorough editing should be conducted before proceeding further. Materials should be subjected to at least three types of editing, including technical accuracy, composition, and applicability. Furthermore, possible ideas for needed improvement can be identified if the materials being developed are evaluated with the Curriculum Materials Assessment Form, which was discussed in Chapter 9.

Technical Accuracy. The purpose of this type of editing is to determine the accuracy of the materials prepared. Editing for technical accuracy may be best conducted by team members who were not involved in the preparation process or by persons external to the curriculum development group. Once the materials have been verified for technical accuracy, any subsequent revisions will need to be reexamined to be sure that the intent of the original content has not been changed.

Composition. Editing for composition focuses upon several areas. These are

> Do the materials appear to be capable of communicating with the intended audience?
> Is the language used suitable for the intended audience?
> Are the materials free of ambiguous, unnecessary words?
> Are explanations, illustrations, and examples clear and concise?
> Are the materials grammatically correct?

Whereas editing for composition serves to eliminate words, phrases, or sections that may lead to difficulty in understanding the technical information, the true value of the materials will be determined during the testing stage.

Applicability. Editing for applicability becomes more subjective, since materials are reviewed in terms of the degree to which applications may be made to learning situations. For example, how well do the materials conform to an approved format, if one exists? Several questions related to applicability include

> Do the materials present information that will aid in meeting the established objectives?
> Are the materials structured according to the approved format?

Do the materials either incorporate sound learning strategies or provide for the inclusion of such learning strategies?

Similar to the editing discussed earlier on composition, the true applicability of materials will not be determined until the materials have been field-tested.

Prepare a Second Draft.   After the materials have been edited for technical accuracy, composition, and applicability, revisions must be made. These revisions are typically based on the suggestions provided by reviewers and are to be made by the same individuals who prepared the first draft. This will help to avoid the possibility of changing the writing style throughout the materials.

Pilot-Test the Second Draft.   The materials should now be ready to be tried with a small group from the intended audience (e.g., teachers and students). Details about the pilot-testing process are provided in Chapter 12. Generally, the group that pilot-tests the materials need not be large. Most important is that persons using the materials have sufficient opportunity to try them out in realistic settings and have the ability to provide meaningful feedback to the developer. Students need to be informed that the purpose of the exercise is to help evaluate the materials and not student performance.

Prepare the Third Draft.   A third draft of the materials is prepared so that any suggestions or recommendations resulting from the pilot-testing can be taken into account. Revision at this point occurs only after all student data as well as teachers' comments from the pilot-testing have been gathered and analyzed.

Field-Test the Third Draft.   As detailed in Chapter 12, field testing should be carried out with several groups in settings representative of those where the materials are to be used. The purpose of this field testing is to assess the materials' quality with a larger number of students and teachers.

Prepare the Final Draft.   Although few major revisions are likely to be needed at this point, the field-testing results should be carefully examined to determine if any steps must be taken to make appropriate changes in the materials so that they can be ready for dissemination.

Duplicate the Materials.   The last stage involves duplication of sufficient numbers of copies needed for those who are to receive the materials. In addition, ample copies need to be on hand for meeting future needs for maintaining a supply until a revision of the materials occurs and, where possible, to take advantage of new educational technology.

Managing the Curriculum Materials Development Process

One has only to review the many stages involved in the development of curriculum materials to realize that this process is quite complex. However, if quality materials are to be developed, all stages must receive due consideration. Thus, it is essential for those who provide leadership in the development of materials to incorporate sound management techniques into the development stages identified earlier.

Accountability

If resources such as money and time are to be associated with the development of materials, then some form of accountability must be employed to ensure that these resources are used wisely. Accountability is necessary regardless of who is providing the resources. For example, if a special proposal has been written and approved for the development of materials with funds from some outside agency (e.g., state department of education), then the sponsoring organization will be expecting quality materials to be developed within the time frame specified in the original proposal.

Another example of accountability deals with materials produced using resources provided at the local level. As mentioned earlier, time is money, and, where the development of materials is concerned, the time devoted by teachers to curriculum development should not be wasted.

Quality Control

Another important consideration in the management of curriculum materials development is quality control. The quality of materials must be considered continuously during the entire development process, with every effort made to help ensure that the final product is of the highest possible quality. The development of quality materials takes two key areas into consideration: standards of quality and management of quality.

The first area concerns factors associated with the materials quality. These factors can be the assessment areas comprising the Curriculum Materials Assessment Form (Appendix A). Such areas include readability, presentation, bias, content, learning, support, and cost-benefit. These and perhaps others must be considered during the development process if the materials produced are to be of high quality. Detailed discussions of each of these factors are provided in Chapter 9 and therefore will not be discussed here.

A second key area of quality control that was briefly mentioned earlier concerns the systematic approach to the development of materials. It is imperative that management techniques be developed and followed to ensure quality control. Two of the many management schemes that may be used will be discussed here. These are a checksheet approach and the Program Evaluation and Review Technique (PERT).

Checksheet Approach to Quality Control. One way of ensuring quality throughout the curriculum materials' development process is to use a comprehensive checksheet. An example of a checksheet is provided in Figure 10–1. Through the use of a form such as this, each stage in the materials' development process can be easily identified. Furthermore, individuals associated with the various stages can be identified and their responsibilities delineated. Provision is made for noting the actual completion date for each stage, which serves as a means of maintaining accountability and also provides information that may be used when planning future materials development efforts. As each development stage is completed, it may be checked off and the completion date recorded. This serves to keep a record of the progress made to date.

The checklist is divided into two major phases. The first phase constitutes the preliminary development plan, which serves to collect information leading up to the decision as to whether materials should be developed. If the decision is made to develop high-priority materials, the second phase serves to list those stages that will lead to the completion of the materials.

Program Evaluation and Review Technique (PERT). Another management scheme that may be used to assist with quality control is the Program Evaluation and Review Technique (PERT). The PERT chart can be used to plot out the various stages in the materials development process. In addition, projected completion dates can be noted for each stage. A PERT chart, using the example depicted in the previously discussed checksheet, is provided in Figure 10–2. Although Figure 10–2 does not indicate which individuals are responsible for which stages, a strategy sheet can be attached to the chart to indicate who these persons are.

These management schemes are but two examples of the many that can be used. The point is that some type of procedure must be formulated to help ensure quality control during the development of materials. The scheme selected must be shared with all those involved in the development to help avoid duplication of effort and to illustrate the importance of each stage in the successful completion of the materials.

FIGURE 10–1. Checksheet for the development of a booklet titled "Interviewing for a Job"

Completed	Development Stage	Person[s] Responsible	Completion Dates*		Comments
			Proposed	Actual	
✓	A. Preliminary Development Plan	S. Long	S	S	
✓	1. Determine curriculum content to be investigated	C. Brown	S+15 days	S+13 days	
✓	2. Determine terminal and enabling objectives	C. Brown	S+1 mo.	S+1 mo.	
✓	3. Identify special materials needed	C. Brown J. Smith	S+2 mos.	S+2 mos.	
✓	4. Review literature to determine what materials are available	C. Brown J. Smith	S+2 mos.	S+2½ mos.	
✓	5. Identify materials lacking in the content area	C. Brown J. Smith	S+3 mos.	S+3 mos.	
✓	6. Establish priorities for needed materials	C. Brown J. Smith	S+4 mos.	S+4 mos.	
✓	B. Finalize Development Plan	S. Long	S+5 mos.	S+5½ mos.	
✓	1. Conduct an intensive literature review	Brown, Smith, Bailey, Jackson	S+5½ mos.	S+5½ mos.	

FIGURE 10–1. *(Continued)*

Com-pleted	Development Stage	Person[s] Responsible	Completion Dates*		Comments
			Proposed	*Actual*	
✓	2. Obtain relevant references and re-sources	Brown, Smith, Bailey, Jackson	S+6 mos.	S+6 mos.	
	3. Prepare a first draft of the materials	Brown, Smith, Bailey, Jackson	S+7 mos.		
	4. Edit the first draft	Black, Griner, Jones	S+7½ mos.		
	5. Prepare a second draft	Brown, Smith, Bailey, Jackson	S+8 mos.		
	6. Pilot test the second draft	Combs, James	S+9 mos.		
	7. Prepare a third draft	Brown, Smith, Bailey, Jackson	S+9½ mos.		
	8. Field test the third draft	Roller, Coffey, Richards, Bass	S+10 mos.		
	9. Prepare the final draft	Brown, Smith, Bailey, Jackson	S+10½ mos.		
	10. Duplicate the materials	S. Long	S+12 mos.		

*S denotes starting date

FIGURE 10–2. *PERT chart for the development of a booklet titled "Interviewing for a Job"*

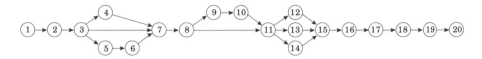

1. Preliminary Development Plan Prepared (S)*
2. Curriculum Content Determined (S+15 days)
3. Terminal and Enabling Objectives Determined (S+1 mo.)
4. Needs for Special Materials Identified (S+2 mos.)
5. Literature Reviewed (S+2 mos.)
6. Materials Lacking Identified (S+3 mos.)
7. Priorities Established (S+4 mos.)
8. Development Plan Finalized (S+5 mos.)
9. Intensive Review of Literature Conducted (S+5½ mos.)
10. References and Resources Obtained (S+6 mos.)
11. First Draft Prepared (S+7 mos.)
12. First Draft Edited–Technical Accuracy (S+7½ mos.)
13. First Draft Edited–Composition (S+7½ mos.)
14. First Draft Edited–Applicability (S+7½ mos.)
15. Second Draft Prepared (S+8 mos.)
16. Pilot Tested (S+9 mos.)
17. Third Draft Prepared (S+9½ mos.)
18. Field Tested (S+10 mos.)
19. Final Draft Prepared (S+10½ mos.)
20. Materials Duplicated (S+12 mos.)

*S denotes starting date.

Disseminating Curriculum Materials

The curriculum materials development cycle is not complete until materials have been disseminated to the intended users. The value of disseminating curriculum materials is quite clear, since valuable and useful material may end up on a shelf and never be used if teachers are not made aware of their worth. Failure to provide plans for dissemination would be a great loss to those who might have benefited from the materials and a great waste of human and monetary resources to those who developed the materials. When devising plans for the dissemination of materials, several factors need to be considered in order to ensure that those who are to be reached during the dissemination are efficiently and effectively informed about how the materials may be used.

Potential Audience

One of the first steps in dissemination is to determine the potential audience for the materials. Since primary consideration has been given to the development of materials in vocational education, the major audience will naturally be vocational educators. In addition to these people, consideration should also be given to applicability in other teaching areas.

Vocational Educators.   Vocational educators who might be interested in curriculum materials could be classified into two groups. One group would be those teachers who are in the vocational specialty areas for which the material was originally developed. If, for example, a group of health-occupations instructors developed curriculum materials in the occupational nurse's aide area, other health-occupations instructors may also have an interest in securing this material.

A second group of vocational educators would be those individuals who are not in the specific vocational area for which the materials were developed. Assume that a group of home economics educators developed curriculum materials in the area of displaying various types and colors of fabrics. Marketing education coordinators might also be interested in the materials. In fact, sharing materials across vocational education specialty areas should be encouraged, since content is often found to be similar in a variety of curricula. Even if the curriculum materials must be adapted or revised in order to make specific application to a vocational area, they may be of help to teachers who are experiencing a void of curriculum materials in a content area being taught.

Other Teachers.   Teachers in other areas constitute another potential audience for vocational curriculum materials, especially with the current emphasis on the integration of academic and vocational instruction. Vocational curriculum materials can serve a useful purpose in this integration, since many of them may be used by academic teachers, especially those materials designed for student use. As an illustration, assume that trade and industrial teachers develop curriculum materials for student use in the area of carpentry and that each student must read the materials. Thus, the materials could be used by reading or English teachers to develop the student's reading ability. Another example would be a set of materials developed in agribusiness management that includes numerous mathematical problems. Mathematics teachers could make use of these problems in their classes. Without a doubt, many of the materials developed for use in vocational education classes could be used by academic teachers in teaching students the skills, knowledges, and attitudes associated with their particular teaching areas.

Geographical Considerations

The size of the potential audience for curriculum materials is difficult to assess. If materials are developed at the local level, local schools may not see the dissemination of materials to other parts of the state as a high priority. In this case, any dissemination that occurs may take place more by accident than through any planned effort. However, if the materials are developed by a university, state educational agency, or other similar group, the dissemination should be targeted to a larger audience. In fact, materials developed through these organizations should be disseminated widely, since this is typically one of their responsibilities. The dissemination might take on a statewide, regional, or even national flavor.

Dissemination in Relation to Cost

One concern that must be made before dissemination is carried out concerns the price of the materials in relation to the mode of distribution. Three modes of distribution are free distribution, cost recovery, and distribution for profit. The first mode is basically when the producer of the material has the ability to absorb the cost of producing the material, or the cost has been covered by a special grant or contract. Cost recovery is when an organization seeks to recoup the expenses incurred during the development of the materials. The last mode, distribution for profit, is usually the approach used by commercial enterprises when a return on their investment is important to the success of the business.

Curriculum Materials Adoption Process

The dissemination and, hopefully, the eventual adoption of materials that are produced represent the true goals of any materials developer. The adoption of materials cannot be left to chance, but should be the culminating step in a well-planned educational program designed to disseminate the materials produced. In planning for the dissemination of curriculum materials, developers need to consider the process people follow to adopt new ideas or innovations. Various stages in the adoption process have been presented in the literature that have relevance to the adoption of curriculum materials. In reviewing these sources, five commonly accepted stages have been identified in the adoption process. The stages, which can guide the dissemination and eventual adoption of curriculum materials in education, include

  Awareness/knowledge. The stage at which an educator or decision maker is exposed to curriculum materials, develops some understanding of their potential value, and visualizes how the curriculum materials might be used.

  Attitude formation. The stage during which an educator or decision maker becomes more receptive to either adopting the materials or rejecting their use.

Decision. The stage where previous experience leads an educator or decision maker to either adopt or reject adoption of the curriculum materials.

Application. The stage at which an educator or decision maker uses curriculum materials in an actual learning environment.

Validation. The stage at which an educator or decision maker continues use of the curriculum materials to either reaffirm the earlier decision to adopt the materials or discontinue use of the materials.

Any dissemination program must include planned activities that will place an educator or prospective user of the materials in contact with them in such a way as to experience these five adoption stages in a positive manner. This dissemination applies to in-service programs as well as preservice programs.

In-Service and Preservice Materials Orientation Programs

As was stressed earlier, the dissemination of materials must include a planned educational program for those who can utilize the materials. Dissemination typically focuses on in-service programs for teachers; however, orientation for preservice students is also vital.

In-Service Level.   The purpose of conducting an in-service program for the dissemination of curriculum materials is to maximize the use of the materials. Although in-service programs may take many different formats, several basic components should be incorporated into any in-service session.

Provide Hands-On, Practical Exercises.   Teachers will be more likely to adopt new materials, especially computer software, if they are provided with the opportunity for a hands-on exercise. This experience should closely parallel the situation the teachers will be facing with their students. In this way, they will be made aware of the skills or procedures needed in order to use the materials effectively in all educational settings.

Provide for Relating Materials to Teachers' Specialty Areas.   Teaching circumstances differ, and thus teachers may need some assistance in adapting the materials to their own particular specifications. Examples should be provided of the ways materials can be used in different situations. Involving teachers in the in-service program who have had experience using the materials is a real benefit to others in attendance, since they will be able to understand how the materials have been used by their colleagues.

Provide Teachers with Examples of the Materials as They Leave. An effective way to end an in-service program is to have something for the teachers to take with them. This could be a complete set of the materials or just a small section. For example, if only part of the materials are to be distributed, then providing the teachers with a form for students to fill out as part of the complete set of materials might encourage the teachers to use the form on a trial basis and eventually to secure and use the entire set of materials. Teachers are more apt to feel the in-service program was beneficial if they have something to carry home with them to use.

Provide for Followup with Teachers. A followup session with teachers (either individually or as a group) who have used the materials on a trial basis may help in their eventual adoption. Some teachers may have experienced difficulty using the materials, especially with compatible computer software, and assistance at this point can aid greatly in finding solutions to problems encountered. Other teachers may actually improve the materials or change the suggested format and make them even more effective. Furthermore, followup activities by curriculum materials developers or their colleagues serve to encourage those who have not used the materials to do so.

Preservice Program. The education provided to preservice teachers regarding the value and use of new curriculum materials should not be overlooked. The discussion relating to in-service education applies equally well to the preservice program. An appropriate time for this orientation is during student teaching. Preservice teachers will be able to see how the materials can assist them to become better teachers and how curriculum materials will better prepare their students for employment.

Updating Curriculum Materials

Once curriculum materials are developed, the curriculum developer must make a conscious effort to update materials as appropriate. This is most important because technological changes occur so rapidly. For example, the recommendation to use a certain pesticide last year may not represent a safe or desirable recommendation for the current year. Although teacher educators and curriculum specialists must share the responsibility for keeping teachers up-to-date, the major responsibility rests with the teacher to ensure that the information being taught is accurate and represents the best knowledge students should be learning.

Summary

Regardless of the materials available on the market today, curriculum specialists and teachers are often faced with the situation of needing certain types of curriculum materials and discovering that none exist in the content area where teaching is to be done. This situation leaves few alternatives for the educator, with the most logical one being to develop the materials needed.

Before the actual decision is made to develop these materials, several important factors must be considered to determine if such development is feasible. These factors include dollars and time available, time needed to develop the materials, and available expertise. Among the decisions that must be made concerning the development of materials are what materials are needed and why, who should develop them, and when and where they should be developed. Other factors to consider are the target population, computer based or not, dissemination planned, support needed, and development alternatives, either through a team or individual approach.

The curriculum materials development process consists of several stages. Once the needed materials are identified, the development stages include obtaining the references and resources needed, preparing the first draft, editing the first draft, pilot testing, revising, field testing, preparing the final copy, and duplicating. Management of the curriculum materials' development process can be guided by use of a PERT chart, checksheet, or other similar management scheme which could be computerized.

The dissemination of materials is a critical and important step. Without teacher adoption and use, materials may be shelved and thus would be useless. For this reason, materials need to be disseminated in an orderly manner to vocational educators and others who may have an interest in them. Before the dissemination is conducted, decisions regarding cost must be made as well as regarding the way materials will be introduced through in-service education to teachers and to preservice students.

Once materials are released and made available to teachers, continuous efforts must be made to keep them up-to-date. Otherwise, materials that have been developed will soon become obsolete.

Related References

Balan, Phyllis. "Improving Instructional Print Materials through Text Design." *Performance & Instruction* 28, no. 8 (August 1989): 13–18.

Bensen, M. James. "High Tech Comes to Instruction." *VocEd* 61, no. 6 (September 1986): 26–27.

Brown, James W.; Lewis, Richard B.; and Harcleroad, Fred F. *AV Instruction, Techniques, Media, Methods.* New York: McGraw-Hill, 1977.

Finch, Curtis R., and Crunkilton, John R. "Is your Curriculum Ready for the Nineties?" *VocEd* 60, no. 2 (March 1985): 31–32.

Gall, Meredith Damien. *Handbook for Evaluating and Selecting Curriculum Materials.* Boston: Allyn and Bacon, 1981.

Greer, Michael. "How to Test Draft Materials." *Performance & Instruction* 28, no. 2 (February 1989): 44–50.

Heinich, Robert; Molenda, Michael; and Russell, James D. *Instructional Media and the New Technologies of Instruction, 3rd ed.* New York: Macmillan Publishing Company, 1989.

Kemp, Jerrold E., and Smellie, Don C. *Planning, Producing, and Using Instructional Media, 6th ed.* New York: Harper and Row Publishers, 1989.

Morgan, Barton; Holmes, Glenn E.; and Bundy, Clarence E. *Methods in Adult Education, 4th ed.* Danville, Ill.: Interstate Printers and Publishers, 1985.

Rogers, Everett M. *Diffusions of Innovations.* New York: Collier Macmillian Publishers, 1983.

Ulmer, Dale. "Interactive Video Changed My Classroom." *VocEd* 61, no. 6 (September 1986):34–36.

11

Trends and Issues in Curriculum Implementation

Introduction

Curriculum planning and development are important; however, they serve as precursors to the curriculum implementation process. For it is during curriculum implementation that plans, programs, courses, and materials are applied to student-learning settings. Many approaches to curriculum implementation are already well known to educators. For example, conventional classroom and laboratory instruction are considered common knowledge to those who teach vocational and technical subjects, and cooperative vocational education, which links the school more closely to the workplace, is utilized by cooperative vocational education coordinators across the United States.

The discussion that follows presents an opportunity to examine implementation approaches that extend beyond traditional practices. Some of these approaches have been used for decades, whereas others are just beginning to be employed in schools and technical and community colleges. As would be expected, some approaches have been well accepted by educators and others have evoked a great deal of controversy. In order that a range of implementation approaches may be viewed, several different approaches have been selected for discussion. These include individualized instruction, modularized instruction, competency-based education, integrating academic and vocational education, Tech Prep, school-based enterprise, customized training, and technology transfer. Although several of these approaches tend to overlap, each one is discussed separately so as to highlight its unique character.

Individualized Instruction

Individualizing instruction has been a concern of educators for a number of years, perhaps beginning in the minds of early teacher-philosophers such as Plato and Aristotle. These scholars, as well as Rousseau, Froebel, and others, relate to a common theme in their writings, that of providing consideration to the needs of the individual within the instructional process.

However, current conceptions of individualized instruction take on a much more comprehensive focus. Individualized instruction as provided in contemporary educational curricula is comprised of at least five basic components. As indicated in Figure 11–1, these components are the student, instructional environments, instructional content, instructional media, and instructional strategies. Of these five components, the student is central, with the others arranged in a manner designed to maximize learning. Obviously, different arrangements might be more appropriate for attaining different instructional objectives or for two students to achieve the same objective. For example, providing a nonreading option (the media component) might be most critical in aiding a poor reader to achieve mastery of a certain competency, whereas another student might be aided to a greater extent by the physical setting (the environment component).

If instruction is to be truly individualized, these components cannot be dealt with one at a time. Instead, they must be examined, organized, and used in concert. The teacher should ensure that all factors that may contribute to student learning are taken into account. Although instructional content, media, environments, and strategies are also taken into account in individualized instruction, the student should always serve as the primary focal point.

Individualization, then, is seen as a means of enhancing instruction so there may be greater assurance of meeting students' individual needs and providing learning experiences that align with personal capabilities. By making a commitment to individualizing instruction, the teacher is saying that he or she will provide whatever arrangements are necessary to ensure that each student will be constantly engaged in learning those things that are of greatest value to himself or herself. This is what makes

FIGURE 11-1. *Basic components of individualized instruction*

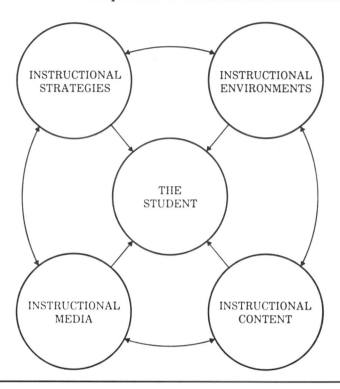

individualization a most meaningful contributor to the goals of vocational and technical education.

Although most vocational and technical educators agree in concept that individualized instruction is a sound approach, concerns are often raised about its implementation. Typical of the questions asked about implementing individualized instruction are Where will I obtain all the instructional materials I need to individualize instruction? Where will I find the extra time needed to design instructional sequences for and work closely with each student? What diagnostic tools can I use to determine which instructional strategies are best for each student? What support will be provided to my classes by special education teachers and school psychologists? These and other questions raised by vocational and technical teachers reflect the perceived need for a variety of support, support that sometimes cannot be provided. However, by its very nature, vocational education emphasizes applied learning in laboratory settings where each student can work and learn at his or her own pace and receive individual attention and assistance. In addition, many vocational education class sizes are limited by the number of laboratory work stations, thus providing teachers with more opportunities to assist students. Finally, the individual educational program (IEP) used with each student with special needs must be prepared by a team that includes representatives from the special education and school psychology areas. For the vocational teacher, this means much of the individualization for students with special needs will be built into IEP preparation.

Modularized Instruction

Traditionally, administrators, curriculum specialists, and teachers have arranged instruction to take place over a designated period of time such as hours, days, weeks, or months. Although this sort of arrangement has proved to be very useful for scheduling purposes, it often leaves much to be desired as far as students are concerned. Distributing instruction over a specified time frame often forces the vocational and technical teacher to organize content and instruction so that the primary focus is on the average learning of class members. The result of this arrangement is obvious. With a lack of opportunity to progress at their own rates, some students may be held back while others are not able to keep up with the pace of instruction.

Conventional instruction is also arranged in a somewhat arbitrary manner. A curriculum often takes the form of courses or semesters that relate more readily to grading periods than anything else. Since this arrangement is usually imposed on teachers, they are required to fit varying amounts of instructional content into rigidly prescribed units of instruction. Consequently, some courses may be too short for the material to be covered while others are too long—the result being that course length and content coverage needed to meet specified objectives are seldom completely congruent.

In recent years, the modularization of instruction has been set forth by certain educators as a viable alternative to conventional instructional arrangements. This approach is based on the premise that students are better able to learn if they do so at their own rates and study those areas that focus directly on mastery of a particular objective or set of objectives. Naturally, persons who are concerned with the establishment of individualized, competency-based curricula have recognized the potential of modularized instruction, since it appears to focus directly on meeting students' needs and development of those competencies that are critical for successful employment. For these reasons, instructional modules are often found in use where individualized, competency-based education has been implemented. Since the instructional module is quite different and distinct from its traditional counterpart, anyone who is contemplating use of the modular approach to instruction should be aware of its characteristics as well as certain advantages and limitations associated with it.

Module Characteristics

In contrast with conventional curriculum design, the modular approach utilizes the module as a basic instructional building block instead of arranging content around a subject, unit, or lesson. This fundamental difference has many implications for anyone involved in curriculum development and implementation. What, then, is an instructional module? Briefly stated, it may be defined as *an instructional package that includes a planned series of learning experiences designed to help the student master specified objectives.* Although modules are not always individualized, this appears to be the rule rather than the exception. Naturally, when one is designing an instructional package, it is fairly simple to incorporate various aspects of individualized instruction into the finished product. It would, therefore, be in order to include "individualized" in the above definition if a developer is intent on assisting all of his or her students to the maximum extent possible.

A clearer understanding of the module may be obtained if its basic characteristics are described. These characteristics focus on the way a module is organized and packaged, as well as how it relates to student needs.

First, the module is self-contained. This means the student does not have to go to the instructor and ask what to do next or what materials he or she should use. Instead, information and directions are provided within the module. Each module should provide explicit guidance with regard to what the student is to do, how he or she should proceed, and what resources and materials might be used. Instructional resource materials are usually either incorporated into the module or made available on a check-out basis.

Next, the module is typically individualized. Although development costs and time constraints may preclude the complete and absolute individualization of a module, the developer should attempt to include as many characteristics of individualized instruction as possible. As a minimum, each module should make provision for self-pacing, feedback, and mastery. Examples of these characteristics, as they apply to modular instruction, would be as follows:

> *Self-pacing:* The student may progress through the module at his or her own rate. Each may set up a working-learning schedule based upon personal capabilities.
>
> *Feedback:* The student receives an assessment of progress as he or she proceeds through each module learning experience. At the end of each learning experience, the student is provided with immediate results of performance.
>
> *Mastery:* The student focuses on attainment of specific, measurable objectives within each module. By taking module learning experiences, attainment of these objectives is enhanced.

Third, the module is a complete package. This reflects a logical and systematic flow of module content with a definite beginning and ending. In other words, the student knows when he or she has begun, progressed to a certain point, and completed a particular module. There is no question as to what must be done to achieve certain objectives and whether or not they have been achieved.

Fourth, the module includes learning experiences and objectives. Experiences are provided to assist each student in mastering specified objectives as efficiently as possible and may make provision for a broad range of student involvement from reading and listening to role playing, simulation, and cooperative work experience.

Fifth, included in each module is some mechanism for assessing the extent to which a student has achieved module objectives. This aspect of the module is extremely important, since it relates quite closely to student feedback and mastery. Equally important, however, is the fact that assessment provides a means of formalizing the criteria or standards associated with module completion.

Although the modular approach may serve as an excellent vehicle for implementing CBE, it should be recognized that just because instruction is modularized does *not* mean it is competency-based. For example, a set of modules might be developed that focuses on improving students' avocational pursuits. These modules may be of great value in their own right, but they do not necessarily focus directly on the development of vocational and technical competencies—tasks, skills, attitudes, values, and appreciations identified as being critical to successful employment. It is extremely important to make this distinction, since time and effort devoted to module development may be wasted if the developer does not give initial consideration to what competencies the module will focus on. Just because certain aspects of a curriculum focus on general education does not mean that they must be taught in a traditional mode. Modules can be developed that assist students in achieving a multitude of objectives. However, it must be recognized that not all modules are competency-based. Only those that focus directly on the development of actual competencies may be classed in this manner. The discussion that follows will, naturally, focus on developing individualized, competency-based modules, since these are of most value to the vocational and technical teacher. Many of the basic development procedures apply equally well to all individualized instructional packages. Developers should find these procedures of value no matter what sort of module is being contemplated.

Formatting

Obviously, locating modules that have already been developed and using them would be the easiest approach. Unfortunately, modules have not

---

FIGURE 11–2. *Typical module format*

Introduction. In this section, the student is told how the module may serve as a means of developing certain skills, knowledges, and attitudes. Specific prerequisites (if any) are detailed and directions for proceeding with the module are provided. Also included are a cover page and table of contents.

Objectives. Provided here are specific statements of performance the student should be able to demonstrate while progressing through the module and when completing it. Terminal and enabling objectives specify the activities to be performed, the conditions under which they are to be performed, and the levels of acceptable performance.

Preassessment. This section is useful in determining student entry performance and provides a means of "testing out" of the module if he or she can demonstrate mastery. Student instructions and an assessment form with explicit criteria are placed here to ensure that there is no question about what constitutes module mastery.

Learning Experiences. Learning experiences are detailed that correspond with each of the enabling objectives. They are designed to provide each student with the best means of mastering module objectives. Each learning experience consists of one or more activities followed by assessment and feedback to the student. Learning experiences may include resource materials such as computer programs, information sheets, references, audiotapes, etc., that serve to enhance the learning process and help individualize instruction.

Resource Materials. This section serves to reference all resource materials used in the various learning experiences so that both teacher and student may locate them rapidly. The resource materials listing aids the teacher in "setting up" for students and ensuring that all materials are available when they are needed.

Postassessment. This section is quite similar to the preassessment and, in many cases, may be exactly the same. The postassessment focuses on the terminal objective and an assessment form is used to determine whether or not it has been met.

---

been developed for all vocational and technical areas, nor does it appear likely that they will be for some time. Realistically, the vocational and technical instructor should plan to become involved in some module development if he or she intends to have an individualized curriculum.

Since formatting is based on both teacher and learner considerations, no attempt will be made to show all of the various formats one might use. Instead, a general format is presented as a useful guide for module development. Figure 11–2 shows a typical module formatting arrangement. It should be noted that provision is made to ensure meeting the individual needs of students. Included are the following:

1. Each student is afforded the opportunity to "test out" of the total module or any of the learning experiences.
2. The student receives feedback as to his or her performance on each learning experience and on the entire module.
3. No specific time limit for module completion is imposed on the student. Instruction is self-paced.
4. There is no question as to what the student should do to demonstrate module mastery.

In some instances, certain portions of the module are included in a teacher's section or guide. If it is felt that assessment keys should not be used by students, the keys may be included in the teacher's guide. Likewise, if a performance examination is to be used, details for its administration would be provided there. Special procedures might need to be included such as methods of organizing for a role-playing situation or planning a field trip. Since details of this nature are relevant only to the instructor, it is best to omit them from the student's material. Formatting is a personal matter, so the module developer may want to experiment with different approaches until one (or more) is found suitable to both instructor and student. Above all, it should be remembered that the format serves as a means to an end—module mastery. If it does not help in this regard, modification is in order.

Competency-Based Education

One approach that has gained much support from vocational and technical educators is competency-based education (CBE). CBE has been shown to be most effective as an alternative to conventional forms of education.

As one might expect, vocational teachers and administrators alike have expressed concern about why a competency-based instructional focus should be any different from that already being used. A vocational teacher may, for example, comment that all of his or her graduates are competent, so why should any changes be made in the curriculum? In a broad sense, any mode of instruction aims at, or should aim at, the competence of students and graduates. However, as will be indicated, CBE does not differ from other modes of education in its goals. Instead, CBE is unique in terms of its underlying assumptions and the approaches that characterize it.

Assumptions Underlying
Competency-Based Education

There are several aspects of CBE that distinguish it from traditional instruction. Although each of these aspects may be found in some conventional curricula, it is their collective use that constitutes a true competency-based program. CBE has been variously described as focusing on several key areas. The areas include the nature of competencies, criteria used to assess the competencies, ways that student competence is assessed, student progress through the program, and the program's instructional intent.

Competencies.   At the core of CBE is competency. It reflects the ability to do something in contrast with more the traditional ability to demonstrate knowledge. Specifically, competencies for vocational and technical education are *those tasks, skills, attitudes, values, and appreciations that are deemed critical to success in life and/or in earning a living.* Just because something is performed by a worker does not mean that it is automatically classed as a competency. The worker must, in fact, find this competency to be a critical aspect of employability in the occupation. Each competency, then, evolves from explicit statements of worker roles, and, since competencies align so closely with an occupation, student competence is ultimately assessed in much the same way as that of a worker. In order to ensure that assessment will be fair to the student, all competencies are detailed and made available for anyone to examine.

Criteria.   In the assessment of student competence, it is not enough merely to call for a global exhibition of performance. The teacher must also have specific criteria available that clarify each competency. For example, it might be that each student in a particular curriculum should be able to complete a job application form. In order to judge student competence in this area accurately, one must know what standards the completed form should meet as well as the conditions under which it should be filled out. Criteria associated with each competency have to reflect both the level of acceptable performance and the conditions associated with this performance. As with competencies, criteria are also made available to each student so there is no question as to what constitutes mastery.

Assessment of Competence.   When student competence is being assessed, primary consideration should be given to application. Although it may not be possible for all vocational students to be assessed as they perform in actual work settings, this is the ultimate evaluation environment one should strive for, since it is the most realistic. Even though it may not be possible to assess competency on the job, each student should be evaluated as objectively as possible using the most realistic applied standards available. Unlike some traditional instructional modes, student competence, not grading, provides the primary evidence of achievement. Consequently, instructional staff are required to move beyond the traditional knowledge type measures such as multiple-choice and essay examinations and focus on assessment that aligns with worker competence in the real world.

Student Progress. A curriculum is typically divided into clearly identifiable time frames such as years, quarters, terms, semesters, and weeks. These serve as starting and ending points for various portions of the instruction and enable an instructor to say that students have completed a certain phase of the curriculum. In fact, students do not always achieve at the same rate. Abilities such as reading, mathematics, and verbal comprehension vary greatly among vocational students, and a time-based curriculum cannot take this wide variance into account to the extent that any instructor would like. In contrast with a time-based mode, competency-based education uses demonstrated competence as a determiner of student progress toward program completion. This enables students to proceed through a program at their own particular rates, based upon their individual abilities, and thus master specified competencies in a shorter (or longer) time period.

Instructional Intent. The explicit intent of competency-based education is to facilitate student achievement of competencies specified in the program. Each instructor is obligated to provide a sufficient variety of learning experiences so that students will be afforded an opportunity to master a minimum set of competencies, and, in effect, the instructor may be held accountable for student achievement. If it is indicated that each student should be able to prepare a résumé that meets certain specific criteria, the instructor cannot just provide basic information on this area and assume that all the learners will be able to perform the task. The instructor is obligated to make available to students those experiences that facilitate the development of résumé writing skills. This might include the use of role playing and other simulation activities, outside resource persons, and other techniques that enhance and aid each student's attainment of competence.

Competency-Based Materials

Successful delivery of CBE is closely aligned with the development and use of relevant curriculum materials. Whereas Chapters 9 and 10 have presented general guidelines for the selection and development of curriculum materials, it is also useful to focus on the more specific aspects of competency-based materials. In a broad sense, any materials can be used in competency-based education. However, it is important that consideration be given to how an item (e.g., book or practice set) contributes to the development of student competence. The extent to which a contribution is made reflects an item's value in the CBE setting. Keeping basic curriculum materials' standards in mind, we can expand the list provided in Chapter 9 to include these CBE-specific questions:

1.   Are competencies stated in the materials?
2.   Have the stated competencies been verified via some research base?
3.   Do objectives provided in the materials contribute to and align with stated competencies?
4.   Is sufficient emphasis placed on teaching for application, not just for awareness and knowledge?
5.   If materials will be used by teachers, are meaningful suggestions provided to help students master stated competencies?
6.   If materials will be used by students, are learning activities/ experiences provided to help each student master stated competencies?

Indeed, there are many different types of competency-based materials, but we have chosen to focus on three representative types: the competency catalog, the competency profile, and the module. Each has its specific purpose within the context of CBE and may have greater or lesser application depending on the particular students, teacher, and level of instruction.

Competency Catalogs. As the name implies, a competency catalog includes an array of competency statements from which may be selected those competencies most relevant for a particular curriculum or program. The catalog concept gives consideration to (1) establishment of verified competency lists, and (2) the selection of a competency subset that satisfies local employment requirements. In the case of exploratory programs, a competency catalog delineates those competencies that maximize development of students' career exploration and decision-making skills.

Employment-Related Catalogs. Perhaps most active in the development of competency catalogs is the Vocational and Technical Education Consortium of States (V-TECS). This consortium has prepared competency catalogs for numerous occupations that are based on extensive task analyses (see Chapter 6). Essentially, the V-TECS catalog consists of separate pages, each of which is devoted to detailing information about a certain competency. This information includes a duty statement, a task statement, a performance objective that aligns with the task, and a performance guide that specifies decisions made and steps followed in the performance of a task. Also included may be a checklist with evaluative statements and criteria related to the task.

It should be kept in mind that a competency catalog is not designed to be a curriculum guide. Instead, it is an employment-referenced data base which may be used for curriculum development, instructional design, and program review. V-TECS lists several suggested uses for data provided in competency catalogs. These include

1. Use the duty category grouping tasks as testing domains.
2. Use the performance objectives as focal points for student learning.
3. Use the performance guides as foundations for operation sheets, enabling objectives, instructional sequencing, test development, module preparation, and identifying prerequisites a student must have before he or she attempts to learn the task.

Catalogs for Exploratory Programs. Similar information may be found in competency catalogs developed for exploratory programs. In this case, the competency focuses to some extent on the educational process (e.g., read, observe, participate). Additionally, not as much emphasis is placed on duplicating standards and conditions associated with employment. Since the focus of programs at the junior high/middle school level is on career orientation and exploration, it is not necessary for students to demonstrate competence at the level of a worker entering the occupation. They should merely be examining and experiencing certain aspects of an occupational area.

Competency Profiles. Persons who begin establishing CBE programs soon find that some means must be devised to communicate what competencies students should learn and to record student progress toward program completion. One creative approach to this situation is through use of a competency profile. The competency profile, which is sometimes called a skill record or employability profile, may be defined as a *document that lists competency areas required in an occupation and provides a means of assessing mastery of specific competencies.* The competency profile does not serve as a substitute for instruction. Rather, it complements and supplements the ongoing instructional process by communicating to instructor and student alike what educational expectations exist and to what extent they are being met.

Although competency profiles may vary in format, several basic elements seem to be included in profiles used in competency-based programs. Basic to each profile is a listing of those competencies deemed essential for the particular program. Many of these competencies might be drawn directly from competency catalogs; however, it is important to recognize that tool, equipment, and work-habit competencies are equally as important as tasks that are basic to an occupation.

Equally important is the inclusion of a rating scale. Such a scale is used to evaluate and record student mastery of competencies in the program. One should keep in mind that a scale should have relevance to teacher, student, and potential employer. Whereas rather extensive criteria may be used to evaluate student mastery of a particular competency, the competency-profile scale serves to summarize this evaluation in such a way that a competency level is communicated.

The competency profile also typically includes student background information. If the profile is used strictly within a school or program, this may be limited to items such as the program title, student's name, and instructor's name. Should the profile be provided to prospective employers, additional information may be of value. This could include attendance information, instructor recommendations, and related occupational experience.

The lab contract may be considered as a competency profile that includes some additional considerations. Although the concept of educational contracts is not new, their application to CBE has great potential. Essentially, the student is asked to sign a contract and by doing so agrees that he or she will work to become competent in a particular area. Even though the contract is not legally binding, it does have great psychological impact. The student's written commitment to learn can serve as a personal motivator. Likewise, if the student's progress falls behind, the instructor can provide a reminder that a contract has been signed. This may serve to jar the student back to reality.

Integrating Academic and Vocational Education

Although teachers have often worked together informally to create linkages across vocational and academic teaching areas, the process of formally linking these areas has tended to be neglected. This is unfortunate since, in actuality, education is neither academic nor vocational. It is instead comprised of two elements, i.e., formal and informal education, and has as its goals preparation for life and preparation for earning a living. As noted in Chapter 1, these two goals are not mutually exclusive; each must give consideration to the other, and each can contribute to the accomplishment of the other.

Recent concern about the artificial distinctions between academic and vocational education as well as reports critical of public education and new federal legislation focusing on integration have combined to create a more urgent need for integrating academic and vocational education. It thus appears that integration of academic and vocational education is more than a passing thought; this approach has been implemented in a number of schools across the nation.

Basically, integration refers to the process by which academic and vocational education teachers work together to ensure that program, course, and lesson content and delivery are more relevant and meaningful to students. This is accomplished by providing academic content in vocational education contexts and vocational content in academic contexts. Potential benefits of integration include students achieving both academic and vocational competencies and graduates being better prepared to enter and succeed in the work world.

Norton Grubb and his associates (Grubb et al., 1991) note that at least eight different models of integration exist in schools across the United States. These models include a variety of practices, reflect a great deal of creativity and innovation, and appear adaptable to the wide range of schools and curricula in American secondary schools. The eight models of integration include

1. Incorporating more academic content into vocational courses.
2. Combining vocational and academic teachers to enhance academic competencies in vocational programs.
3. Making the academic curriculum more vocationally relevant.
4. Curricular "alignment": modifying both vocational and academic courses.
5. The senior project as a form of integration.
6. The academy model.
7. Occupational high schools and magnet schools.
8. Occupational clusters, "career paths," and occupational majors.

Grubb notes that no single model may be applied to all schools. He indicates that "each school can examine its existing programs, its local labor markets, and the needs of its students and fashion its own approach to integration" (Grubb, 1991, p. 24). According to Grubb, the most successful programs appear to be ones where administrators and faculty have established a vision of what integration should be, decided together how the task should be accomplished, and worked cooperatively to ensure that the vision becomes reality.

Since the integration of vocational and academic education is a relatively recent movement, a number of questions can be raised about its implementation in the schools. Among these are How might integration be best defined for a particular state, region, or school? Which integration model is most appropriate for a particular school system or school? In what ways might integration operate successfully at the postsecondary level? How can the success of such a fuzzy reform be assessed? (Stasz & Grubb, 1991). It is clear that the concept of integration has a great deal of appeal. However, a number of key questions must be answered as the movement evolves from concept to widespread implementation.

Tech Prep

Tech Prep is a phrase that denoted *Tech*nical career *Prep*aration programs that employ creative linkages between high schools and community and technical colleges. The objective of Tech Prep is to merge the last two years of high school and two years of community or technical college study into a comprehensive educational experience that includes greater amounts of and more relevant mathematics, science, communication skills, and technical studies. Several outcomes associated with successful Tech Prep programs are (1) greater opportunities to make academic and technical studies more relevant to students' needs, (2) greater retention of at-risk high school and community/technical college students, (3) greater numbers of high school graduates going on to postsecondary technical education studies, and (4) community and technical college technical degree graduates being better prepared to meet business and industry demands for employees who can adapt to technological advances in the workplace.

Tech Prep can include articulation agreements between secondary and postsecondary institutions that focus on advanced placement and time-shortened programs. However, articulation is just one of Tech Prep's several components. Tech Prep may be distinguished from basic articulation agreements between institutions in that it includes extensive cross-institutional collaboration in curriculum planning and implementation. This planning and implementation involves secondary and postsecondary administrators, counselors, and faculty members and business and industry representatives in a curriculum-building process that results in a program extending across two or more different educational institutions. The program, which tends to be four years in length and typically culminates in award of the associate degree, is designed to provide students with more extensive mathematics, science, communication skills, and technology-based knowledge and skills than would be possible if two separate two-year programs were offered.

How then may a Tech Prep program be initiated? Although more and more Tech Prep programs are being established each year, the initiation process is still quite fluid. Debra Bragg and Allen Phelps (1990, pp. 3–4) have assembled a useful list of strategies for initiating Tech Prep programs. Among the recommended strategies are gaining state support for the program; ensuring that leadership and commitment exist for the program; preparing a joint articulation and program implementation plan; establishing student eligibility standards for admission, placement, and advanced standing; conducting a joint curriculum review and development process; preparing student advisement and counseling guides; developing strategies for promotion of the program; providing shared secondary and postsecondary advisory committee membership for the program; planning joint faculty teaching assignments between institutions; and involving business and industry representatives in program planning and implementation. As noted in this strategy list, establishing a Tech Prep program can be quite complex and includes the combined efforts of professionals from many sectors. In effect, Tech Prep exemplifies the movement in education toward involvement of professional teams of people from a range of institutions, agencies, and companies in important curriculum development decisions.

Implementing a Tech Prep program is not without its potential concerns. Considering the time and effort that institutions may spend articulating, coordinating, and collaborating Tech Prep, it is important to address various issues and concerns before they evolve into unsolvable problems. Among the issues and concerns that may be faced include How can faculty members, counselors, and administrators be prepared to work as part of a professional Tech Prep implementation team? What special support services will be needed for students enrolled in Tech Prep (e.g., developmental/remedial studies, English as a second language instruction)? How can the cooperating institutions each overcome a tendency to maintain complete ownership over a program? What are the best ways to recruit students into the Tech Prep program? How may educators and the general public be convinced that Tech Prep can be a win-win experience? (Hull & Parnell, 1991). Providing answers to these questions can be a useful starting point on the road to successful Tech Prep program implementation.

School-Based Enterprise

School-based enterprises (SBEs) bring realistic occupational preparation activity into the school by involving students in the operation of an enterprise such as a restaurant, store, factory, or repair service. SBEs may be defined as formal activities under the auspices of a school that involve students in producing goods or providing services to persons other than the students themselves. Historically, SBEs have operated as meaningful components of many vocational education programs. For example, automotive technician and auto body repair programs may accept customers' cars for service; building construction programs may involve students in building a home for sale to the public; marketing education programs may operate a school store; agricultural programs may operate a greenhouse or farm that grows and sells produce; and cosmetology programs may provide haircutting and styling services to people in the community.

By including SBEs in these programs, students can be provided with a number of benefits. These include

1. Exposure to ways that the business world operates and gaining a first-hand view of entrepreneurship in action
2. Reinforcement of what is learned in the classroom
3. Learning and enhancing applied team-building and group problem-solving skills
4. Providing greater opportunities for integrating vocational and academic studies
5. Developing individual personal and social skills
6. Development of skills that may later contribute to community economic development

A specific SBE may not include all these student benefits. However, as the SBE is being established and later when it is operating, student benefits may be used as a gauge to judge how useful the program has been or will be.

Flexibility, creativity, and utility best describe the successful SBE. Because SBEs need not be course-credit driven, school officials can have great latitude with an SBE's organization and operation. In some instances, students operate enterprises such as restaurants or stores in high-customer/traffic locations that are far removed from the school campus. Often, SBEs are available to all students in the school; involvement need not be limited to those enrolled in vocational classes. Clearly, benefits can accrue for all students regardless of their personal goals and aspirations.

The establishment and operation of SBEs force school administrators to deal with a range of concerns. These concerns include What resources are needed to manage the SBE's fiscal complexities? Which faculty member or members will serve as SBE managers, and what qualifications must they have? How can the school deal with the public's perception that the SBE is "stealing" customers away from businesses in the community? What should be charged for SBE-produced goods and services? How can the school be sure that the enterprise and "profit" aspects of the SBE do not overshadow the need to provide learning experiences for students? There may be other questions that emerge as the SBE is being established and operated. But these basic questions should be addressed early in the planning process to ensure that the probability of SBE success is maximized.

Customized Training and Technology Transfer

In recent years, some vocational and technical education institutions have, in addition to teaching individual students, begun providing "customer service." This customer service has taken several forms, but has shown up most often as customized training offered to employees of businesses and industries in the local community. Customized training may be considered as the human resource dimension of economic development. As such, it focuses on meeting the specific, targeted training needs of business and industry, needs that employers feel should be met so their companies will be more competitive. The basic purpose of customized training is meeting targeted rather than general employment needs. Customized training may be on a credit or noncredit basis and may take a few hours or many months to complete.

Customized training is often closely linked with technology transfer services. Technology transfer services focus on providing technology-related consultant assistance and are designed to help businesses and industries solve technological problems in the workplace. Technology transfer has as its aim assisting establishments in becoming more productive, competitive, and profitable. Typically, when technical or community college representatives prescribe a solution to a company's technological problem, they recommend that certain employees receive specialized training that aids these persons in implementing and maintaining the technological change. The educational institution often provides this training as part of the total technology transfer agreement.

As educational institutions become more entrepreneurial, several questions may be raised about how far institutions should reach beyond the traditional education mode. These questions, which apply to both philosophical and implementation issues, are as follows: Is providing direct services to businesses and industries a valid function of public educational institutions? If it is a valid function, what amount of time and effort should be devoted to this function? How much equipment and training do faculty members need to keep them on the "cutting edge" of technology? What qualifications should faculty members have before they participate in customized training and technology transfer activities? How much should businesses and industries be charged for these services? How are overhead or indirect charges computed? How can the educational institution be sure that "customer service" activities do not erode its basic educational mission? These are the types of questions that should be asked as an institution becomes engaged in customized training and technology transfer activities.

Summary

Curriculum implementation is equally as important as curriculum planning and development. For it is during the implementation process that curricula, programs, and materials are actually applied to educational settings. The curriculum may be implemented in a variety of ways. In addition to curriculum implementation in more conventional classroom, laboratory, and cooperative ways, educators may employ other approaches to ensure that students achieve curriculum objectives. Individualized instruction centers on providing learning experiences that align with students' individual capabilities. Modularized instruction can provide students with opportunities to learn at their own rates and focus on mastery of specific objectives.

Competency-based education's direct emphasis on the development of tasks, skills, attitudes, values, and appreciations critical to success in life and/or in earning a living makes it very relevant to vocational and technical education. CBE is often individualized and packaged into modules. The integration of academic and vocational education is a relatively recent concept that has potential to make curriculum content more relevant to all students.

Creative linkages between high schools and community and technical colleges can be created via Tech Prep. This approach relies on cross-institutional collaboration to plan and implement the curriculum. School-based enterprises bring realistic occupational preparation activities to the school by involving students in the operation of an enterprise such as a restaurant, store, factory, farm, or repair service.

Customized training is designed to meet the specific, targeted training needs of industry and business, whereas technology transfer involves educators in seeking solutions to companies' technological problems. Customized training is often provided to a company as part of a technology transfer agreement.

Even though a host of concerns may be raised about approaches to curriculum implementation that vary from tradition, these approaches have great potential to improve instruction and student learning. It is for this reason that educators must explore the range of curriculum implementation possibilities that exist and select from them the ones best suited for their particular educational setting, needs, and locality.

Related References

Blank, William E. *Handbook for Developing Competency-Based Training Programs*. Englewood Cliffs, N.J.: Prentice-Hall, 1982.

———. "A Statewide System for Competency-Based Instruction." *Journal of Industrial Teacher Education* 24, no 4 (Summer 1987).

Bragg, Debra, and Phelps, L. Allen. *Tech Prep: A Definition and Discussion of the Issues*. Champaign, Ill.: University of Illinois Office, National Center for Research in Vocational Education, 1990.

Cunningham, Daisy L.; Hillison, John; and Horne, Ralph A. "Adoption of an

Innovation: Monitoring the Concerns of Vocational Educators." *Journal of Vocational Education Research* 10, no. 1 (Winter 1985): 15–28.

Finch, Curtis R., and Faulkner, Susan L. "The Occupational Education Administrator's Role in Developing a Competent Workforce: Case Studies of Success." *Journal of Studies in Technical Careers* 12, no. 4 (Fall 1990): 341–351.

Grubb, W. Norton. "The Challenge to Change." *Vocational Education Journal* 66, no. 2 (February 1991): 24–26.

Grubb, W. Norton; Davis, Gary; Lum, Jeannie; Plihal, Jane; and Morgaine, Carol. *"The Cunning Hand, The Cultured Mind"; Models for Integrating Vocational and Academic Education*. Report MDS-141. Berkeley, Cal.: National Center for Research in Vocational Education, July 1991.

Hoerner, James L. "Tech Prep: A Viable Solution for the Forgotten Half." *ATEA Journal* (April–May 1991): 18–20.

Hull, Dan, and Parnell, Dale. *Tech Prep Associate Degree*. Waco, Tex.: Center for Occupational Research and Development, 1991.

Scott, Robert, W. "Making the Case for Tech Prep." *Vocational Education Journal* 66, no. 2 (February 1991): 22–23, 63.

Stasz, Cathy, and Grubb, W. Norton. *Integrating Academic and Vocational Education: Guidelines for Assessing a Fuzzy Reform*. Working Paper MDS-375. Berkeley, Cal.: National Center for Research in Vocational Education, July 1991.

Stern, David. *Combining School and Work: Options in High Schools and Two-Year Colleges*. U.S. Department of Education, Office of Vocational and Adult Education, March 1991.

12

Evaluating the Curriculum

Introduction

There can be no doubt that the way a curriculum is planned and established has great impact on its quality. However, the process used to define and determine that quality is of at least equal importance. The role of evaluation in curriculum development cannot be overemphasized. When utilized properly, evaluation can help ensure that the curriculum is of a high quality and that deficiencies are identified before they cause major problems to arise.

What, then, constitutes evaluation? Within the context of curriculum development, evaluation may be defined as *the determination of the merit or worth of a curriculum (or portion of that curriculum). It includes gathering information for use in judging the merit of the curriculum, program, or curriculum materials*. Obviously, the task of evaluating an entire curriculum is quite complex and time-consuming. Thus, evaluations often tend to focus on *programs* and *materials*. Although programs and materials are indeed closely related, the evaluation of each takes on a somewhat different air. This may be easily seen in the evaluation literature, where a clear distinction is made between the evaluation of educational programs and materials. Programs are often viewed as being synonymous with curricula; however, they more logically focus on formal aspects of education and typically on a specific course or instructional area (e.g., agribusiness, reprographics, child care). Materials, on the other hand, are typically instructional items such as guides, modules, computer software, texts, or multimedia packages that the developer feels have utility beyond a single teacher.

Anyone who intends to conduct an evaluation should recognize that numerous evaluation techniques are available. These techniques tend to be categorized as being either quantitative or naturalistic. Quantitative techniques are perhaps exemplified by this chapter, with its focus on specific evaluation outcomes, criteria, and objective measures. Naturalistic techniques, on the other hand, place less emphasis on outcomes and more emphasis on process. Inquiry is conducted in a nonjudgmental manner with those under study serving as collaborators in the evaluation process (Williams, 1986a). Examples of naturalistic techniques are participant observations and life history interviews. The decision to use quantitative or naturalistic evaluation techniques is, in large part, a function of the evaluator's philosophy and expertise. Ideally, it is best to select techniques based on *potential utility* rather than personal perspective. Realistically, this does not always occur. If the curriculum evaluator is to be truly effective, he or she should be schooled in *both* quantitative and naturalistic techniques, have a broad perspective about what evaluation is, and focus on the real concerns of stakeholding audiences.

Whereas it is recognized that an entire text could be devoted to curriculum evaluation, the information presented in this chapter should provide the curriculum developer with a foundation for conducting meaningful evaluation activities. Initial emphasis is given to the presentation of an evaluation framework that aligns with curriculum development. Next, various aspects of planning for evaluation are discussed, including evaluation objectives and the development of an evaluation plan. The conduct of a program evaluation is then described. This is followed by a description of curriculum materials evaluation. Finally, thought is given to the ways evaluation results may be used to effect curriculum improvement.

A Framework for Evaluation

Curriculum evaluation in vocational and technical education is often dreaded and avoided. Although many give lip service to evaluation by making comments such as "Every time I meet with a student I am evaluating" or "We evaluate whenever it is appropriate," the fact remains that few curricula are actually subjected to rigorous, systematic evaluations. The reason for this is quite simple. Educators often feel they have neither the time, the expertise, nor the inclination to carry out the type of comprehensive evaluation actually needed. Unfortunately, few realize that an evaluation does not have to take up much extra *time*. In fact, much of the curriculum development work that is already taking place can easily be part of an evaluation effort if meaningful standards and measures are used. In terms of *expertise,* there should be at least one person in a school district, community college, or area vocational school who is knowledgeable about evaluation and can bring his or her expertise to bear on this area. Likewise, professionals at the state level as well as college and university faculty may be in a position to provide needed assistance with evaluation plans. With regard to *inclination,* attitudes must change if evaluation is expected to have more than minimal impact on the curriculum. Administrators, deans, division chairpersons, supervisors, department heads, and teachers must all recognize the value of evaluation and integrate evaluation efforts into ongoing curriculum development and refinement activities.

One way this integration may take place is through the acceptance and use of a comprehensive evaluation framework. Just as curriculum development activities must be systematic, curriculum evaluation must, likewise, follow some sort of meaningful structure. Since the contemporary curriculum is quite comprehensive, evaluation must also be comprehensive, taking into account the various aspects of curriculum initiation, structuring, and operation. The diagram presented in Figure 12–1 serves to illustrate various aspects of evaluation that relate to curriculum initiation, structuring, and operation (Finch and Bjorkquist, 1977). It portrays an evaluation scheme that is both comprehensive and systematic. The four elements of evaluation include

> *Context evaluation,* which deals with whether or not to offer a curriculum and, if so, what its parameters will be including focus, goals, and objectives.

FIGURE 12–1. *A framework for curriculum evaluation*

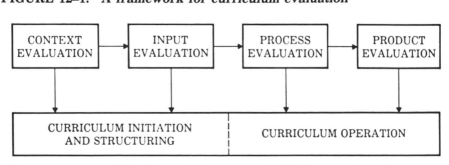

Input evaluation, which relates to deciding what resources and strategies will be used to achieve curriculum goals and objectives.

Process evaluation, which focuses on determining what effect the curriculum has on students in school.

Product evaluation, which deals with examining the curriculum's effects on former students.

Context, input, process, and product (CIPP) have been espoused by Stufflebeam and others (Stufflebeam et al., 1971; Webster, 1981; Armstrong, 1989) as the key elements of a comprehensive evaluation, particularly when information is gathered and used for decision making. As emphasized in previous chapters, proper decision making is a key to the development of quality curricula. Thus, it is most appropriate to use these four elements as a foundation for meaningful curriculum evaluation. Context and input evaluation are employed as the curriculum is being initiated and structured. These two elements focus on gathering information and making decisions relative to curriculum planning (e.g., whether or not to offer a curriculum), curriculum development (e.g., what content should be included in a curriculum), and curriculum materials' development (e.g., whether or not materials are of a sufficient quality). Process and product evaluation relate to curriculum operation. Process evaluation focuses on decisions associated with curriculum effects on students (e.g., whether or not content is learned by students), whereas product evaluation is more closely aligned with decisions about curriculum effects related to former students (e.g., whether or not the curriculum affects graduates' employability).

Context Evaluation

Context evaluation is basic to the curriculum development process, since it is closely associated with decisions about whether or not the curriculum should be offered and what goals and objectives should be used. Realistically, a comprehensive planning effort may include the essential elements of context evaluation. Specifically, context evaluation may define and describe the environment in which a curriculum will be offered, identify needs that have been used as criteria, and pinpoint any constraints that keep these needs from being met. The aggregate data and information gathered serve as a basis for curriculum decisions and the subsequent development of objectives (Stufflebeam et al., 1971; Webster, 1981).

The following are representative of the numerous curriculum questions one might seek to answer in relation to context evaluation:

Should the curriculum be offered?

What student population will the curriculum serve?

What business or industrial population will the curriculum serve?

What content will be included in the curriculum?

What goals should the curriculum have?

What objectives will be used in the curriculum?

A variety of strategies and measures are associated with context evaluation. Among those discussed in previous chapters are needs assessment, task analysis, and introspection. By its very nature, context evaluation is quite speculative, particularly when a new curriculum is being initiated. Decisions are mostly subjective, since "hard" data may not always be available. Naturalistic evaluation techniques may have great potential for use in this setting because a clearer description of the curricular environment is sought.

Input Evaluation

Input evaluation, with its focus on resource and strategy decision making, has important implications for the curriculum developer. As a curriculum is being structured, every effort should be made to ensure that the best resources are chosen and that provision is made for their proper use. Decisions made in this regard are all too often based upon conjecture rather than data. Input evaluation serves to aid the developer in making more objective decisions about the ways content might be provided to students. This is accomplished by systematically identifying and assessing relevant capabilities of the educational agency, resources for achieving curriculum objectives, and alternate plans for their implementation (Stufflebeam et al., 1971; Webster, 1981). Resources can range from media, modules, and learning environments to teaching strategies and learning experiences. Information based on this identification and assessment is used to select specific resources and strategies to meet stated curriculum objectives.

The use of input evaluation is somewhat restricted, with a basic prerequisite being that a decision has been made to offer a vocational or technical curriculum. Since input evaluation is used to determine how resources might be best utilized to achieve curriculum objectives, the evaluator should be aware that data-based decisions are somewhat more arbitrary than their counterparts in process and product evaluation. The logic for this is simple: input evaluation focuses on *intended* rather than actual outcomes. Thus, the extent to which input evaluation is meaningful depends on its true relationship to curriculum process and product (Finch and Bjorquist, 1977). For example, a decision might be made to utilize team teaching in a curriculum because there is some feeling it will enable students to meet a greater number of objectives. This decision obviously is classed as tentative until such time as data show team teaching to be a significant contributor to student achievement.

Curriculum questions related to input evaluation include (but are by no means limited to)

What curriculum materials might be most useful in a particular educational setting?

Which materials are most acceptable to teachers and students?

How might instruction be best implemented?

What are the relative effects of different materials on student achievement?

Data gathering for input evaluation can range from relatively simple to complex, with instruments representing varying degrees of objectivity. Techniques utilized in the data-gathering process may include group consensus, expert judgment, literature and curriculum examination, management by objectives, and pilot experimental and quasi-experimental efforts (Finch and Bjorkquist, 1977).

Process Evaluation

Process evaluation is most closely aligned with instruction. Whereas all evaluation ultimately needs to focus on how the curriculum actually helps students, process evaluation appears most appropriate when the immediate effects of instruction are being examined. Since process evaluation deals directly with the operation of the curriculum, the information associated with this element is most meaningful for the instructional staff. In the traditional sense, process evaluation is what many think of as being evaluation. However, it is but one part of a total evaluation framework. Certainly, the student's success in school is very important, but it is meaningful only to the extent that inferences may be drawn to out-of-school success. Thus, although conclusions drawn from process evaluation are useful for curriculum improvement, they may not align very closely with employment-related outcomes.

Process evaluation can be used to examine a variety of areas. For example, it might be appropriate to determine the extent to which students have achieved certain curriculum objectives or whether a certain innovative program is operating properly. Examples of curriculum questions that could be associated with process evaluation include

How well are learners performing?

What is the quality of instructional and support personnel?

What are the costs associated with operating the curriculum?

To what extent are students satisfied with their instruction?

Which (if any) of the curriculum components are deficient?

Process evaluation measures are numerous. They may include rates of completing certificates, diplomas, or degrees; course completion rates; program completion rates; and student achievement on standardized tests (Hoachlander, 1991).

The ways that process evaluation data may be gathered are numerous. These include the use of teacher behavior measures, teacher rating measures, standardized achievement measures, expert referenced measures, and teacher constructed knowledge and performance instruments.

Product Evaluation

Evaluation must accomplish more than just putting the focus on the student in school. Major consideration must be given to ways the curriculum has aided former students. Product evaluation uses the former student as a focal point in determining this aspect of curriculum quality. The end product of any curriculum is the graduate, and this product (as well as his or her counterpart who did not graduate) needs to be studied if realistic statements are to be made about the worth of the curriculum.

Product evaluation typically takes place "in the field," with information gathered from sources such as employers, supervisors, and incumbent workers (former students). These sources of information are extremely important, since process evaluation only deals with short-range in-school effects (Wentling, 1980). In terms of curriculum questions associated with product evaluation, the following are illustrative:

What is the mobility of former students?

How satisfied are former students with their positions?

How do employers view the performance of former students?

How adequately is the curriculum preparing individuals for job entry?

Measures associated with product evaluation must be selected with care to ensure that an accurate assessment is made of curriculum effectiveness. Among those measures most frequently utilized in product evaluation are the skills survey, job satisfaction, job satisfactoriness, and value of the curriculum. Information gathered may include time needed to locate and secure employment, placement rates, entry-level salary, rate at which quarterly earnings increase, and employer and employee satisfaction (Hoachlander, 1991). Consideration should also be given to use of naturalistic techniques such as ethnography, historiography, and biography to capture the thick descriptive information associated with this area.

Planning for Evaluation

Some may feel that evaluation just happens; this is far from the truth, however. The quality of any evaluation is closely related to the amount and type of planning that go into it. Planning to conduct a meaningful curriculum evaluation usually involves a great deal of time as well as systematic effort. The planning process is composed of several key elements. These include the establishment of sound evaluation objectives and standards and the development of a comprehensive evaluation plan.

Evaluation Objectives and Standards

Most curricula being developed today include performance objectives that specify the activity to be accomplished, the conditions under which the activity is to be performed, and the level of acceptable performance. These types of objectives have been detailed in Chapter 8. Although performance objectives are excellent from an instructional standpoint, they do not relate directly to the curriculum evaluation process.

It appears most efficient to focus initially on evaluation objectives and standards as they relate to curriculum quality. Assume that a curriculum developer is interested in evaluating some materials such as modules that are hopefully of a "high quality." Translating this rather vague statement into more explicit standards related to quality, the curriculum developer might first ask the following broad questions:

1. Do students master the modules?
2. Is each module accepted?
3. Can the materials be used in the regular school setting?

The next logical step would be to develop more detailed questions related to each of these areas. Some of the questions that might be included under these broad areas are as follows:

Do students taking each module achieve mastery of learning experience objectives?

Do students have positive attitudes toward modularized instruction?

Do teachers perceive the modules as making a meaningful contribution to the teaching-learning process?

Will use of the modules require special facilities?

Will use of the modules require special equipment?

Will use of the modules require other resources?

Next, taking the first question and combining it with performance objectives, we can develop an evaluation objective and standard such as

Of the students taking each module, 70 percent must complete each learning experience attempted and must master the objective in a given learning experience on the first trial.

This level of specificity is important when curriculum materials are being assessed, since it provides a clearly defined quality-control level and cutoff point for recycling purposes. That is, if the standard was not met, the module would need to undergo revision and then be assessed again. The 70 percent is somewhat arbitrary, being based primarily on the type of subject matter involved, characteristics of the students, and the expected error associated with the testing process.

The next two questions might be translated into the following assessment objectives:

Of the students completing each module, 80 percent must score 160 or higher on the Instruction Attitude Inventory.

Teachers administering the modular instruction must react favorably to at least 80 percent of the items on the Teacher Reaction Form.

Each of these evaluation objectives and standards is combined with an instrument to ensure that accurate assessments can be made. The attitude objective utilizes a summated rating instrument, with individual items on the inventory being combined to form a composite attitude score. The perception objective utilizes a form with items that are individually scored. In this case, items are not summed, they are examined individually with the 80-percent minimum for each teacher serving as a standard.

The three final questions might possibly be answered by merely reading the modules and speculating that special equipment would or would not be needed. However, since the real test of quality takes place when materials are being used, the following assessment objectives or standards might be developed:

None of the teachers using the modules indicate that materials required the use of special facilities.

None of the teachers using the modules indicate that materials required the use of special equipment.

None of the teachers using the modules indicate that additional resources were required.

Information associated with these objectives might be gathered via personal interviews with teachers or by way of items inserted on the Teacher Reaction Form. No matter how this information is gathered, it is important that instructors are given an opportunity to provide their personal views about the curriculum materials.

Similar types of evaluation objectives and standards may be developed when a program evaluation is being planned. Let us say that it is desired to examine the effects of a cosmetology program on its graduates (product evaluation). Although the determination of actual program effects may be quite difficult, it is possible to pinpoint some indicators in this regard via the following broad questions:

1. Did program graduates pass the state license examination?
2. Are program graduates employed as cosmetologists?
3. Are program graduates' supervisors satisfied with their work performance?
4. Are program graduates satisfied with their work?

The first question could be converted into a meaningful evaluation objective or standard such as

95 percent of the 19X4–19X5 graduates successfully pass the state license examination within six months of graduation.

Although standard one does not represent employability, passing an examination in a technical field may be a prerequisite to employment and success on the job. The 95 percent and six-month figures may certainly be adjusted; however, there are reasonable limits to this. For example, would there be much value in continuing a cosmetology program where only 10 percent of the graduates ever pass the state license examination?

Translating the second question into a meaningful evaluation objective, we might come up with the following:

Of the 19X4–19X5 graduates who are available for employment as cosmetologists, 80 percent have positions in this occupational area.

Note that the objective specifies a certain employment percentage. This is important to spell out so that quality is clearly defined. Additionally, the group is clearly identified (19X4–19X5 graduates available for employment) to ensure that there is no question about the data source. If it were merely stated as "19X4–19X5 graduates," persons might be included in the group who were currently in the military service or who were physically incapacitated. The figure of 80 percent is merely illustrative, since the actual percentage would be determined through group consensus or some similar process.

The third question could be developed into the following evaluation objective:

> Of the 19X4–19X5 graduates employed as cosmetologists, 90 percent are rated at or above the mean by their supervisors on the Job Satisfactoriness Scale.

In this case, supervisors play an important role in determining quality, since they would be asked to complete Job Satisfactoriness scales for 19X4–19X5 graduates. By specifying a standard (90 percent at or above the mean), there is no room for ex-post-facto standards to be established. In the absence of explicit standards, persons have occasionally been known to let the results form the standard. Thus, by providing a clear, measurable standard *before* data have been gathered, there is much greater assurance that an expected level of quality is not modified at a later date.

An evaluation objective based on the fourth question might consist of

> Of the 19X4–19X5 graduates employed as cosmetologists, 75 percent rate their work at or above 42 on the Job Satisfaction Index.

This objective allows the graduates to serve as a data source. Each graduate employed as a cosmetologist is afforded an opportunity to indicate his or her job satisfaction by completing a standardized instrument. The actual level of quality (in this case, 42 or above) would most likely be determined through group consensus (e.g., the cosmetology advisory committee). As with the other objectives, standards are established before data are gathered so the evaluator will be sure of what constitutes a measure of program quality.

There are a host of additional evaluation objectives and standards that could be presented; however, the ones provided serve to illustrate the range of possibilities a curriculum evaluator might use. Whether the task is to evaluate curriculum materials, a specific program, or an entire curriculum, it is extremely important that evaluation planning include meaningful, measurable evaluation objectives. Otherwise, there is not much point in conducting any evaluation at all.

Developing the Evaluation Plan

After evaluation objectives and standards have been developed, a framework for gathering and examining data may then be established. This framework, which is called the evaluation plan, details the evaluation procedures to be followed and helps assure that a thorough, accurate evaluation will be conducted.

Need for the Evaluation Plan. There are several reasons for using an evaluation plan. The first relates to the general value of planning. If an evaluation were conducted without any prior planning, the result might be a faulty design for data gathering, missing data, or invalid results. From a practical standpoint, time spent in the planning process pays large dividends in helping to determine curriculum quality accurately. Planning can assist the curriculum developer in overcoming a number of potential problem areas such as scheduling, data gathering, and data analysis.

A second need for the evaluation plan may be associated with documentation. As an example, although many curriculum materials are "tried out," the user seldom sees the detailed results of this tryout. What the evaluation plan does in this regard is to help the curriculum developer document procedures that were followed and results that were drawn for the data analysis. This documented evidence, together with the ways that the evidence was gathered, may be used by others who want to know just how well the curriculum materials are suited to their needs.

Evaluation Plan Components. The plan for evaluation typically consists of four components. Each component serves a useful purpose in the clarification of evaluation by detailing what is actually going to be evaluated, why it will be evaluated, and how it will be evaluated. Certainly some curriculum evaluation may be conducted without first developing a detailed plan, it is nonetheless important to keep the plan's content in mind when preparing to evaluate. The typical components of an evaluation plan are the overview; curriculum program, or materials description; evaluation design; and evaluation report description. An example of a table of contents from an evaluation plan is provided in Figure 12–2.

Overview. In this section of the evaluation plan, a need for the evaluation is specified. It is imperative that the need be clearly established so others will know exactly why the particular curriculum should be evaluated. Since an evaluation plan may be used to help sell people on the idea or convince them to allocate resources in this direction, the rationale section can serve as an introduction to the evaluation process and encourage the reader to read further. In addition to a specific statement of need, the general evaluation approach should be stated. This helps the reader obtain a feel for the evaluation's overall scope. A final item in this section consists of detailing the benefits derived from conducting the evaluation. These benefits should focus on the groups served (e.g., teachers and students) and how the evaluation will actually help them.

This section also includes the evaluation objectives. Precise evaluation objectives are provided so that there is no question about standards the curriculum should meet. In some cases, the objectives may not yet

FIGURE 12–2. *Table of contents from an evaluation plan*

have been developed. If this situation exists, the plan should detail procedures that will be used to generate these objectives and standards.

Curriculum Description.   At this point in the plan, it is important to describe thoroughly the curriculum, program, or materials being evaluated. The instructional objectives are provided and content is described. Any unique aspects of the content are explicated. Items such as media and personnel that must be available to support the curriculum need to be described; and finally, details are given about the types of students who will use the curriculum and the settings in which it will be used.

Evaluation Design.   The evaluation design is the heart of the plan. It builds on the rationale, objectives, and description in such a way that relevant data can be gathered and valid results generated. In this section, a general organizational design for the evaluation is provided. This design should take into consideration the specific curriculum being evaluated as well as evaluation constraints. If, for example, there are certain factors such as time, dollars, or legal barriers that might limit the scope of the evaluation, these should be detailed so the reader may see exactly why the evaluation is being conducted in a particular manner. Information needed to determine whether or not objectives have been met is detailed. This would include information sources and collection methods as well as a collection schedule. Whether the evaluation involves a simple survey of users or a complex experimental design, the exact process used to collect information must be specified. Techniques for analyzing the collected information are also provided. Although the actual data analysis process might be somewhat dependent on its specific nature, it is most meaningful to have in mind the various ways data may be used. Also included in the design section is a proposed budget for the evaluation. This budget should detail expenditures that are directly associated with the evaluation process. Items that might conceivably be related to evaluation efforts include printing, travel, data processing, typing, and personnel costs. Instruments that will be used to gather information about curriculum quality are generally included in an appendix so that the reader may see exactly what will be used in this regard. This might include standardized measuring instruments and/or initial drafts of instruments that will undergo validation before the evaluation is conducted.

Evaluation Report.   This section is useful as a means of planning for the eventual development and distribution of a formal evaluation report. The report should be such that the quality and the process used to determine this quality are clearly indicated. In many instances, the evaluation plan can serve as a basis for the report. With minor modification, the first three sections of the evaluation plan can make up the first part of a comprehensive evaluation report. This, together with sections dealing with evaluation results, conclusions, and recommendations, constitutes a report that should be most acceptable to administrators and/or sponsors. An outline of the evaluation report to be eventually produced is provided in this section so that the reader will know what to expect with regard to documentation of the evaluation effort. Also of value would be an indication of those who are tentatively scheduled to receive copies of the report. This information need not be of a specific nature (i.e., actual names) but should include classes of persons who might find the report to be of value (e.g., teachers in specific schools, administrators at certain levels, and other curriculum developers).

Conducting the Program Evaluation

The actual conduct of a program evaluation varies in relation to a number of operational constraints. Although it would be most profitable to examine the program context, input, process, and product, this is not always feasible. Say, for example, it is desired to evaluate a program that is already in operation. In this particular situation, it would be quite difficult to conduct a context and input evaluation. However, if a program is being initiated or revised, these two evaluation areas might be quite easily examined as a part of the total evaluation effort.

Once the scope of the evaluation has been determined, it is necessary to examine what evaluation roles will be assumed by various staff members. Whereas basic consideration is given to this in the evaluation plan, it is imperative that activities be initiated to ensure that staff members are supportive and will do their part. Consideration might be given to faculty and administrator orientation, staff input sessions, and the provision of incentives for involvement. Even though there will be those few who do not accept evaluation, every effort should be made to bring these persons "into the fold."

As the program evaluation is being conducted, staff members should be kept informed of progress that is being made and have an opportunity to participate in the evaluation to the extent that their schedules permit. For example, it might be most appropriate for a power sewing machine operator instructor to visit local industries and conduct a personal follow-up of former students. A marketing education coordinator might feel that it is best to combine evaluation of former students with visits to students who are involved in cooperative work experience activities. In the case of input evaluation, staff most definitely should play an active role in the establishment of program goals and objectives. Process evaluation, with its close relationship to school-related success of students, cannot be conducted unless teachers are involved in the assessment of student performance. Thus, it is evident that staff members should know what the evaluation entails and be given every opportunity to become partners in the assessment process.

Once data have been gathered and compared with established evaluation objectives, results should be immediately conveyed to all staff members. Delays in this regard could give rise to thoughts of suppressed information and might otherwise adversely affect staff morale.

Although each program evaluation is closely aligned with its particular evaluation plan, there are a number of concerns that cannot be easily committed to paper. These have to do primarily with interpersonal activities. Above all, it should be recognized that evaluation is not a mechanical procedure one follows to get from point A to point B. The most meaningful evaluation effort is one that is founded on sound objectives and standards, that has a clear framework within which it is to be conducted, and that gives major consideration to staff input and involvement.

Evaluating Curriculum Materials

Traditionally, the curriculum materials writing process has served as a setting for establishing curriculum materials quality, with the writer or writers serving as the sole means of quality control. After a decision is made to develop a particular item, an individual or group writes it and then the material is reproduced and distributed to appropriate teachers and students for their use. Although the writer is a key figure in the development process, he or she may not always be capable of determining exactly how teachers or students might react to use of the materials. Obviously, the writing environment is different than the teaching environment, and because of this difference, each situation serves a useful role in the determination of curriculum materials quality.

Chapters 9 and 10 have dealt extensively with the processes of determining which materials to select and developing materials in a systematic manner. Each of these areas is of considerable value to the individual who is selecting or preparing curriculum materials for vocational and technical education. Chapter 11 has provided detailed information about developing a special type of curriculum material—the individualized, competency-based package or module. This type of material places further emphasis on the need for precision in the curriculum materials' development process. It must be noted, however, that systematic development is only the initial step in the establishment of curriculum materials quality. The contemporary curriculum developer goes beyond materials selection and preparation to actual testing in realistic educational settings.

Need for Curriculum Materials Evaluation

In recent years, educators have placed greater and greater emphasis on the area of curriculum materials evaluation. Whether this emphasis has evolved from administrative pressure, public displeasure, a shrinking funding base, or professional concern is dependent upon the particular educational environment; however, the fact remains that educators are increasingly aware of the need to gather information about the worth of materials they use.

When giving consideration to the evaluation of curriculum materials, it is important to distinguish between two levels of evaluation: formative and summative. *Formative evaluation* is used to improve materials while they are being formulated and developed. This sort of evaluation is typically conducted by someone such as a curriculum developer who is familiar with the materials and/or has worked closely with them. *Summative evaluation,* on the other hand, involves the examination of a completed item to determine its impact on the potential consumer. An unbiased person or persons from outside the organization is brought in to conduct the summative evaluation (Brandt, 1981). Although much of the remainder of this chapter applies equally well to formative and summative evaluation, the focus will be on the formative type, since this level of evaluation is seen as a major role of the curriculum developer.

Why, then, is there a need to determine curriculum materials quality? The need appears to parallel determination of any curriculum's worth. This includes the contribution materials make to student growth, curriculum materials' credibility, and practical considerations associated with their use.

Contribution to Student Growth.   Although development and review by experts serve as useful means of gathering information about the worth of curriculum materials, these experts do not deal directly with the concern about how students are actually helped. No matter how much writers or reviewers praise a particular item, their praises may be in vain if it is not of value to the students for whom it has been designed. This factor represents the single, most important aspect of curriculum materials quality, for if an item is not able to affect some positive change in students, it is certainly of little value as a component part of the vocational education curriculum.

Credibility.   A second need for determining curriculum materials quality lies in the area of credibility. Not only should the materials be tangible contributors to the student growth but they must also be readily accepted by both teachers and students. No matter how useful curriculum materials are in effecting student learning, they may be considered worthless if teachers and their students will not accept them as being meaningful ways to learn. One must recognize, however, that credibility does not substitute for a contribution to student growth. This is merely one of several dimensions that must be closely scrutinized if quality materials are to be developed.

Practical Considerations.   Any curriculum materials that may be easily introduced to the classroom and laboratory setting and can be utilized by teachers and students with a minimum of effort will most likely be used again and again. Conversely, materials must fit well in the educational setting to be of genuine value. Even though teachers and students may accept the materials as being worthwhile and as helping students to learn, they must have practical utility as well.

Establishing Evaluation Standards

When one is faced with the task of evaluating curriculum materials quality, initial consideration must be given to the development of meaningful evaluation standards. Quality has numerous interpretations, but the curriculum developer's job is to spell out exactly what quality is in relation to his or her particular materials. Quality, then, is operationally defined for each of the materials that undergoes development, with standards for some being different than standards for others. The variation in standards from item to item is typically a function of time and associated resources available to the developer; however, each standard must be one that professional educators can live with. Otherwise, the evaluation results will not be accepted by them. In many cases, standards may be established before development begins. If this were always the case, there would be no need to deal with setting up standards at this juncture. However, since some materials have their standards established on a post-hoc basis, information about the process is presented here rather than in Chapter 10.

The establishment of evaluation standards typically follows a three-step process. Initially, a definition of quality is developed for the particular curriculum materials. Next, evaluation objectives are prepared, each of which aligns with the definition of materials quality. Finally, instruments are identified that focus on the various evaluation objectives. Two of these steps are detailed in the sections that follow. The third step, preparing evaluation objectives, was presented earlier in this chapter as part of the overall planning process.

Defining Curriculum Materials Quality

The quality of curriculum materials can be viewed as multidimensional. Any materials used by teachers and students must meet a number of practical standards, each of which represents a unique dimension of their overall quality. The specification of materials quality can only be limited by one's creativity. As long as the curriculum developer can ensure that objectives are specified and instruments identified, there is virtually no limit to the set of specifications one may associate with quality. There is, however, a practical problem of time and resources available to assess the various aspects of materials quality. One solution to this problem involves selection and evaluation of those dimensions that appear to be the major contributors to materials quality. For example, a curriculum developer might identify twenty areas of quality that relate to a particular set of materials but may have sufficient resources to assess only three of these areas. He or she would then select the three areas felt to be most critical to quality and evaluate the materials on these dimensions. In the selection process, consideration should be given to use of a professional team consisting of vocational teachers and curriculum developers who are charged with the responsibility of ranking the various quality areas and selecting those that are most important to evaluate.

Evaluators have given much thought to the various aspects of curriculum materials quality. Although a discussion of all these areas is beyond the scope of this volume, it may be of value to deal with several that should be considered when materials are being evaluated. These dimensions are materials effectiveness, efficiency, acceptability, practicality, and generalizability.

Effectiveness. This area of quality deals directly with assessing the effects of materials used. Questions that might be raised about materials effectiveness include Does use of the materials change student behavior? What changes occur with what types of students? Do the materials effect a greater change than other materials?

Efficiency. Efficiency is concerned with materials effectiveness as it relates to time and cost. Materials may be deemed effective but at an increased cost or with a greater time allocation. If this is the case, vocational educators might find it more beneficial to remain with the original instructional arrangement. Efficiency may be represented by either greater effectiveness than materials now in use with no increase in time and/or cost, or equal effectiveness to other materials with a decrease in time and/or cost. Questions that can be raised about materials efficiency include Do the materials effect a greater student success rate than alternate modes of instruction while not being greater in time or cost? Does it cost less to achieve a specified student success rate with the materials than with other materials? Does it take less time to achieve a specified student success rate with the materials than with other materials?

Acceptability. The area of acceptability deals with students and teachers who use the materials. Concern here is with the users' acceptance of materials as a useful contributor to the teaching-learning process. Questions one might elicit about materials acceptability include Do students perceive the materials as making a meaningful contribution to the teaching-learning process? Do students have positive attitudes toward instruction received via the materials? Do teachers perceive the materials as making a meaningful contribution to the teaching-learning process? Do teachers have positive attitudes toward instruction via the materials?

Practicality.   This area of quality is associated with materials use in the school environment. It is concerned with potential constraints that might restrict materials use even though they show up well in other quality areas. Questions related to materials practicality might include Will use of the materials require special facilities or equipment (e.g., laboratories, audiovisual aids, references)? Is the cost-per-unit price of the materials prohibitive? Will in-service teacher education be required before the materials may be used? If so, how extensive will the in-service program be?

Generalizability.   The generalizability area focuses on curriculum materials potential to be used by students in other schools, school districts, community colleges, or subject matter areas. Since a number of materials go through an extensive and costly development process, it is important to know if an item can be used by students other than those for whom it was initially designed. A parallel concern is the gathering of evidence about possible new applications for the materials. Questions one might raise with regard to generalizability include To what extent may the materials be used with students in other educational settings? To what extent may the materials be used by students with different characteristics than those whom they were originally intended? To what uses might the materials be put that have not heretofore been identified?

Instruments for Curriculum Materials Evaluation

A most important aspect of curriculum materials evaluation involves identifying instruments that can be used to determine whether or not the specified standards have been met. It becomes obvious that some evaluation objectives cannot be developed unless immediate consideration is given to instruments that will be used in the evaluation process. Thus, the curriculum developer must sometimes consider the kind of instruments he or she will use concurrently with the development of evaluation objectives.

Instrument selection can be a rather personal matter, since the curriculum developer needs to be sure that an accurate evaluation is being made of his or her materials. The actual selection is based on an instrument's alignment with a particular quality question and evaluation objective. This alignment often presents problems, since numerous standardized instruments do not align well with many of the evaluation objectives developed for curriculum materials. If, for example, one desires to determine the effectiveness of a particular learning package that focuses on development of skills in using the metric system, a standardized general mathematics test might be inappropriate, since it may not be sensitive enough to any change produced by the package. In this case, the curriculum developer might utilize tests that focus directly on the package's objectives. These tests could already be a part of the package; otherwise, they would need to be developed locally for use in the evaluation process.

The types of instruments used to evaluate materials quality are numerous, and with so many possibilities to choose from, the curriculum developer may find it quite difficult to select an instrument that is appropriate. In order that the developer may be provided with a better picture of how instruments align with areas of materials quality, the following discussion focuses on instrumentation as it relates to assessing various aspects of quality.

Knowledge Instruments. If the objective is to produce a change in the cognitive area, a knowledge examination might need to be developed for use in evaluating materials effectiveness. As was mentioned earlier, a curriculum developer is often faced with the task of developing instruments, since there appear to be few commercially produced instruments that closely align with materials outcomes.

Numerous books are available that describe the procedures used in developing knowledge instruments. The curriculum developer would do well to locate a good applied measurement book and use this as a guide in the development process. Of course, central to instrument development is the concept of relevance. Any instrument that is developed must focus directly on the curriculum materials outcomes. If this is not done, the materials probably will not fare very well when being evaluated. Equally important concerns in the development of knowledge instruments are the establishment of *validity* (the extent to which an instrument measures what it is supposed to measure) and *reliability* (the extent to which it measures something consistently). These elements can also affect the success of an evaluation and should, therefore, be an important aspect of the instrument development process. Whether a knowledge instrument is selected or developed, it is extremely important to have validity and reliability information available so that no questions will be raised about the instrument's value.

Attitude and Opinion Instruments. Attitude and opinion instruments focus directly on the affective aspects of curriculum materials quality. These instruments align most closely with materials acceptability; however, they can also be used to gather information about materials practicality. The attitude instrument is especially difficult to develop, since attitudes are generally measured by indirect rather than direct means. This necessitates the use of more subjective procedures than would be associated with the knowledge instrument. In the development of an attitude instrument, one does not simply write down items, give them to students, and then come up with a composite score for each individual. The attitude instrument must be a valid and reliable measure that meets basic educational measurement standards. An example of an attitude instrument, together with information about the supporting data, is provided in Figure 12–3. Note that the instrument is of the Likert-type with item scores being summed to produce a composite score. Other types of item arrangements such as the Thurstone and Semantic Differential approaches might work equally well for a variety of curriculum materials assessment situations.

The opinion-type instrument or opinionnaire serves as a useful means of gathering information about specific user concerns. The opinionnaire may include a variety of items, each of which focuses on a different aspect of quality. Each item then becomes a somewhat separate entity; items are not summed to produce a composite opinion score. The value of using an opinionnaire rests in its ability to gather information that might otherwise "fall between the cracks." Although an attitude instrument may be extremely useful in determining whether or not materials are basically acceptable to students, it does not usually tell where certain specific deficiencies may exist. The opinionnaire enables a curriculum developer to obtain feedback from users about specific aspects of the materials. For example, items might be included that ask students how clear the objectives were or ask teachers how relevant the learning experiences were. An additional advantage of the opinionnaire is that it has the capability of soliciting the degree of user commitment to materials. If instructors were asked, "Would you use these materials again with another class?", their collective responses such as "Yes," "Yes with revision," and "No" would give the developer a good idea of how the materials would fare with regard to continued use. Additionally, opinionnaires allow the user to provide free response information about how well the materials are accepted. Even though this information is very difficult to code, it may provide useful ideas about the materials specific strengths and weaknesses. These particular ideas may then be discussed with users to help determine exactly where revisions should be made.

The opinionnaire works equally well with students and teachers. Realistically, it is important to obtain opinionnaire-type information from both of these groups, since they may each see the materials in a different light. The student may view a particular set of materials in relation to his or her learning a certain aspect of the vocational education curriculum, whereas the instructor might see the same materials as one of several ways students can be assisted in mastering certain specified objectives. Examples of opinionnaires that are useful for gathering in-

FIGURE 12–3. *Example of an attitude instrument*

Instruction Attitude Inventory [IAI]

LAST NAME   FIRST   INITIAL   DATE

COURSE   INSTRUCTOR

DIRECTIONS: Below are several statements about the period of instruction which you have just completed. Read each statement carefully and indicate how much you agree or disagree with it according to the following scale:

SD = STRONGLY DISAGREE   D = DISAGREE   N = NEUTRAL   A = AGREE   SA = STRONGLY AGREE

USE A #2 PENCIL FOR MARKING. DO NOT USE BALL POINT PEN OR RED PENCIL. ERASE ALL UNINTENDED MARKS.

1. I would like more instruction presented in this way
2. I learned more because equipment was available for me to use
3. This instruction was very boring
4. The material presented was of much value to me
5. The instruction was too specific
6. I was glad just to get through the material
7. The material presented will help me to solve problems
8. While taking this instruction I almost felt as if someone was talking with me
9. I can apply very little of the material which I learned to a practical situation
10. The material made me feel at ease
11. In view of the time allowed for learning, I felt that too much material was presented
12. I could pass an examination over the material which was presented
13. I was more involved with using equipment than with understanding the material
14. I became easily discouraged with this type of instruction
15. I enjoy this type of instruction because I get to use my hands
16. I was not sure how much I learned while taking this instruction
17. There are too many distractions with this method of instruction
18. The material which I learned will help me when I take more instruction in this area
19. This instructional method did not seem to be any more valuable than regular classroom instruction
20. I felt that I wanted to do my best work while taking this instruction
21. This method of instruction makes learning too mechanical
22. The instruction has increased my ability to think
23. I had difficulty reading the written material that was used
24. I felt frustrated by the instructional situation

25. This is a poor way for me to learn skills
26. This method of instruction does not seem to be any better than other methods of instruction
27. I am interested in trying to find out more about the subject matter
28. It was hard for me to follow the order of this instruction
29. While taking this instruction I felt isolated and alone
30. I felt uncertain as to my performance in the instruction
31. There was enough time to learn the material that was presented
32. I don't like this instruction any better than other kinds I have had
33. The material presented was difficult to understand
34. This was a very good way to learn the material
35. I felt very uneasy while taking this instruction
36. The material presented seemed to fit in well with my previous knowledge of the subject
37. This method of instruction was a poor use of my time
38. While taking this instruction I felt challenged to do my best work
39. I disliked the way that I was instructed
40. The instruction gave me facts and not just talk
41. I guessed at most of the answers to problems
42. Answers were given to the questions that I had about the material
43. I seemed to learn very slowly with this type of instruction
44. This type of instruction makes me want to work harder
45. I did not understand the material that was presented
46. I felt as if I had my own teacher while taking this instruction
47. I felt that no one really cared whether I worked or not

formation from students and teachers are provided in Figures 12–4 and 12–5. The student opinionnaire deals with reactions to use of a microcomputer learning package, whereas the teacher opinionnaire focuses on feelings about the use of a microcomputer in an instructional setting. These two examples represent the range of information that might be gathered about curriculum materials. Depending on the type of information desired, it may be possible to develop some items that reflect common concerns of both teachers and students. Then, after data have been collected and summarized, an examination may be made of similarities or differences that exist between these groups.

Performance Instruments.   The performance instrument may be used when materials have been designed to develop student capability to perform certain tasks or activities in applied settings. A key aspect of performance instrument development is its content validity. That is, does the instrument's content accurately portray the performance required in applied settings? If this standard is not met, the instrument will not give a true picture of student performance. An additional aspect of instrument development involves determining how easily the instrument may be administered to students. Even the most valid performance instrument will cause a curriculum developer problems if it cannot be administered to students with relative ease.

Performance instruments may already be a part of curriculum materials. If this is the case, instrumentation problems are solved, since the evaluation of performance can take place as students complete their required instruction. If a product does not include a performance instrument, performance may have to be evaluated during a special testing session. Either situation requires that the examiner ensure control over the testing environment so each student is given an equal opportunity to do his or her best work. Areas that performance tests may be developed for include (but are not limited to) marketing, treating, diagnosing, adjusting, building, displaying, selecting, calculating, planning, drawing, administering, preparing, repairing, developing, and compiling.

Questionnaires.   The questionnaire serves a useful purpose in gathering information about curriculum materials users and the educational setting. Questionnaires may be used to identify the teachers' and students' personal characteristics, such as age, occupational experience, teaching experience, and education. This kind of information is important when the curriculum developer wants to determine how different groups of teachers might react to the materials or how different types of students might perform after having received the instruction. Other kinds of information that can be gathered via questionnaires include student grade level, location of the evaluation, and time required to complete the materials.

FIGURE 12–4. *Example of student opinionnaire*

Microcomputer Learning Package Opinionnaire

I. SPECIFIC REACTIONS

INSTRUCTIONS: Please read each of the following statements. Circle the term on the right of each statement that most nearly represents your opinion of this microcomputer learning package. The terms on the right are defined as follows:

SA   A   D   SD

Strongly Agree   Agree   Disagree   Strongly Disagree

Your carefully considered responses will definitely be used in our revision of this microcomputer learning package!

1. I easily understood each of the learning package objectives before I began working with the learning experience: .... SA A D SD
2. Each learning experience assisted me in achieving its related objectives .... SA A D SD
3. I was well aware of my progress (or lack of progress) as I worked through this learning package .... SA A D SD
4. The evaluations (self-tests, rating sheets, checklists) measured my achievement of the objectives .... SA A D SD
5. The learning experiences made the best use of my time in achieving objectives............................. SA A D SD
6. I felt that the instructional materials helped me achieve the learning package objectives .... SA A D SD
7. I feel that the performance objectives included in this learning package are important to my success in this program .... SA A D SD

II. GENERAL REACTIONS

INSTRUCTIONS: In this section we want your reactions to *any* aspects of the microcomputer learning package that you like or dislike.

1. What did you like *best* about this learning package?
   A.
   B.
   C.
2. What did you like *least* about this learning package?
   A.
   B.
   C.
3. Any additional comments?

FIGURE 12–5. *Example of a teacher opinionnaire*

Microcomputer Opinionnaire

Name: _____ School: _____

DIRECTIONS: Below are several statements about the microcomputer that you have been using with your classes. Read each statement carefully and indicate the extent to which you agree or disagree with it according to the following scale:

SD–Strongly Disagree; I strongly disagree with the statement.
D–Disagree; I disagree with the statement, but not strongly so.
A–Agree; I agree with the statement, but not strongly so.
SA–Strongly Agree; I strongly agree with the statement.

CIRCLE YOUR RESPONSE

1. The microcomputer requires a great deal of maintenance   SD D A SA
2. The microcomputer provides my students with a good
   way to learn skills ....   SD D A SA
3. The microcomputer should be used in conjunction with
   instructional materials such as booklets and instruction
   sheets ....   SD D A SA
4. The microcomputer should be located in the classroom ...   SD D A SA
5. The microcomputer should be used instead of classroom
   instruction ....   SD D A SA
6. Microcomputer breakdowns did not occur very frequently   SD D A SA
7. The microcomputer should be located in the school
   laboratory area ....   SD D A SA
8. Instructors should be provided with time to develop instructional materials that can be used with the
   microcomputer ....   SD D A SA
9. Students should work on the microcomputer in groups ...   SD D A SA

Although questionnaires can be developed and administered separately from other instruments, they are often combined with opinionnaires, with each taking up one or more parts of a composite instrument. This procedure makes the evaluation process go more smoothly by reducing paperwork and allowing the user to feel that he or she is not burdened with so many pages of material to complete.

Conducting the Curriculum Materials Evaluation

Once sufficient planning has been done, including the establishment of meaningful evaluation objectives and instruments, the curriculum developer is ready to carry out the evaluation. This is a relatively simple task if proper steps have been detailed in the evaluation plan and one that is most rewarding, since the developer now has an opportunity to find out just how well materials fare in realistic educational settings.

The extent to which one can actually evaluate curriculum materials is dependent on available resources. Dollars or time available to evaluate materials destined for use at the local level may be considerably less than for evaluating materials to be used by state and national audiences. Thus, the developer may be faced with decisions about how extensive an evaluation can be accomplished for a given set of materials. Ideally, the evaluation is a two-phase process consisting of pilot testing and field testing. Realistically, this might be limited to pilot testing if time and/or dollars are unavailable, with the recognition that both pilot and field testing are necessary in order to make a meaningful check of materials quality.

Pilot Testing

The pilot-testing activity consists of trying out materials in school environments and with students who are similar to those who will eventually use the materials. Since the pilot test represents an initial tryout effort, testing is usually limited to one location.

Pilot testing focuses on the acceptability and practicality aspects of curriculum materials' quality. Whereas it is recognized that materials effectiveness, efficiency, and generalizability are of equal if not greater importance, the pilot test serves as an initial trial that does not usually allow the evaluator sufficient time to deal directly with these key areas. The pilot test might be said to serve as a prerequisite to field testing. Since any product must be deemed functionally sound before additional tryouts are conducted, the pilot test is an important means of obtaining this sort of information.

A pilot test typically involves one or more regular classes of vocational students who can benefit from the materials. The evaluator must first identify a site where the test may be conducted and then coordinate the efforts with appropriate school administrators, teachers, and students. Groups should know exactly what their respective roles will be and procedures to be followed during the test. Even though information gathered is of a more descriptive nature, it is important for all teachers to recognize that accuracy of information is paramount. If it is not possible for teachers to gather data, the evaluator may choose to gather his or her own data. This course of action must meet with teachers' and administrators' prior approval.

Field Testing

Field testing involves the trial of materials in several realistic settings. The field-testing process builds on pilot testing and typically focuses on all five aspects of curriculum materials quality: effectiveness, efficiency, acceptability, practicality, and generalizability. Acceptability and practicality have already been examined during the pilot testing; field testing provides an additional opportunity to gather data about these areas and see how the materials fare with other students and teachers.

The field test is characterized as being more rigorous than the pilot test and may include one or several rather sophisticated designs. Most of the basic approaches one can use to conduct field tests are drawn directly from research and evaluation in the behavioral sciences, and with so many possibilities available, it sometimes becomes difficult to decide which design or combination of designs will be best for a particular situation. When designing the field-test process, it is best to give initial consideration to internal and external validity. This, in effect, means a close look should be taken at the field-testing process to ensure that test results will be interpretable and that they can be generalized to appropriate populations, settings, and so forth. Obviously, a true experimental design would be the best means of obtaining internal and external validity. Its use enables the curriculum developer to control for sources of invalidity in an efficient manner. The developer should recognize, however, that experiments cannot always be conducted when evaluations are done.

Other factors such as available time and dollars work against the use of experiments in field testing. Because of these restrictions, developers often turn to quasiexperimental and nonexperimental or preexperimental designs. Although these designs are acknowledged as lacking in terms of internal and external validity, they are typically used by evaluators. Since field testing is often a compromise situation, these designs seem at least to align with the basic evaluation constraints of a vocational and technical education setting. It should be emphasized that if the preexperimental design is used, serious consideration must be given to conducting a number of field tests. Satisfactory performance over repeated testing with different students should indicate that the materials are of a high quality in terms of both effectiveness and generalizability.

When considering the sample size to use in a field test, it is best to keep in mind that a random sampling of students just cannot be accomplished. It is impossible to take a completely random sample from all present and future populations to which the field-test results are to be inferred. The logical alternative is to conduct the field test with students whose personal characteristics are representative of those who will eventually use them. This helps to ensure that, when the materials are implemented on a large scale, they will be as effective as when they were field tested.

The question is often raised as to what size a sample of students should actually be. A rather vague answer to this question would be to use as large a sample as can be afforded. In experimental research, a minimum of ten to fifteen subjects is usually assigned to each group. This minimum number is perhaps a good one to use. However, before numbers are actually firmed up, the curriculum specialist should ask an important question about sample size: How much difference will one student's performance make to the composite evaluation results? If one student represents 10 percent of the field-test sample, success or failure by that individual will have much greater impact on results than would a student who is part of a forty-student sample.

Site selection and coordination of the testing effort are equally as important in field testing as they are in pilot testing. In fact, since field testing includes the use of multiple test locations, it is imperative that detailed arrangements for testing be worked out as the evaluation plan is being developed. When multiple-location testing is being conducted, it is too late to back up and make major revisions to the process. This is why testing arrangements should be thought out and committed to paper far in advance of the time testing begins.

Utilizing Evaluation Results for Curriculum Improvement

Curriculum evaluation is only useful to the extent that results have a positive impact on the curriculum, program, or materials. Although it may be necessary on occasion to conduct an evaluation to comply with some external mandate, the real strength of evaluation lies in its potential to effect educational improvement. Whether concern is with a total curriculum, a vocational program, or curriculum materials used in that program, it is essential that evaluation results serve as a basis for determining if and when appropriate educational changes should be made.

Program Improvement

The vocational program, which represents a substantial portion of the curriculum, can certainly benefit from sound evaluation. Benefit is, of course, relative and tends to parallel the comprehensiveness of evaluation. Logically, an evaluation that only focuses on the educational process is not going to produce as much meaningful data as one that deals directly with context, input, process, and product.

Context evaluation data may be used to help improve the educational environment and refine a program's goals and objectives. Input evaluation data can assist the curriculum developer in determining which resources and strategies have the greatest potential as well as how content might be arranged. Process evaluation data may be utilized to focus on improving both teaching and learning, whereas product evaluation can aid in determining which programs are more successful in producing work force members.

With regard to the aforementioned areas, it is important to ask the following questions:

Have the specified evaluation objectives and standards been met?

If the objectives and standards have not been met, what program changes can be made to ensure that they are met in the future?

If the objectives and standards have been met, is it worthwhile to raise the specified quality standards?

These questions are based on the assumption that realistic, measurable evaluation objectives have been established. Obviously, anything less than this will not enable questions to be answered. Vocational program improvement, then, is most dependent on the objectives used in the evaluation effort. If objectives are vague, it may never be known whether they have been met, much less what action should be taken to effect program improvement.

Program improvement is typically incremental. Certain changes are made based on evaluation results and then future evaluations focus on the results of these changes. Since it is usually not feasible to make wholesale changes in a program, only those changes are made that will benefit students the most. Program evaluation has the potential to assist vocational educators in making meaningful improvements. However, the extent to which these improvements may actually be made depends on the quality and comprehensiveness of the evaluation effort.

Curriculum Materials Improvement

Once an evaluation of curriculum materials has been conducted, how can a curriculum developer best utilize the results? Although this question appears easy to answer, the testing process does not always provide the clear results that one might like to have. For example, when testing a particular set of curriculum materials, the data might indicate that the materials are effective and acceptable but not efficient or practical. In this situation, the burden of responsibility rests with the curriculum developer to decide whether materials should be either discarded, revised and retested, or allowed to be released with deficiencies clearly documented. The decision made in this situation might depend on how serious the deficiencies are or how much revision time is available. In either case, the developer is faced with making a decision, and, hopefully, this decision will be based on data gathered during pilot and field testing.

If deficiencies do exist, it is important to identify exactly where they are so that appropriate revisions may be made. One fruitful approach is to examine individual opinionnaire items and determine if the specific problem areas may be pinpointed. An item indicating that a high number of students felt their time was wasted might lead to revision of content such as eliminating nonrelevant material. Students' negative reactions to reading assignments might lead the developer to provide nonreading alternatives. Whatever the deficiency may be, it is important to identify exactly where the problem is and make necessary revisions.

In some cases, it may be obvious that materials have major deficiencies that cannot be resolved. If this situation occurs, the developer could be faced with terminating a development effort and admitting that work has been unsuccessful. This is certainly a difficult task but a necessary one if the need should ever arise. All too often, curriculum materials are made available to the public that do not meet standards of the profession. The curriculum developer's role is clearly one of controlling materials quality and, if necessary, he or she should be ready to point out identified shortcomings. Evaluation is more than simply confirming materials quality; it involves determining their worth and reporting that worth to the public. The curriculum developer should be prepared to report what this worth is, regardless of the evaluation findings.

Summary

This chapter has focused directly on curriculum evaluation in realistic educational settings. Comprehensive evaluation of the curriculum may best be achieved if focus is on curriculum context, input, process, and product. The evaluation process is initiated with the establishment of evaluation standards. This includes actually defining what quality is as well as developing evaluation objectives.

A key to the success of any evaluation effort is the development of a practical evaluation plan. This plan serves as a framework for gathering and examining evaluation data. Included in the plan should be a rationale for the evaluation as well as a description of the curriculum and the evaluation design that will be utilized. After the evaluation has been carried out, provision must be made to use the results for curriculum improvement. It is only in this way that the evaluation effort will have fulfilled its purpose.

Related References

Armstrong, David G. *Developing and Documenting the Curriculum.* Needham Heights, Mass.: Allyn & Bacon, 1989.

Asche, F. Marion. "Indicators of Quality for Virginia Vocational Education Programs." Paper presented at the Conference for Virginia Vocational Administrators, October, 1990.

Brandt, Ronald S., ed. *Applied Strategies for Curriculum Evaluation.* Alexandria, Va.: Association for Supervision and Curriculum Development, 1981.

Buttram, Joan L.; Kershner, Keith M.; Rioux, Steven; and Dusewicz, Russel A. "An Evaluation of Competency-Based Vocational Education in Pennsylvania: Five Years Later." *Journal of Vocational Education Research* 12, no. 4 (Fall 1987): 35–55.

Finch, Curtis R., and Bjorkquist, David C. "Review and Critique of Context and Input Measures in Evaluation." *Journal of Industrial Teacher Education* 14, no. 2 (Winter 1977): 7–18.

Hoachlander, E. Gareth. "Designing a Plan to Measure Vocational Education Results." *Vocational Education Journal* 66, no. 2 (February 1991): 20–21, 65.

Hoachlander, E. Gareth. *Systems of Performance Standards and Accountability for Vocational Education.* Berkeley, Calif.: National Center for Research in Vocational Education, 1991.

Miles, Matthew B., and Huberman, A. Michael. *Qualitative Data Analysis.* Beverly Hills, Calif.: Sage, 1984.

Raab, Robert T.; Swanson, Burton E.; Wentling, Tim L.; and Clark, Charles D. *Improving Training Quality: A Trainer's Guide to Evaluation.* Rome, Italy: Food and Agricultural Organization of the United Nations, 1991.

Rae, Leslie. *How to Measure Training Effectiveness.* New York: Nichols, 1986.

Stufflebeam, Daniel Z., et al. *Educational Evaluation and Decision-Making.* Itasca, Ill.: F. E. Peacock Publishers, 1971.

Webster, William J. "CIPP in Local Evaluation." In R. Brandt, ed. *Applied Strategies for Curriculum Evaluation.* Alexandria, Va.: Association for Supervision and Curriculum Development, 1981.

Wentling, Tim L. *Evaluating Occupational Education and Training Programs.* Urbana, Ill.: Griffon Press, 1980.

Williams, David D., ed. *Naturalistic Evaluation.* San Francisco: Jossey Bass, 1986a.

———. "Naturalistic Evaluation: Potential Conflicts Between Evaluation Standards and Criteria for Conducting Naturalistic Inquiry." *Educational Evaluation and Policy Analysis* 8, no. 2 (Spring 1986b): 87–99.

Appendix A

Curriculum Materials Assessment Form

Curriculum Materials Assessment Form

Section I.   General Information

1. **Title and ISBN number** (If applicable):_____

   _____

2. **Author(s):** _____
3. **Source:** (Publisher name, address, telephone, and fax number)

   _____

   _____

   _____

4. **Publication date:** _____   5. **Cost:** _____
6. **Potential teaching area(s), subject(s), and courses where resource may be used:** _____
7. **Potential students:** (e.g., grade level, postsecondary, adult, handicapped, disadvantaged, special needs) _____

   _____

8. **Description:** (e.g., content, purpose, size, time allocation)

   _____

   _____

   _____

   _____

   _____

9. **Format:** (Check all that apply)

_____ Textbook	_____ Workbook	_____ Guide
_____ Diskette	_____ Audio tape	_____ Videotape
_____ Game	_____ Simulation	_____ Film
_____ Transparencies	_____ Pamphlet	_____ Manual
_____ Other (Specify) _____		

10. **Instructional application(s):** (Check all that apply)

_____ Laboratory	_____ Lecture/ Discussion	_____ Classroom
_____ Individualized	_____ Work Simulation	_____ OJT
_____ Content Integration	_____ Other (Specify)	

Section II. Assessment Areas

Descriptive comments by each area reflect an acceptable level. Describe deficiencies for areas that are not acceptable. Code each area as follows:

A = Acceptable
? = Questionable
U = Unacceptable
D = Does not apply

11. _____ **BIAS** (The material is free of gender, racial, age, religious, ethnic, cultural, and employment bias)
Deficiencies: (Explain) _____

12. _____ **READABILITY** (The reading level of the material is satisfactory for all intended students)
Reading level: _____ Formula applied: _____
Deficiencies: (Explain) _____

13. _____ **CONTENT** (The content is technically accurate, up-to-date, and presented at a level that is appropriate for all intended students)
Deficiencies: (Explain) _____

14. _____ **PRESENTATION** (The content is presented in an easy-to-use format, contains sufficient illustrations and examples, and has good visual appeal)
Deficiencies: (Explain) _____

15. _____ **LEARNING** (The material is organized and sequenced in such a way that it contributes to student learning)
Deficiencies: (Explain) _____

16. _____ **SUPPORT** (Technical, equipment, and human resource support required to utilize the material in educational settings are available, accessible, and of a reasonable nature in relation to objectives to be achieved)
Deficiencies: (Explain): _____

17. _____ **COST-BENEFIT** (Based on the cost of the material, its perceived value to instruction and learning compares favorably with other materials)
Deficiencies: (Explain) _____

Section III. Strengths and Limitations

18. Provide below one or more of the material's **strengths.**
_____
_____
_____

19. Provide below one or more of the material's **limitations.**

    _____

    _____

    _____

20. Provide **additional comments** about the material below.

    _____

    _____

    _____

Section IV. Assessment Summary

Area	Acceptable	Question-able	Unaccept-able	Does Not Apply
Bias	_____	_____	_____	_____
Readability	_____	_____	_____	_____
Content	_____	_____	_____	_____
Presentation	_____	_____	_____	_____
Learning	_____	_____	_____	_____
Support	_____	_____	_____	_____
Cost-Benefit	_____	_____	_____	_____
Other Factors	_____	_____	_____	_____
Overall Assessment	_____	_____	_____	_____

Assessor _____ Date _____

Appendix B

Microcomputer Software Evaluation: Application Software

MICROCOMPUTER SOFTWARE EVALUATION:
Application Software

Description:

Package Title _____

Version _____ Cost_____

Producer _____

Subject Area _____ Grade/Ability Level _____

Purpose:

Medium of Transfer: ☐ 5¼" Flex. Disk   ☐ Tape Cassette

            ☐ 3½" Flex. Disk   ☐ Other _____

                                             (Specify)

Required Hardware:

Required Software:

Type of Package:

☐ Single Program

☐ Integrated Series_____

_____   _____
                                 (Explain)

Source: Schmidt, June B. "Procedures for Evaluating Microcomputer Software Used in Vocational Education." *The Journal of Vocational Education Research,* Winter 1984: 10–23. Used with permission of author.

I. Name _____ Year Graduated _____

   Address _____

II. What is your current employment status?

   ☐ Employed full-time   ☐ Or part time (Check one)

   Current job title _____ Employer _____

III. Did you continue your education? ☐ Yes ☐ No

   If yes, answer the following:

Type of School	Currently Enrolled	Completed Program	Major Field of Study
Community college	_____	_____	_____
Technical school	_____	_____	_____
Four-year college	_____	_____	_____

IV. Why did you continue your education? (Check all that apply)

   ☐ Preparation for job

   ☐ Upgrading in present job

   ☐ Maintaining competency for present job

   ☐ No occupational objective

   ☐ Other reason (specify) _____

V. List all jobs held since graduation from high school.

Dates	Job Title	Employer
_____	_____	_____
_____	_____	_____
_____	_____	_____
_____	_____	_____

Evaluation:

Rating

Strongly Agree / Agree / Disagree / Strongly Disagree / Not Applicable

Impor-tance (Opt) — *Higher / Lower*

Rating: Circle the letter abbreviation which best reflects your judgment. (Use the space following each item for comments.)

Impor-tance Circle the letter which reflects your judgment of the relative importance of the item in this evaluation.

☐ Check this box if this evaluation is based partly on your observation of student use of this package.

	Rating	Importance	Item
DOCUMENTATION	SA A D SD	NA	H L	1. The documentation is clear and unambiguous.
	SA A D SD	NA	H L	2. Technical terms are adequately explained.
	SA A D SD	NA	H L	3. The documentation is accurate.
	SA A D SD	NA	H L	4. The documentation uses a logical, tutorial approach.
	SA A D SD	NA.	H L	5. The directions are easy to follow.
	SA A D SD	NA	H L	6. Information in the documentation is consistent with the hardware.
	SA A D SD	NA	H L	7. Menus are carefully documented.
	SA A D SD	NA	H L	8. Interrelationships of menus are explained.
	SA A D SD	NA	H L	9. A comprehensive index is provided.
USE QUALITY	SA A D SD	NA	H L	10. The screen is effectively used.
	SA A D SD	NA	H L	11. Commands used are logical and easily remembered.
	SA A D SD	NA	H L	12. Corrections are easily handled at all stages of operation.
	SA A D SD	NA	H L	13. Procedures exist for escaping from all stages of operation.
	SA A D SD	NA	H L	14. Minimum time is required to move from operation to operation.
	SA A D SD	NA	H L	15. Judicious use is made of the printer.
	SA A D SD	NA	H L	16. Intended users can operate the program without unwarranted assistance.
TECHNICAL QUALITY	SA A D SD	NA	H L	17. The program performs reliably (i.e., the result can be consistently achieved).
	SA A D SD	NA	H L	18. The program logically achieves its intended purpose.
	SA A D SD	NA	H L	19. The program appropriately uses computer capabilities.
	SA A D SD	NA	H L	20. Maximum capability is delivered at minimum cost.
	SA A D SD	NA	H L	21. Procedures used are comparable to those that business would use.

22. ☐ I would use or recommend use of this package. (Note suggestions for effective use in Item 25.)

☐ I would not use or recommend this package.

23. Describe the major strengths of the software package:

_____

24. Describe the major weaknesses:

_____

Package Title _____ Version _____

Reviewer's Name_____ Date _____

25. Describe the potential use of the software package in classroom settings. (Note: Complete items 1–21 before completing this item.)

_____

Index